THE COMPLETE
BOOK OF
WOODWORKING
AND
CABINETMAKING

THE COMPLETE BOOK OF WOODWORKING AND CABINETMAKING

Byron W. Maguire

USAF, Ret.
Engineer, Litton Industries

RESTON PUBLISHING
COMPANY, INC.
Reston, Virginia 22090
A Prentice-Hall Company

50186

Library of Congress Cataloging in Publication Data

Maguire, Byron W.   1931-
     The complete book of woodworking and cabinet-
making.

     1. Furniture making.   2. Woodwork.   I. Title.
TT194.M33   684.1'04   73-22158
ISBN 0-87909-153-3

© 1974 by
Reston Publishing Company, Inc.
A Prentice-Hall Company
Box 547
Reston, Virginia 22090

10   9   8   7   6   5   4

Printed in the United States of America.

*The writing is meaningful
because of the personal experiences
that have gone into its preparation
by my wife and children.*

CONTENTS

PREFACE

The most impelling reason for anyone to work with wood is probably the satisfaction you get from seeing the finished product. So much of our everyday work is often cloaked in mass production methods that we never see an end product created by ourselves. Each of us may perform a single step or a group of steps in this manufacturing process, and often our work is fatiguing and dull. So we look for an escape.

Woodworking often fills this need. In addition to its function as a relief valve for tension, it produces a product—lasting and often quite beautiful. By careful selection of materials and designs, the finished product takes on its beauty. It incorporates the qualities of the materials and the skill of the craftsman.

This book provides you with basic knowledge of woodworking joinery so you can increase your skill, fashion a finer product, and create furniture that is structurally sound, is functional, and has lasting quality and beauty.

The book is divided into five homogeneous units that examine parts of the woodworking field. Unit I explains, and attempts to develop an interest in, the shapes, styles, and characteristics of furniture and cabinetry. Unit II develops methods of making individual cabinet joints in a variety of ways so that those who have only hand tools can make the joints. There are also descriptions for those who have some portable tools and for those with a full or partial shop of bench tools. Unit III details and illustrates how to combine the usual joints into combination joints that ultimately go into many cabinets. Each chapter in this Unit includes full-page preferred sequence instructions and illustrations so that the book may be set on the work bench as a ready reference. Unit IV presents a methodology for cabinet construction. In hopes of making the study more meaningful, a sample project is designed, planned, assembled, and finished. Unit V is a gathering of reference data that should prove very useful. A short chapter on fine woods is presented, followed by an appendix containing tables showing screws, nails, plywood, and other common building needs, and by a glossary of terms.

I wish to express my sincere thanks to all of those persons in the industries for their assistance in providing me with data and illustrations that have made this book more meaningful. I especially want to thank Mr. Greenway of Drexel, Inc. for his help, as well as Mr. A.J. Schaak of the 3M Company, Mr. B.F Jameson of the Hitchcock Chair Company, and Mr. R.W. Campbell of the Stanley Tool Company. In addition, let me personally thank the following for their interest in helping me by supplying illustrations: The Temple Stuart Company, for their beautiful Early American furniture illustration; The Lane Company, for their beautiful illustrations of modern contemporary furniture; and The Louvre in Paris, the Rijksmuseum in Amsterdam, and the Henry Ford Museum and Greenfield Village. I also extend my thanks to the Forest Service, U.S. Department of Agriculture, for the literature obtained from the Superintendent of Documents in Washington, D.C.

BYRON W. MAGUIRE

UNIT I

Unit I consists of three chapters, which, when combined, attempt to develop a sensitivity for the beauty of fine woodworking. We start by examining the history of woodworking, with particular emphasis on the styles of joinery that are used today. Following this, each major style, six of which are featured, is examined in detail. Each basic type of joinery is described in sufficient depth to permit rapid identification. Following this, a chapter is devoted to defining cabinet shapes. Shop methods are generally used rather than engineering methods. Some of the featured tools are the square, dividers, twine, and straightedge.

1
THE HISTORY OF WOODWORKING

You may wonder why a book like this includes a review of the history of woodworking. You may ask: "What use can I make of this material? Will it make me a better craftsman?" When a person enters a field that is new to him, he will progress more rapidly if he has prior knowledge of all its aspects. He can become more skillful in woodworking if he applies the principles of woodworking that have been developed in the past. Trees do not grow in the forms in which we need them (as tables, for example, or as boxes), yet people must have storage places, homes to live in, and places to sit. We must learn how the tree has been fashioned in the past to meet man's needs.

As early in history as Egypt during the time of the Pharaohs, wood has been joined together to make functional objects. Beginning our discussion there, we will endeavor to provide you with a broad overview of the methods of joinery used by civilized man.

1.1
EGYPTIAN TO
RENAISSANCE
PERIOD

1.1.1
EGYPTIAN
INFLUENCE

When preparations were started for the burial of a Pharaoh, craftsmen were assigned the task of constructing a variety of storage devices, the largest of which were, of course, the pyramids. No less important were the building of boxes and the making of urns, both of which were used to store the personal belongings of the Pharaoh. The boxes, of course, varied in size because of the types of articles they were to hold. This purpose, identified in modern woodworking as a design-element "function," was used in ancient times. In Figure 1-1 is shown a box with inlays, created in the time of which we are speaking. As you perhaps know, the work was performed by hand with hand tools made of bronze and hardened copper. The craftsman who created such beautiful objects did work that was to be copied for centuries.

Now look at Figure 1-2. The *mortise and tenon* joint shown here, which has been one of the most successful of all joints, was developed

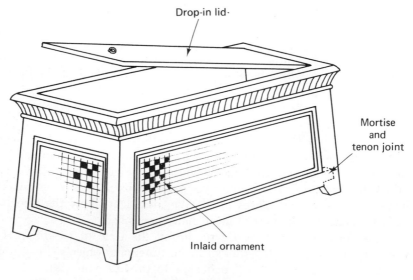

Drop-in lid·

Mortise
and
tenon joint

Inlaid ornament

FIGURE 1-1   EGYPTIAN BOX

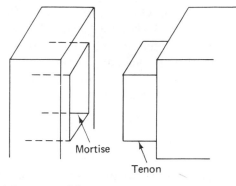

FIGURE 1-2   MORTISE AND TENON JOINT

by the Egyptians. This joint was and still is used when two pieces of wood are being joined at any angle other than parallel. As we review history you will see how this joint has stood the test of time. Simply put, a mortise and tenon joint requires two specific acts. First, a mortise must be made in one of the two pieces to be joined. Figure 1-3 shows a craftsman making a joint by hand. You see that he is

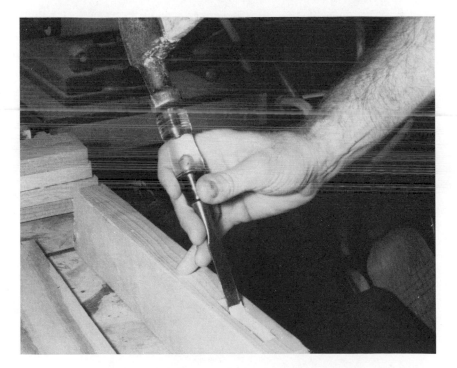

FIGURE 1-3   HOW TO CHISEL A MORTISE BY HAND

chiseling out stock from a previously marked area, thereby creating
a rectangular hole in the stock. He must make the walls of the hole
straight and parallel to the outer surfaces of the board. In Figure 1-4
the man is using a mortising machine to accomplish the same task.
Although the joint is formed more easily by machine, the end product
is the same. (In Unit II we shall give you step-by-step procedures for
making this and other joints.)

When the mortise had been completed the craftsman could begin
to make the tenon. He placed the board on which the tenon would be
made over the mortise as shown in Figures 1-4 and 1-5, and he made
a number of pencil marks. First, as in Figure 1-5, he made marks to
establish the thickness of the tenon. Second, as also shown in Figure

FIGURE 1-4   MORTISING MACHINE

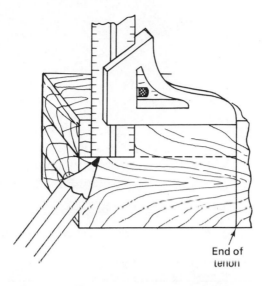

End of
tenon

FIGURE 1-5   HOW TO MARK A TENON

1-5, he laid the board with the mortise over the board that was to have the tenon and marked the latter board. He then connected all his lines and with saw or chisel or both cut away the excess material, as shown in Figure 1-6. Craftsmen performed the task in this manner for centuries, but since about 1780 machines have been available that could make the necessary cuts. Figures 1-7 and 1-8 show two school or home shop tools that can be used to make a tenon. In Figure 1-7 a radial arm saw with dado heads installed cuts away the material. In Figure 1-8 a table saw is used to make the two vertical cuts in the stock. Not shown, but next, the table saw would be reset to a different saw depth and fence position for the flat cut.

The mortise and tenon is not the only joinery method we credit to the Egyptians. Another, and most useful device associated with their craftsmen is the *dowel*. The dowel shown in Figure 1-9 is a modern machined pin. In Egypt and throughout the ancient period the dowel was probably handcrafted with knife and chisel. It could also have been fashioned on a hand-opearted lathe. Such dowels were probably not as round as the one illustrated. However, they would all serve the same purpose, to provide a link between two pieces of wood that were to be joined. It is probable that the dowel was used widely, for it could be employed as a holding device with little restriction on the positioning of the stock to be joined. Figure 1-10 illustrates some of its applications. As we proceed through our study of woodworking we shall see more and more uses of this device.

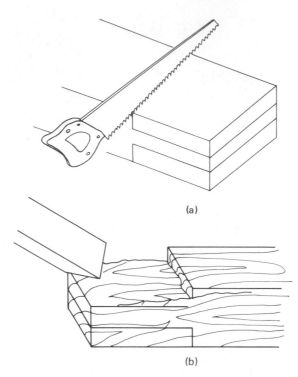

(a)

(b)

FIGURE 1-6   HOW TO CUT A TENON

FIGURE 1-7   HOW TO MAKE A TENON WITH A RADIAL
ARM SAW

FIGURE 1-8   HOW TO MAKE A TENON WITH A TABLE SAW

FIGURE 1-9   MACHINED DOWEL

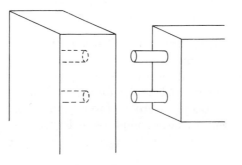

FIGURE 1-10   DOWEL JOINT

One other commonly used joinery method, the *rabbet,* also dates back to the Egyptian period. One rabbet or rabbeted joint is shown in Figure 1-11, where you see a portion of the side or edge of the board removed to make ready for the joining of the board to another piece. The rabbet joint used during this period of time and to the present day was coupled with the use of the mortise and tenon to make a frame and panel. The rabbet made possible the insertion of the panel within the frame yet did not reduce the interior dimensions of the box.

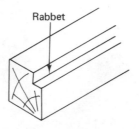

FIGURE 1-11   RABBET JOINT

Clearly these developments in joinery have established lasting principles. It is proper to acknowledge that these joints were used by these craftsmen when performing carpentry skills, too. At this time and well into the reign of Queen Elizabeth I there was no separation between the carpenter and the cabinetmaker: they were all woodworkers.

Review Figure 1-1 and examine the inlays in the sides of the box. These were fashioned by hand and had extremely simple lines. As history moves closer to us, other peoples influenced the craft and made it more complex. The first of these were the Greek and Roman craftsmen.

1.1.2
GREEK AND ROMAN
INFLUENCES

Because of the long history of the Greek people from 2600 B.C. until (and after) the fall of the Roman Empire, the Greco-Roman influence on woodworking is heavily weighted on the side of the Greeks. Many factions invaded, conquered, and ruled Greece and the surrounding areas. Many of the people were seafarers and traveled widely. Thus woodworking—furniture and cabinets—was largely an expression of the architect of the times and contained ideas the travelers brought back with them.

Many characteristics of Greek design have survived the test of time. These features have been used throughout the history of wood-working and are still in use. It is difficult to state which is the most important or useful, and it probably does not matter anyway. But if one looks through pictures of the furniture of yesteryear and walks through the furniture stores of today he finds extensive use of the flute. The most extensive use of the concave flute was made during the building of the temples in early Greece. The columns shown in Figure 1-12 were carved with fluting spaced every few degrees apart around

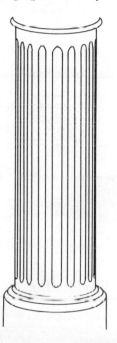

FIGURE 1-12   GREEK FLUTED COLUMN

the circumference and extending from the base to the top. The front legs on the Grecian settee sketched in Figure 1-13 show fluting. Fluting was used extensively throughout the Greek and Roman Empires. It is used in the manufacture of Mediterranean and Italian provincial furniture and cabinets today. The flute is a decoration made in a piece of wood in which part of the wood, in the form of an arc, is chipped away. Figure 1-14 shows a woodworker making a flute in a table leg with a router. After positioning the leg, the woodworker slides the router with its veining bit to the next position and repeats the routing. Each step is repeated until the leg is complete.

Ornamental characteristics abound in which architecture and furnishings are studied. Most of the design features use various char-

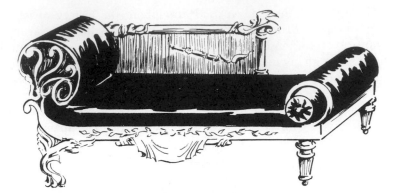

FIGURE 1-13   GRECIAN SETTEE

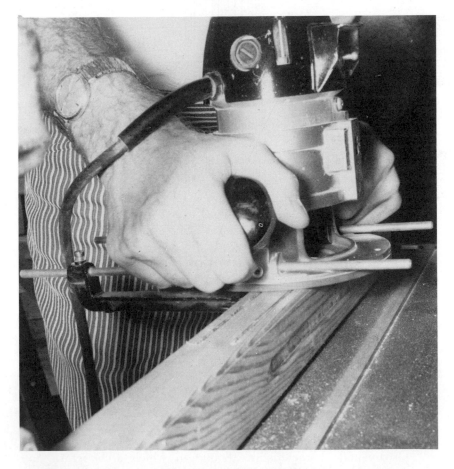

FIGURE 1-14   HOW TO MAKE A FLUTE WITH A ROUTER

acteristics of living species. The wings of birds are used as decoration in every form of created object. Refer to the settee in Figure 1-13 and note the wing of the bird on the left foot. Also observe the carving of plumes above the foot at the upholstered end of the settee. Another example of the use of the wing is shown in the chair in Figure 1-15, where the carved angel with wing is supporting the arm. In addition to these examples of the use of the wing (or its feathers), many buildings had carved birds as statues along the eaves, ridges, and cornices.

FIGURE 1-15   ARM CHAIR WITH ANGELS

Another ornament that found prominent use during this period and is still widely used today is the fret. The fret is defined in the dictionary as an "interlaced work." It may be called by more descriptive phrases, such as open fret or closed fret, but it still maintains its interlaced-work characteristic. Figure 1-16 shows an open fret as used by Hepplewhite (English designer) in one of his chairs. Another type of fretwork, used frequently during the ancient Greek and Roman civilization and still in use today, is shown in Figure 1-17. The strip of

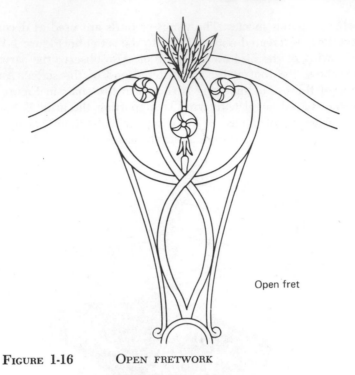

Open fret

FIGURE 1-16   OPEN FRETWORK

FIGURE 1-17   INTERLACED FRET MOLDING

molding shown in the figure may be as narrow as ½ inch to as wide as 3 feet, depending upon its use. The interlace is determined by the fashion of the lines as they pass each other. The first example shows fretwork using curves. The second example uses straight lines in rectangular form. The latter example of the fret is closely aligned with what we often call *"molding."* There are other shapes of ornament obtained from the Greeks and Romans that were incorporated into moldings.

The rope and the egg and dart are two more examples. The rope design shown in Figure 1-18 has been widely used in spindles, where, as shown in Figure 1-18, the wood is carved in spiral fashion around the circumference. In Figure 1-18b a molding made of a half of a circle has a rope design carved in its round surface. The flat surface makes for easy gluing to flat surfaces of cabinets and furniture.

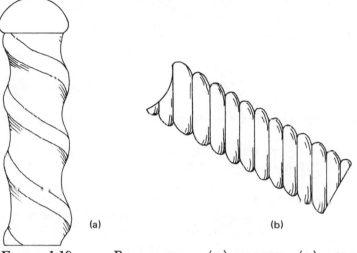

(a)   (b)

FIGURE 1-18   ROPE DESIGN: (A) SPINDLE; (B) ROPE

The egg and dart, shown in Figure 1-19, is commonly used to decorate frames and furniture as well as Greek and Roman architecture.

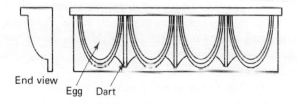

End view

Egg   Dart

FIGURE 1-19   EGG AND DART

Probably one of the most beautiful of all overlay and inlay ornamented designs attributed to Greek workmen was the carving and use of the Anathus plant. This vine of Mediterranean origin had large leaves and prickles. It is shown being used in the settee in Figure 1-13 and again in Figure 1-20, which shows its characteristics more clearly. This design feature gave craftsmen the opportunity to relieve straight, plain areas of wood with the gentle curved winding of the vine and the vine adorned with leaves and prickles and flower buds. This characteristic of Greek design was also used in the most ornate of the three

FIGURE 1-20   ANATHUS

primary design orders of the empire, on the columns of Corinthian capitals.

Refer to Figure 1-21, which shows the three architectural orders of the Greek Empire. Figure 1-21a shows an example of the Doric capital column. Notice its plain simple lines. Figure 1-21b shows the capital column of the Ionic order. Notice the extensive use of the egg and dart in this column and head. Also distinctive is the use of the scrolls at the outer corners. The use of the flute for the main column is slightly different from the Doric because a flat part of the column circumference remains, whereas in the Doric the outer edge of the flute comes to a point. Figure 1-21c shows a Corinthian capital, which is the most ornate. It contains many characteristics that are used in the modern manufacture of homes and furnishings. The cove design is used in ceilings in homes. The cove was combined with bead (one-quarter round) to make crown moldings on Early American, French, Spanish, traditional, and Mediterranean cabinets. Ionic scrolls incorporated with carved leaves often decorate corners of ornate picture frames and are sometimes used in the crowns of French provincial cabinets. Parts of other living species have been used in woodworking by these and other peoples. Look again at Figure 1-13 and notice the birds used in the leg and at the arm. Also note the angel holding up the arm in Figure 1-15. Other animal features that have been used include the goat leg. Used some in Egypt and again in Greek and Roman style, it became known later as the cabriole (cab'-ree-ol) leg. It is slender at the ankle, as shown in Figure 1-22. As shown in Figure 1-22, it is frequently made from more than one piece of wood. The craftsman of England (1800) used it extensively and incorporated into it Corinthian carving.

Before leaving the subject of Greek influence on woodworking, look at one more example of Grecian furniture. Figure 1-23 shows a

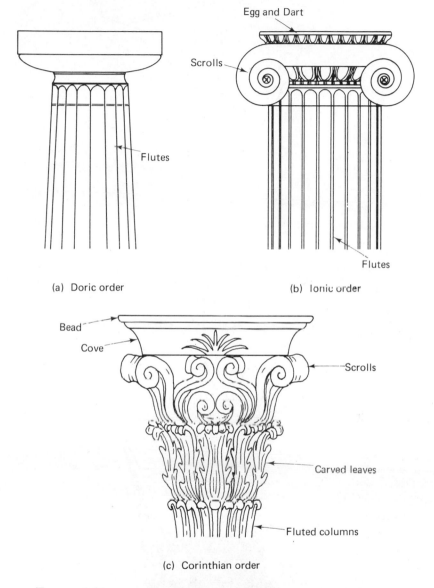

(a) Doric order

(b) Ionic order

(c) Corinthian order

FIGURE 1-21   DORIC, IONIC, AND CORINTHIAN COLUMNS

chair with a deep seat. The most distinctive feature of its design is the use of the scroll in legs, arms, and back. It is very similar in appearance to Ionic style.

Roman Empire craftsmen borrowed extensively from the Greeks

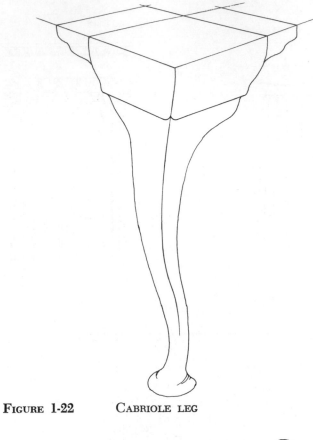

FIGURE 1-22   CABRIOLE LEG

FIGURE 1-23   GRECIAN CHAIR

and Egyptians. They used the capital column designs, incorporated animals into their design, and made extensive uses of geometric pat-

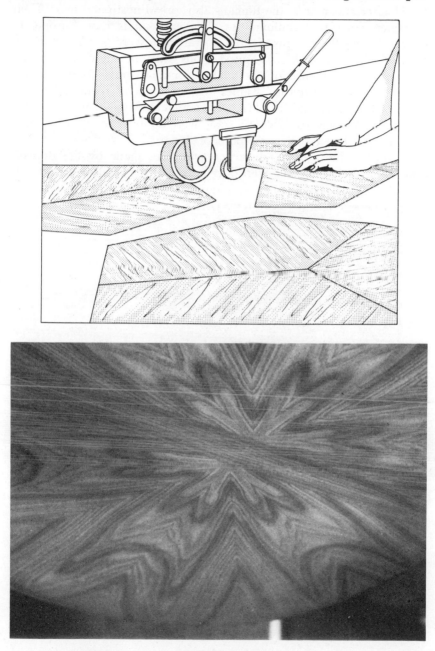

FIGURE 1-24   HOW TO APPLY VENEER

terns. Geometric patterns—squares, rectangles, cones, and others—have influenced much of craftsmen's work. Whereas the Greeks roamed only the Mediterranean area, the Romans also spread north and west. Their craftsmen developed communities all over what is now Europe. In most instances the designs of Roman craftsmen were geometric. However, where honeysuckle was used, buds and open flowers were included. Some evidence of the wicker common today in chairs was found in Roman furniture. Tables with round and rectangular tops supported by three and four legs were common. Some of the legs were turned, others were straight, and some were double-carved or cabriole. All generally had the claw or the hoof design.

One of the most significant contributions made by the Romans came from the Venetians, who developed the art of veneering hard-

FIGURE 1-25   VENEERED CABINET (*Courtesy of Drexel*)

woods onto tables, caskets, and chests. Records show that, although the Egyptians used a similar method to some degree, the Venetians developed the techniques that have endured. Veneering is the skill of gluing selected pieces of paper-thin wood into design patterns onto a surface. The surface may be large or small and the veneer may cover all or part of the surface. Figure 1-24 shows a craftsman applying veneer, and Figure 1-25 shows a cabinet that has been veneered.

1.1.3
MEDIEVAL
EUROPEAN
INFLUENCE

From the fall of the Roman Empire until the fifteenth century, much of the skill and artistry of the woodworking craft was lost. But, during the fifteenth century a number of developments took place that restored the wealthy class, and the churches became increasingly aware of finer things. The rich traveled. As a result, furniture was built in such a way that it could be transported. The items included

1 / Folding stools
2 / Trestle tables
3 / Folding chairs
4 / Beds with collapsible frameworks

Along with these objects were items used in churches. These included

1 / Desks
2 / Lecterns
3 / Benches (pews)
4 / Altars

Also significant to woodworking was the revival of use of the *frame and panel*. The skill in using this woodworking feature reduced the need for sawing large planks of lumber, which often split. This made for stronger, lighter cabinets. Together with the frame and panel, shown in Figure 1-26, was the development of the miter. A miter, shown in Figure 1-27, can be incorporated at any angle desired. The choice depends upon the number of sides in a cabinet. However, it generally is 50 percent of the total number of degrees at the joint. Figure 1-27

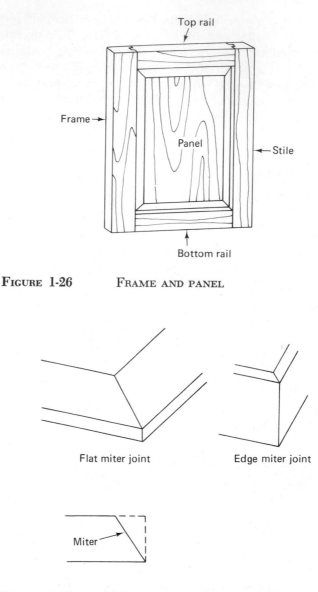

FIGURE 1-26   FRAME AND PANEL

FIGURE 1-27   MITER AND JOINT

shows a corner with a 90-degree turn that has a *miter* of 45 degrees on each piece. Until the cupboard came into existence in the fifteenth century, the chest was the mainstay for storage of personal items. However, with the building of the cupboard came the building of drawers, and later the incorporation of the drawer into other caseworks.

1.2
THE
RENAISSANCE
PERIOD

During the Renaissance, the Italian influence in woodworking was similar to their architecture—beautiful and simple with straight lines and simple carvings. Once again the carver made use of cupids, scrolls, foliage, and fretwork. Because of the Italian craftsmen's influence, French craftsmen were quick to absorb their ideas, especially as a result of the influence of Italians imported to France by French royalty.

Some French furniture is Gothic in style, with cupids, medallion heads, and grotesque decorations. However, this style soon gave way to the lighter, delicate, graceful lines common during the reigns of Louis XIV, Louis XV, and Louis XVI. Pieces of furniture and cabinets were inlaid with marble, semiprecious stones, and woods of various colors. Oak was the primary wood in use.

During this period the Moors occupied Spain. Although wood-

FIGURE 1-28   TRESTLE TABLE (*Courtesy of Drexel*)

working remained Western, the Moors lent it Eastern influence through use of wrought iron, massive locks, drawers, and velvet cloth for linings.

The sixteenth century brought much change to Europe and England. The Gothic influence that had begun in the Medieval era gave way to the Renaissance and lighter forms of woodworking. Beds, chests, cabinets, and chairs were made lighter and showed more of their wooden frames. The trestle table shown in Figure 1-28 gave way to the joined table with its fixed top. The trestle table became common during the Medieval era when landowners traveled between their homes. Each move required the taking of all furniture. In England the trestle table was first used in the great halls in castles. At mealtime servants would bring the tables into the halls and erect them. After the meal was over, the servants would disassemble the tables and store them until the next meal. Trestle tables again became popular in Colonial America.

1.3
THE POST-RENAISSANCE PERIOD TO COLONIAL TIME

With the arrival of the seventeenth century, little advancement was made in developing new joinery, but great steps were made in incorporating the joinery and characteristics of design carried over from early civilizations. Influences from the Orient and from the Moors, Goths, Danes, and others were combined by masters of woodwork, and some very beautiful design features resulted.

Characteristics such as fluting, reeding, carving, inlay, and veneering were commonly used. Not for the common man, though, only for the aristocrat. Work was primarily performed by hand with craftsmen carving pieces individually. Figures 1-29, the Dutch cupboard, and 1-30, the Dutch table, exemplify the art of the woodworker.

During the reigns of Louis XIV, Louis XV, and Louis XVI, French provincial as we know it today came into prominence. Gilding, a process of overlaying a cabinet with silver or gold (now done with gold paint), was used extensively. Fine silks from the Orient were used for upholstery, and delicate S curves were incorporated into almost every piece. Extensive use of the cabriole leg can be found in most

FIGURE 1-29   DUTCH CUPBOARD OF OAK WITH EBONY
VENEER AND IVORY DECORATION (*Courtesy
of the Rijksmuseum, Amsterdam*)

FIGURE 1-30   DUTCH TABLE OF OAK, FIRST HALF OF
SEVENTEENTH CENTURY (*Courtesy of the
Rijksmuseum, Amsterdam*)

design patterns and pieces. Figure 1-31, the "bureau du roi" made for
Louis XV, shows many of these characteristics.

FIGURE 1-31   BUREAU DU ROI (*Courtesy of the Louvre,
                   Paris*)

The most famous English designers—Chippendale, Sheraton,
Hepplewhite, and Robert Adam—did their work during the same
period. Their artistry dictated much of the design used by English
royalty. Characteristics of their furniture, shown in Figure 1-32, can be
related to earlier civilizations. However, their work exemplified most
the art and skill of the craftsmen of their time. Their use of carvings,
reeding, fretwork, and joinery exemplified the highest state of the
woodworkers' art.

(A) CHIPPENDALE DRESSING TABLE WITH CARVED SHELL ON KNEE, FOUR CLAW-AND-BALL FEET, INSET QUARTER COLUMNS, AND CARVED SHELL AND LEAF DRAWER FRONT

FIGURE 1-32   CHARACTERISTICS OF THE WORK OF CHIPPENDALE, HEPPLEWHITE, AND SHERATON (*Courtesy of Henry Ford Museum and Greenfield Village*)

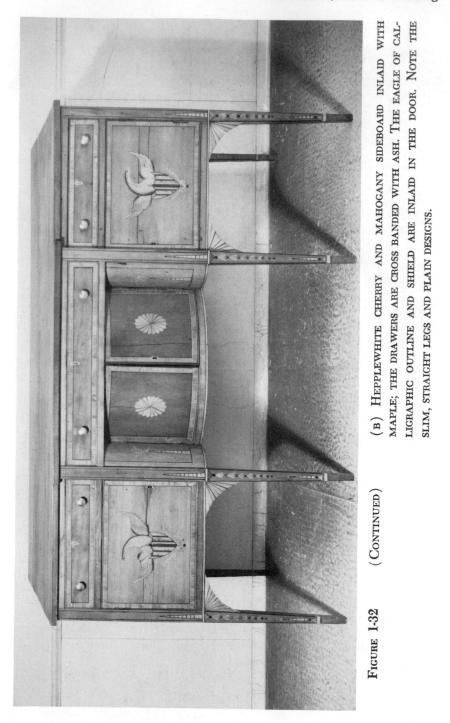

FIGURE 1-32   (CONTINUED)

(B) HEPPLEWHITE CHERRY AND MAHOGANY SIDEBOARD INLAID WITH MAPLE; THE DRAWERS ARE CROSS BANDED WITH ASH. THE EAGLE OF CALLIGRAPHIC OUTLINE AND SHIELD ARE INLAID IN THE DOOR. NOTE THE SLIM, STRAIGHT LEGS AND PLAIN DESIGNS.

(c) SHERATON MAHOGANY SIDEBOARD WITH BIRD'S EYE MAPLE INLAY, FLUTED LEGS, AND BEVELED DRAWER EDGES

FIGURE 1-32   (CONTINUED)

1.4
EARLY
AMERICAN
TO MODERN
DAY

Migration to America by the English and others produced a regression in the art of woodworking. The wilderness required immediate use of simple homes and furnishings. This need gave rise to the bench, trestle table, and dry washstand. But soon there was a demand for more elaborate furnishings. The wealthy class imported fine furnishings from Europe with which to decorate their homes. But the common people needed furniture, too; so Duncan Phyfe and others came to America and opened shops in which simple furniture was designed and built. At one time, Phyfe employed over 100 woodworkers in his New York factory.

Exemplifying the American woodworker, a man named John Hitchcock established a chair factory in New England. He designed and built furniture with simple lines and decorated the chairs with various ornaments. Figure 1-33 shows the factory where some of the

FIGURE 1-33   HITCHCOCK FACTORY, 1826 (*Courtesy of Hitchcock Chair Company*)

chairs were made. This company is representative of many that had their start early in the Colonial period. Some of the other work from earlier days is shown in Figure 1-34. This type of furniture supplied the needs of Americans and contained fine joinery.

FIGURE 1-34   EXAMPLE OF DREXEL FURNITURE—EARLY
                   AMERICAN (*Courtesy of Drexel*)

Americans move fast and so does its woodworking industry. Machines replaced man's manual skills and mass-produced fine, well-made furniture. Figure 1-35 shows some pictures of factory setups for mass production.

With modernization of the industry, not many innovations resulted. Joinery is still made using the

1 / Mortise and tenon

2 / Dowel

3 / Miter

4 / Frame and panel

5 / Rabbet

and it is still decorated with ancient characteristics, such as

(A) PRECUTTING STOCK TO NEEDED LENGTHS

(B) LAYING OUT STOCK FOR MULTIPLE PIECES/CUTS

(C) MARKING ALL PIECES OF STOCK

(D) MAKING END TENONS

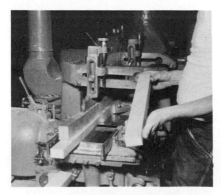

(E) SHAPING STOCK

(F) SANDING SHAPED STOCK

FIGURE 1-35   FACTORY SETUPS

1 /   Leaves and vines

2 /   Fretwork

3 /   Living species

4 /   Cabriole legs

5 /   Ball and claw

6 /   Rope

7 /   Egg and dart

8 /   Designs from capitals

One element did evolve in the twentieth century—plastic—and with it entered contemporary furniture. However, the plastics used in woodworking are most frequently overlays, usually poured into forms in the molten state, dried, then stained as wood, with distressed finishes often incorporated in the design. Figure 1-36 presents an example of molding and overlay made from plastic for use in woodworking.

FIGURE 1-36   MOLDED OVERLAY

Our trip through history should have provided you with two pieces of knowledge. First, the state of the art changes slowly, and most of the joinery techniques used in ancient societies are still in use today. Second, by learning the italicized terms common to woodworking described in the chapter, you have begun to accumulate a new vocabulary.

QUESTIONS |

1 / How does the word "function" relate to the Egyptian era?

2 / What joint is one of the most used and successful of all joints developed by the Egyptians?

3 / What is one useful joinery method associated with Egyptian craftsmen?

4 / What events influenced the woodworking of furniture and cabinets during the period of Greek influence?

5 / What are the various concave flutes used on the temples of Greece?

6 / What is a design feature or ornamental characteristic used by Greek and Roman architects that is related to honeysuckle?

7 / Can you give a definition of "fret."

8 / During the Medieval period in Europe, what feature was revived that was significant to woodworking?

9 / What is the major material evolved in the twentieth century that has influenced woodworking?

PROJECT |

Locate a piece of antique furniture in your community and make a report about it. Determine which period it belongs to by comparing the data in Chapter 1 with the data you obtain in your research.

2

FEATURES OF
CABINETS AND
FURNITURE

Studying the features and designs of cabinets requires a lot of training and practice and consideration of a number of factors. One important element relates to styles, some of which are modern, traditional, provincial, and Early American; another encompasses the selection of materials, colors, and finishes; and a third involves building techniques, which aid in creating a style.

The beginner can make a successful product with just a few tools and machines and a minimum of experience. This chapter explains significant features of design that can be identified and used to make a beautiful cabinet for any room in a home.

2.1
HOW TO
BUILD THE
CABINET
WITH A
PURPOSE

The first and probably the greatest single thought that initiates a cabinet project is its *purpose*. What will the cabinet do for the family or person who will use it? What will it house? Where will it be located? Will it be portable or built in to the wall? The dictionary defines purpose as "the object or end for which a thing is made, done, used, etc." Clearly, then, the purpose of a cabinet is the primary consideration.

You may recognize that all cabinets are primarily boxes. The shapes and sizes vary with their purpose, but the box structure remains. If the cabinet is an end table, for instance, it is roughly 16 inches wide, 26 inches deep, and 20 inches high. Note that these dimensions create a rectangular box. The shaded area surrounding the end table in Figure 2-1 shows the basic box. Now look at the octagon (eight-sided) cabinet (Figure 2-2); its outer surfaces create an octagon-shaped box.

FIGURE 2-1   END TABLE IN BOX SHADOW (*Courtesy of Drexel*)

FIGURE 2-2   OCTAGON CABINET (*Courtesy of Drexel*)

We can imagine that if boxes were used for all cabinets, there would be little feeling of beauty. More important, though, there would be no organization of materials that are to be stored. All one could do is stack things on top of each other. To help make the cabinet successful for its purpose, two major improvements are incorporated. The first is the *drawer* and the second is the *shelf*.

The drawer provides a detail that allows for specific organization and easy access. Its size, depth, and height are dictated by its purpose. For example, a drawer that will be used to store clothing will be 6 to 10 inches high, whereas a drawer used to store silverware will be 3 to 4½ inches high.

The shelf also allows for organization of products that are to be stored. If the shelves are fixed (not adjustable), their position must be thought out carefully. If, for instance, a cabinet is to be used to store dishes, a service for 12 would require spacing between shelves greater than that for a service for 8. Drinking glasses of 8, 12, 16, and 20 ounces are common, and each is a different size. Shelves of varying space allow for greater storage within a specific cabinet size. Figure 2-3a shows a basic wall cabinet for the kitchen. Notice its equally spaced shelves. If glasses are to be stored, much space will be wasted. Now look at Figure 2-3b. With shelves positioned according to the height of the products to be stored, the wasted space is converted to usable shelf space.

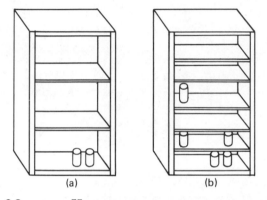

(a)   (b)

FIGURE 2-3   HOW TO USE SHELVES TO MAXIMIZE SPACE

We have made suggestions for the use of drawers and shelves for specific purposes. These characteristics are ultimate and primary, but they do not make for an attractive cabinet. What is needed is an understanding within the beginner's limited capability of how to coordinate a cabinet with other pieces of furniture in the room.

2.2
HOW TO COORDINATE THE CABINET WITH OTHER FURNITURE

Before beginning to cut up expensive wood, consider that besides the purpose of the cabinet, it must also represent a particular style. A nondescript box adds nothing to a room already furnished; on the contrary, it detracts from the room's furnishings and causes a feeling of distaste by anyone entering or staying in the room. Therefore, as the builder and designer you must use caution in selecting the features of the cabinet. Later in the chapter we shall study the six basic styles of cabinetry and furniture found in American homes today. These studies will identify each style by its features, materials, finishes, and other characteristics. This is very important information, for it will dictate the designs you may add to your cabinet.

Before studying styles and their features, let us remember that limitations exist: the skill of our hands and variety of tools and materials that are available. You may recognize that it is beyond the scope of your abilities to copy a piece of cabinetry that you have in your home. In that case, consider the following ideas, which may aid you to decide the design you will use. Build an *accent piece* of furniture or a cabinet using an *accent feature,* or use an *accent color,* or design a *contrasting cabinet.* In any case, read and consider these ideas, then proceed to study each style of furniture so that you understand it from its characteristic features.

2.2.1
ACCENT PIECE

Make a study of the furniture in a room in your home. Determine its style, then ask yourself what you could use in this room that would

FIGURE 2-4   OCTAGON OCCASIONAL CABINET USED AS A
BOOKCASE (*Courtesy of Drexel*)

FIGURE 2-5   MEDITERRANEAN LAMP TABLE (*Courtesy of Drexel*)

FIGURE 2-6   CONTEMPORARY NIGHTSTAND (*Courtesy of Lane*)

provide a useful function and also add beauty. Consider the following ideas for starters. Build an occasional table for the living room or den. If your furniture is square or rectangular and Mediterranean, you might decide on an octagon table or stand. The stand could be designed to hold books (Figure 2-4) or it may be a lamp table (Figure 2-5).

An end table or cabinet for the bedroom is another idea. Observe the furniture within the room and decide on its style. Then build your accent piece in that style. Note the contemporary nightstand in Figure 2-6.

Probably one of the most frequently made projects for the dining room is the rolling serving cart. A project of this nature is difficult to build, but when it is done well, it is certainly worth the effort (Figure 2-7).

FIGURE 2-7   EARLY AMERICAN SERVING CART (*Courtesy of Temple Stuart*)

Having decided on your project, you may find that the designs used in other pieces in the room are beyond your resources and capabilities. Stand back and study the pieces. Ask yourself: What one characteristic design feature stands out most? Could it be an accent feature?

2.2.2
ACCENT FEATURE

An accent feature may be a piece of *molding* anywhere on the cabinet. It may be *trim* near the floor, around the top edge, or decorative trim on doors. If molding is the special feature, study it closely and determine if it is made from one piece or made of two or more pieces glued together. Next, determine if you have the resources (tools and skill) to make it. Or can you buy it? If you can make it or buy it, then consider that the rest of the cabinet may be simple in construction, and the accent molding feature will make it blend with the other furniture in the room.

Shape may also be used as an accent feature. If the other pieces are square, your new cabinet should be square and harmonize; if round, make yours round.

Finally, accents may not be physical but *feeling*. The proper selection of *color and finish* may provide harmony where similar physical characteristics are missing.

2.2.3
ACCENT COLOR

If the room's furniture is white lacquer, for instance, consider finishing any pieces in white lacquer. If soft brown tones are needed, perhaps maple or medium-brown walnut will provide the harmonizing color.

If staining is to be done, study the grain of the wood in your new piece and that of the room's furniture. Are they similar, or different? If your piece has more grain, you may want to tone it down with shellac or a similar material before you apply the stain.

Next, consider the overall finish. Are the other pieces in the room very shiny (high-gloss finish), lustrous (satin finish), or dull (flat finish)? Once you know, plan that your finish will be the same. You may spray lacquer in any of the three finishes, or you may varnish in any of the three finishes.

Do you begin to see how the project you do for your home or office must be carefully planned? It is best to make an accent piece using one or more of these suggestions. If possible, select a feature, a shape, and a color, and use them all. Accent pieces always coordinate with room furniture, but sometimes a contrast piece adds drama to a sedate room.

2.2.4
CONTRASTING
PIECE

A contrasting piece of furniture must be carefully selected. It must be so designed that the eye will see it immediately and recognize it as different. In addition to fulfilling its purpose, its most important characteristic must be its *quality*. The quality of materials, workmanship, and finish must equal the other furnishings. A cabinet made of fir would not be compatible with one made from pecan or oak, nor would a lauan piece look well surrounded by maple furniture.

You may be able to successfully mix the modern and Early American styles. You may also select a nonornate French provincial piece and use it with Early American. Certain pieces of Mediterranean can be used in contrast with Italian or French provincial or Queen Anne. When you design and/or build your contrasting piece, consider these factors and also consider color.

Color is a very important factor in choosing a contrasting piece. All the careful work and the best materials may be ruined by the selection of the wrong color. A safe rule is: When the other pieces are stained, stain yours; when the other pieces are painted, paint yours. The design features will usually be the contrasting feature. However, if you are careful you may stain your cabinet dark brown when the rest of the room's furniture is light to medium brown; or you may do the opposite.

When making a contrasting piece of furniture, many avenues are open. Carefully select one, or at most two, of the areas of accent feature, style, and color, to feature in your piece. If you elect to use all three areas, you will probably be dissatisfied and others will think your project awkward.

Coordinating a new piece of furniture with others that are already in the room can be difficult. The ideas and suggestions provided here are just that, ideas. If possible, work with the accent idea until you become proficient in woodworking. Then, develop a style for the contrasting piece. If you follow this procedure, your chances for success and satisfaction should be enhanced greatly.

Now let us study each of the six styles of furniture that are found in American homes today.

2.3
FURNITURE
STYLES

The six basic styles of furniture used in American homes are Early American, traditional, French and Italian provincial, Spanish Mediterranean, and modern, which consists of three substyles, Danish modern, contemporary, and Oriental. If you study the illustrations while reading the text you will discover that certain features are used many times within a particular style. When they are used in another style, their character changes.

2.3.1
EARLY AMERICAN
STYLING FEATURES

Furniture of Early American design is probably the easiest for all of us to recognize. It is distinctive to our country, although, as we read in

FIGURE 2-8   EARLY AMERICAN COLLECTION (*Courtesy of Temple Stuart*)

Chapter 1, Europeans, especially the English, influenced its design. Early American designs were established during the period 1608–1830 and have been refined ever since.

Figure 2-8 shows a collection of Early American furniture. See how many times a feature is used over again by examining the figure and using the following list of features.

sturdiness	Each piece appears to stand firmly. There is bulk to each section, whether it is a panel style or a rail or a leg. Large flat areas create the mass appearance.
molding designs	*Legs:* legs are *turned.* Most legs have square tops and tapered (feminine) calf sections with use of the ball near the floor. All sharp edges are rounded. *Edges:* edges of tops, drawers, and doors are either tapered straight or tapered one-quarter round. Some *ogee* curving is used. *Bases:* bases on cabinets are massive, but frequently sections are cut away to lighten the mass look.
plugging	Plugging is frequently used to create an authentic look. Usually the plugs are decorative and under them screws bind the jointed pieces.
hardware	Hardware varies from the black-wrought-iron hammered look to fine-polished dull brass. Its shape is varied also.
spindles	Simple dowels are used in Windsor chairs. Turned spindles mark Early American furniture and are frequently used in hutches.
types of furniture	The most distinctive types of furniture and cabinetry are the trestle table with its two dropleafs, the Windsor chair, the open hutch top with paneled base doors, and the butterfly table (variation of the trestle).
woods used	The principal woods used are maple, birch, pine, ash, and oak.
color and finish	Colors range from a very light brown (maple) to russet brown (fruitwood). The finishes are almost always satin, hand-rubbed-effect lacquer, polyurethane, or varnish.

Traditional furniture was developed primarily by the English masters Chippendale, Hepplewhite, Sheraton, and the Adams brothers, in the eighteenth century. These men used many shapes and forms to create their pieces. Most frequently the design characteristics can be traced to the early periods discussed in Chapter 1. However, these designers' individual abilities enabled them to join two or more distinctive characteristics to create beautiful work. American designers duplicate the work of these masters, adding their touches of variation carefully and delicately to prevent an off-balance appearance. Traditional furniture and cabinetry does have a few distinctive features, but it may sometimes be difficult to identify. Since much of the styling uses designs from all over Europe and the Mediterranean, you may see many provincial characteristics included. However, if a piece is not distinctively

FIGURE 2-9   TRADITIONAL GROUPING (*Courtesy of Drexel*)

provincial you can make a fairly safe assumption that it is classified as traditional.

Figure 2-9 shows a collection of traditional furniture. From the following list identify as many features as you can from Figure 2-9.

legs	Many leg shapes are used; cabriole and Queen Anne legs are two prominent ones. Almost all legs are tapered and have curves. Few are turned as in Early American.
carvings	Many carvings are used and may be found anywhere. For instance, carvings are used around mirrors, on drawer facings, in doors, in legs, and in chair backs.
veneers	Use of veneers is extensive. They are found everywhere large flat areas are seen, for example, in drawer fronts, cabinet tops, door fronts, and side panels. The veneers were seldom laid in plain sheets. Most frequently designs were created by using the natural wood grains. One of the pieces in Figure 2-9 shows a table top with decorator veneering.
openings	Most chairs of this period have open backs. Many have carving and interweaving in their designs.
woods	Three woods are used most frequently: mahogany (most extensive), oak, and walnut (least extensive).
color and finish	All brown colors are used as well as dark red mahogany. Finishes vary from the dull, hand rubbed effect to a polished gloss.

2.3.3
FRENCH
PROVINCIAL
STYLING FEATURES

French provincial furniture is very distinctive in its features. It can be found in many homes, sometimes as an accent piece and sometimes in a particular room, such as a bedroom. Much of the style is associated with the reign of Louis XIV, Louis XV, and Louis XVI. French aristocrats of this period had strong desires for beauty and could afford beautiful furniture. Probably the most distinctive characteristic of this furniture is its use of the *curve*. The cabriole leg shown in Figure 1-22 is a good example of the use of the curve.

FIGURE 2-10   FRENCH PROVINCIAL GROUPING (*Courtesy of Drexel*)

Once again you are urged to take your list of features of French provincial and the two following styles, Italian provincial and Spanish Mediterranean, to a furniture store and identify the various styles. But first use Figure 2-10 to identify the characteristics of French provincial, which are as follows:

dainty, fragile appearance   Much of the furniture is very delicate in appearance. Legs (cabriole) are slender and feminine. Hardware is light. Doors with glass have slender rails and styles between glass panels.

carvings   Elaborate, delicate carvings are used with great care but in abundance. You will see them

used on crowns of chests (tops), on skirts of
dressers, on doors and drawers, and on legs.

veneers   Sometimes entire cabinets are veneered. Veneers may be as simple as straight grain or
as elaborate as geometric patterns. Other
applications are found in stripping, where a
bias-cut veneer strip is embedded for accent
near or within other veneer.

woods   Fruitwood and cherry are the two primary
woods used. However, you may find antiques
made from mahogany, oak, and walnut.

finishes   Stained finishes range from light tan to African
mahogany (red). White and black furniture
trimmed in gold (gilded) is common. Hand-
painted flower arrangements are also quite
common. The distressed finish, a finish that appears to have been applied over a resurfaced
piece of furniture that has seen a lot of abuse,
is frequently used.

2.3.4
ITALIAN
PROVINCIAL
STYLING FEATURES

Italian provincial styling differs from French provincial in many respects but uses similar techniques. *Straight lines* are used primarily in
this style, whereas curved lines are used in French provincial. Italian-
styled furniture is bulkier and slightly more massive than French. Most
pieces are built close to the floor with very short legs, or the bases act
as legs. Much Italian-styled furniture is similar to French styles because Italy and France are neighboring countries and many Italian
craftsmen migrated to France, returning later to Italy with knowledge
of French techniques. Compare the following list of characteristics
with those used in the various pieces shown in Figure 2-11.

straight lines   Italian-styled furniture is designed using
straight lines. Cabinets are designed using
straight rails and styles. The fronts of cabinets are straight. Legs on tables and beds are
straight and frequently tapered.

FIGURE 2-11   ITALIAN PROVINCIAL GROUPING (*Courtesy of Drexel*)

fluting

Almost all Italian-styled furniture contains fluting, which may run in any direction. A table leg will often have fluting in the upper part (Figure 2-11) with the pattern repeated in the longer, stem portion of the leg.

hardware

Hardware is usually quite ornate and made with brass and bronze finishes. All types are used, including buttons, pulls, drop pulls, handles, and a variety of hinge styles.

veneer

Much of this style of furniture uses veneer for large areas as well as for small areas. A primary example is shown in Figure 2-11. Matching veneers are used on doors and drawer fronts, which create a rhythmical effect. A rhythmical effect is one in which a particular pattern is repeated. Veneers may be either *inlaid* (flush with the surface) or *overlaid* (veneer glued on top of the panel, causing a raised area).

proportioned

Italian Provincial furniture is almost always designed to exact proportions, the most notable of which is the golden mean rectangle (to be discussed in Chapter 3). The furniture cabinet, especially, will have a balanced appearance and the balance will usually be formal. This means that the left and right halves of the cabinet are mirror images of each other. For instance, a triple dresser will have the left and right one-third with the same design and size of drawers. The center one-third will be the same or an accent design.

woods

Primary woods used are cherry, walnut, and selected fruitwoods.

finishes

Most is finished in light tan to soft brown.

2.3.5
SPANISH MEDITERRANEAN STYLING FEATURES

Because of a mixture of two different types of people—Moors from Africa and the Goths—a very distinctive style of furniture developed The Moors used simple geometric shapes and lines in their furniture. The Goths added the classic styling with carvings and moldings. The resultant outcome was (and still is) a style of furniture that uses almost no expressions of living plants or animals but does make use of a variety of geometric shapes, two primary forms being the horseshoe and the crescent. Spanish Mediterranean furnishings are usually massive. The bold bases on cabinets and heavy-looking crowns (tops) give this feeling. So do the deep carvings on usually thick cabinet drawer fronts and doors. As with Italian provincial, Spanish Mediterranean is well proportioned. The balance may be either formal or informal. With the exception of modern furniture, Spanish uses the most variety of material. Use Figure 2-12 to distinguish the following features:

boldness

Most pieces of Spanish Mediterranean furnishings are bold in appearance. Cabinets usually have large molded bases and often have large crowns. Large flat areas are usually broken up with design features such as overlays, plant-ons, and interlace work. Look for the octagon and hexagon features in the legs and overlay shapes.

carvings

Much bold carving is used, but it is all made from arcs, curves, and French curves (double-S shape). No carvings represent animal or vegetable likenesses.

materials

Except for the modern style, Spanish Mediterranean makes use of the greatest variety of materials. Some of the most commonly used materials are wrought iron; wood of pecan, oak, and some mahogany; ceramics, especially on table tops; and glass. Cane webbing is frequently found in chair backs of this style.

color and finish

Colors range from pecan to walnut; a bleached or antique brown finish is often used. Finishes are frequently distressed and are then polished to a rich, semigloss luster.

FIGURE 2-12   SPANISH MEDITERRANEAN GROUPING
                   (*Courtesy of Drexel*)

The sixth style of furniture is called "modern." It is made up of three distinct substyles: (a) *Danish*, (b) *contemporary*, and (c) *Oriental*. Although the three substyles are all in use, each has had a period of greater prominence than it enjoys today. Danish was very popular in the 1950s, contemporary was in greatest demand during the late 1940s and is currently in vogue, and Oriental has again become popular after losing its popularity during World War II.

Figures 2-13, 2-14, and 2-15 show groupings of each style.

FEATURES OF DANISH STYLING

appearance

Danish modern furniture has at a glance a simple sculptured appearance. For instance, it appears as if the arms grow out of the back piece. Close examination of chairs and tables quickly verifies that jointing is found in many unusual places.

lines

The lines are graceful. Pieces frequently show a slender portion at each end with gentle swelling at the middle. Occasional tables frequently incorporate this styling. Even tops of tables and cabinets tend to be styled along this line.

fragile

This furniture appears to be very fragile, and some of the cheaper pieces are. However, good-quality Danish furniture and cabinetry is sturdy, well constructed, and frequently is doweled.

woods

The primary wood used to make Danish furniture is teak. This wood, which is found primarily in southeastern Asia (Burma, in particular), ranges in texture from very soft to very hard. It is easily shaped, and its grain is very straight. It tends to splinter, however.

finishes and color

Danish modern furniture is usually finished in natural teakwood tones. Light staining may be

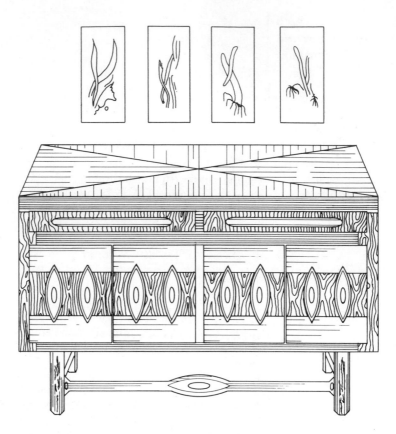

FIGURE 2-13   DANISH MODERN STYLE

used for blending and high-lighting. Almost all pieces of good quality are rubbed to a satin sheen with oil and a tiny bit of lacquer.

FEATURES OF CONTEMPORARY STYLING

appearance

Contemporary styling varies from the informal built-in units often seen in children's rooms to modern furniture built with selected traditional features. This may account for some confusion as to just what contemporary is. It is a style that allows designers to use any and all types of material, including plastic, glass, and metal, in addition to wood. Where specific shapes cause limitations in the other styles previously studied, contemporary has few. The basic box is seen repeatedly. Informality (little rhythm or repetition of design) is customary. Large wall areas are adorned with varied shapes and openings. This style uses very little hardware. Hidden handles and hinges are common.

materials

Such metals as brass, chrome, and nickel are used frequently. Glass of various colors is used, generally in panels and cabinet doors. Plastic of the laminated types is used everywhere. It is used on doors, in doors, on cabinet facings, in shelves, and on countertops.

finish and color

A wide range of color, from blonde to walnut, is used. In addition, painted surfaces are often used. Stained furniture can be found with highly polished surfaces.

FIGURE 2-14   CONTEMPORARY GROUPING (*Courtesy of Lane*)

FEATURES OF ORIENTAL STYLING

appearance

In the Orient, where many people carve by hand, elaborately carved pieces are common. However, mass-produced furniture tends to retain geometric shapes. Much of the design is balanced. Proportion is a very important characteristic. What probably distinguishes Oriental furnishings from other styles is the elaborate use of painted figures and scenes. These may be found anywhere: for instance, on doors, table tops, drawer facings, and even on cabinet trim. Colored lacquer finishes in deep high gloss are common.

materials

In addition to woods such as teak and mahogany, many other products are used in the

FIGURE 2-15   ORIENTAL CABINET (*Courtesy of Drexel*)

making of Oriental furniture. Glass is frequently used. Gold leafing and edging adorn many cabinets. Hand-painted figures and birds decorate doors and table tops.

finishes

Lacquer is the primary material used. It is customary to find black and white lacquered cabinets. The finish is usually high in gloss.

You have just been briefly introduced to the six basic styles of furnishing used in America today. If this text were to teach you how to be a designer, we would have had six volumes to study. That is not our purpose, of course. We just want you to understand enough about the styles so that you can recognize each one.

As a woodworking enthusiast you may find enjoyment in doing a sample study, as we suggested previously. Maybe a group of classmates could do a study. The results could develop an understanding of design.

QUESTIONS |

1 / What is the primary idea that initiates a cabinet project?

2 / What are two major improvements that help to make a cabinet successful?

3 / What are the considerations regarding use of an accent piece?

4 / What are "accent feature" and "accent color"?

5 / What is the major purpose of a contrast piece and what is its most important characteristic?

6 / What are the six basic styles of furniture used in American homes?

7 / What six characteristics of Early American furniture can you name?

8 / How were Chippendale, Hepplewhite, and Sheraton able to create distinctive and beautiful work?

9 / What is the most distinctive characteristic used in the French provincial style?

10 / What is the primary feature of Italian provincial woodworking?

11 / What are the primary features of the Spanish Mediterranean style?

12 / What are the three substyles of modern styling?

PROJECT |

After reading Chapter 2, go into a room in your home and look at the
furniture. Make a list of the different styles you see. Compare them with
the descriptions in the chapter feature for feature.

3

SHAPES AND
ACCENTS

In this chapter we present material in a different style from Chapters 1 and 2. In this chapter you will participate in learning skills by actual performance. Since most of the chapter is devoted to explaining the shapes of cabinets, details are provided so that you can apply *shop methods* of laying out the various shapes.

Only a few tools are needed: a folding 6-foot ruler, a string, and a board called a straightedge. The one most relied-upon tool used in making most shapes is the framing square. Since the framing square may be new to you, a brief explanation of how to use it and its scales and tables is given.

Following the projects that concern laying out the various shapes by the shop method, there is a discussion of types and uses of moldings. In this discussion, examples are provided of common moldings, plant-ons, and moldings that can be made with a router. But let us first ex-

amine and learn what the basic shapes of cabinets are and how to
lay them out.

Figure 3-1 shows the usual basic shapes of most cabinets and tables.
They are identified in the figure as the square, the rectangle, the octagon, the hexagon, the triangle, the round, the diamond, and the ellipse. These shapes are usually those of the top of a table or cabinet.

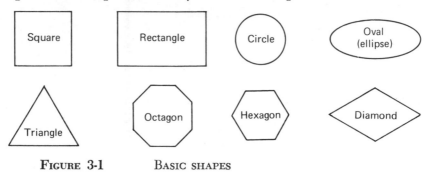

FIGURE 3-1   BASIC SHAPES

For instance, the serving cart shown in Figure 2-7 is, as viewed from
the top, a basic rectangle. Almost all cabinets and tables viewed from
the side are basic squares or rectangles. Note that the side view of the
round table in Figure 3-2 is that of a rectangle. This is almost always
true. Therefore, any cabinet that is being described is almost always
described by the shape of its top.

A point about the hexagon and octagon shapes used as basic designs: We know that in order to make a square, each corner must equal
90 degrees. Tools such as the *framing* and *combination square* are
manufactured with 90-degree sides. The combination square (shown
later) also has one part that can be used to obtain a perfect 45 degrees.
Two 45-degree cuts on two boards result in 90 degrees when placed
together. Machines are also made to cut 90 and 45 degrees with precision.

To make an octagon or a hexagon requires more experience in
the use of different tools. A miter square, shown in Figure 3-3, is used
along with a protractor to obtain the necessary miter angles. In a
hexagon each corner must equal 60 degrees (six corners × 60 degrees

FIGURE 3-2   ROUND TABLE WITH OUTLINED SIDE VIEW

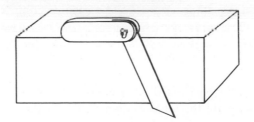

FIGURE 3-3   MITER SQUARE IN USE

= 360 degrees = a circle). Therefore, two miters of 30 degrees when placed together make one corner of a hexagon.

To make an octagon requires even more attention to mitering, because each corner only equals 45 degrees (eight × 45 degrees = 360

degrees). One-half a corner equals 22½ degrees, and cutting boards to
a ½-degree accuracy takes great skill.

You begin to see that it is impractical to make cabinets or tables
in polygons greater than octagon because cutting wood with ¼-, ⅛-,
or even 1/16-degree accuracy is extremely difficult. But before we start
the first project of laying out a square, let us examine a tool that we
shall use frequently, the framing square.

3.2
FRAMING
SQUARE

Note that the square shown in Figure 3-4 is made of one piece of metal
but that each leg is named differently. As shown in Figure 3-4, the
body is the wider and longer (2 by 24 inches) and the tongue is the
shorter (1¼ by 18 inches). Also as shown, the square has a face side

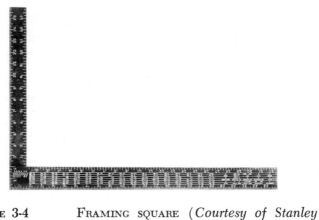
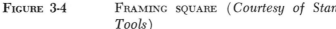

FIGURE 3-4   FRAMING SQUARE (*Courtesy of Stanley
                    Tools*)

and a back side. The parts used in cabinetmaking on the face and back
sides of the square are the measurement scales of the

1 / Face of body outside edge; inches and sixteenths.
2 / Face of body inside edge; inches and eighths.
3 / Face of tongue outside edge; inches and sixteenths.
4 / Face of tongue inside edge; inches and eighths.
5 / Back of body outside edge; inches and twelfths.
6 / Back of body inside edge; inches and sixteenths.

7 /   Back of tongue outside edge; inches and twelfths.

8 /   Back of tongue inside edge; inches and tenths.

9 /   Also on the face side is the *octagon scale.*

This is located on the tongue and looks like a series of dots.

Not used in cabinetmaking is the rafter table, located on the body of the face side. Also not often used are the two tables on the back side: the board foot table on the body and the brace table on the tongue.

This identification of the square is given so that you may easily understand some of its properties. During the next six or seven projects, you will learn to handle and use the framing square as well as some of its tables. Now let us start the first project, which is to make a square layout.

3.3 **HOW TO** **MAKE A** **SQUARE** **LAYOUT**	

The example project in the illustration shows the craftsman making a 36-inch-square layout.

3.3.1 **TOOLS NEEDED**	*Framing square* *Ruler, 6 foot* *Combination square*

3.3.2 **PROCEDURE**	

Take a piece of wood to be used for the project and proceed as follows:

STEP 1 /   Straighten one edge with a plane (if there is not one that is straight already).

STEP 2 /   Place the body of the framing square against the edge of the board as shown in Figure 3-5. Notice how the tongue is laid on the surface of the board.

STEP 3 /   Trace a line with a pencil along the outer edge of the tongue.

FIGURE 3-5   CRAFTSMAN USING A SQUARE

STEP 4 / Continue the line until the desired length of the side of the square is reached. Either of two methods can be used to extend the line when the tongue of the square is not long enough.

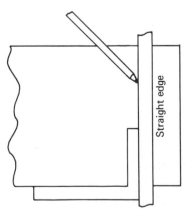

Straight edge

FIGURE 3-6   HOW TO EXTEND THE SIDE OF A SQUARE
WITH A STRAIGHTEDGE

How to Extend the
Line: Method 1

In Figure 3-6 the man knows that the square table top that he is laying out has sides longer than the length of the tongue on the framing square. So he takes a straight-edged board (in this case 4 feet in length) and places the straightedge alongside the tongue's outer edge. Next, he carefully removes the square, sets it aside, and makes a line along the edge of his 4-foot straightedge. NOTE: *This method is best accomplished by two people.*

How to Extend the
Line: Method 2

In Figure 3-7 the man is extending the line of a side by using the body (or tongue, if possible) of the square. First he used the square as shown in Figure 3-5. Then he turned the square around and carefully placed the edge of the body along the line. When it is parallel to the line (no board shows between the existing line and square's edge as viewed straight down), he carefully scribes a line that joins the one already there.

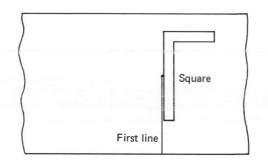

FIGURE 3-7   How to extend a line with a square

STEP 5 / With the first line drawn to the desired length, repeat the process and make the other line (left in our example) at the proper place and of the proper length.

STEP 6 / Finally, lay the square along either line previously drawn and draw the final connecting line. If the side length exceeds the length of the tongue or body, use either method previously explained to extend the line (see Figure 3-8).

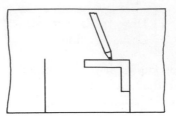

FIGURE 3-8   HOW TO CLOSE THE SQUARE OUTLINE

How To Prove That
Your Square Layout
Is Accurate

To prove that your square is accurate, take the 6-foot folding ruler and measure diagonally as shown in Figure 3-9. Be exact! Record or memorize the length to the nearest 1/16 inch. Then reposition the ruler and measure the other diagonal length. If both are equal, the square is perfect. If not, an error exists because you have a parallelogram but not a square. Recheck your work and measurements.

For small squares up to 10 inches on one side, the combination square can be used effectively. Use steps 2, 3, 5, and 6. Check your work.

A plastic triangle may be substituted for the square but is the least reliable tool to use, especially when making squares the size of table tops.

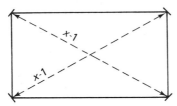

x-1 = both must be
exactly the same
length

FIGURE 3-9   HOW TO CHECK A SQUARE LAYOUT

3.4
HOW TO
MAKE A
RECTANGULAR
LAYOUT

Have you ever given any thought to what makes a good rectangle? One that has been used for many hundreds of years is the golden mean rectangle.

3.4.1
GOLDEN MEAN
RECTANGLE

Before showing you how to obtain a golden mean rectangle, consider this. Television screens originally were circular and people didn't like them, so now they are rectangular. Photos are made in many sizes, but the most popular sizes are 5 by 7, 8 by 10, and 11 by 14 inches. Consider also paintings, china cabinets, home movie screens, and wide-angle screens in theaters. You can see that man enjoys many things that have a particular rectangular shape. One rectangle is especially appealing, the golden mean rectangle. To lay one out requires certain basic steps.

Study Figure 3-10; observe the basic shaded square shape. If we measure along the base of the square shape to a point (X) that is 50 percent along the length, we find the starting point of the radius we shall make. Take a compass or pair of dividers and place one point at X and the other at an opposite corner of the square (a). Draw an arc to the baseline outside the square (b). Next, use a framing square and

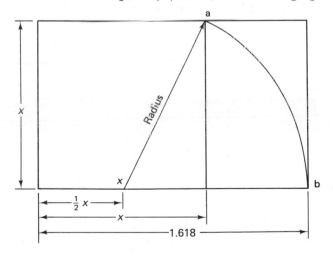

x = length of one side of rectangle
1.618 = length of adjacent side of rectangle times x
Ratio of sides is 1:1.618

FIGURE 3-10   GOLDEN MEAN RECTANGLE

pencil to form a 90-degree corner at point (b) and close in the rectangle across the top. You have just made a golden mean rectangle.

Confused? Don't be; here are step-by-step instructions. Refer to Figure 3-10 as often as you need to.

3.4.2
How to Draw
a Golden Mean
Rectangle

Step 1 / Take a sheet of paper and with pencil and framing square or drafting angle make a square 12 by 12 inches. *Be accurate!*

Step 2 / With a ruler, measure along the base from either corner out to 6 inches. Make a small line or dot.

Step 3 / With a pair of dividers (string can be used), place one point at the center line or dot.

Step 4 / Place the other point of the divider at the upper right-hand corner of the square.

Step 5 / Make an arc with the divider using the point at the upper corner as a start. (*Do not move the lower, center-placed pointer.*) Bring the arc to the right and below an imaginary extension of the base line.

Step 6 / Lay the divider down and with the square

　a / Continue the base line to the arc just completed.

　b / Make a 90-degree corner upward from the base line at the arc's intersection.

　c / Extend the top line of the square to close the rectangle.

　d / Prove your work. The ratio of the sides of a golden mean rectangle is 1 : 1.618. You started out with a 12-inch square. Your longest side on the rectangle should now measure 19⅜ inches.

Now make a project of laying out a full-sized rectangle using the shop method and shop tools.

3.4.3 | *Framing square*   *Straightedge*
Tools Needed | *Ruler, 6 foot*

3.4.4
HOW TO LAY OUT A RECTANGLE

STEP 1 / Select a straight side on the piece to be used. (Plane or cut and dress the piece if required.)

STEP 2 / Place the blade edge of the square along the straightedge, and draw a line along the tongue of the square from the edge of the board.

STEP 3 / Measure from the line drawn in step 2 for the desired length of side of the rectangle and repeat step 2.

STEP 4 / Measure in from the edge with either the square or the ruler along the pencil lines to a point equal to the width of the rectangle and mark.

STEP 5 / Join the two marks to complete the rectangle.

STEP 6 / Prove that the rectangle is accurate by measuring diagonally from corner to corner.

If only one length (side) of a rectangle is known and a golden mean rectangle is desired, refer back to the instructions to make such a rectangle.

3.5
HOW TO MAKE A TRIANGLE LAYOUT

3.5.1
TOOLS NEEDED

Framing square   *Straightedge*
Ruler, 6 foot

3.5.2
HOW TO LAY OUT A TRIANGLE

STEP 1 / Determine the length of one side of the triangle (see Figure 3-11).

STEP 2 / With a square or ruler make a mark (b) halfway between the ends (length) along a straight edge of the piece being used. A 20-inch table, as shown in Figure 3-11, has a mid-point of 10 inches.)

STEP 3 / At the midpoint (the 10-inch point) place the tongue of the square on the side as shown in Figure 3-11 and draw a line along the body from approximately 20 to 24 inches.

STEP 4 / With the square place one point at the end of the base line and intersect line *b* at the 20-inch mark on the square (Figure 3-11).

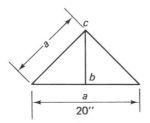

FIGURE 3-11   HOW TO MAKE A TRIANGLE LAYOUT

STEP 5 / Repeat step 4 for the opposite side and complete the triangle.

STEP 6 / Your work requires little proofing since each side is measured already and is equal.

3.6
**HOW TO
MAKE A
DIAMOND-
SHAPED
LAYOUT**

3.6.1
TOOLS NEEDED

Framing square   *Ruler, 6 foot*
Straightedge

3.6.2
HOW TO LAY OUT
A DIAMOND

STEP 1 / Determine the entire length and width of the table. For a perfect diamond the ratio must be 1 : 2, where 1 = width and 2 = length.

STEP 2 / On the piece to be used, mark a midpoint (*a*) as shown in Figure 3-12.

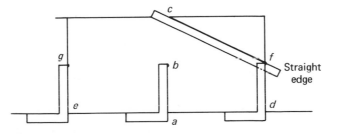

FIGURE 3-12   HOW TO MAKE A DIAMOND LAYOUT

STEP 3 / With a framing square held as shown in Figure 3-12, draw a light line along the tongue or make a point *b* midway across the width and another *c* at the other side. Be accurate.

STEP 4 / If you drew a line, mark a midpoint on it. This equals one-half the width of the layout.

STEP 5 / Move the square to points *d* and *e* (the ends of the layout) and scribe a line as shown. These are the length points of the layout.

STEP 6 / With a ruler, measure a distance equal to *ab* in from the edges at points *d* and *e*. These points are labeled *f* and *g* in Figure 3-12.

STEP 7 / With the straightedge, connect points *af*, *ag*, *cf*, and *cg*.

3.7
HOW TO MAKE AN OCTAGON LAYOUT

An octagon layout consists of an eight-sided figure. Although there are many methods that can be used to obtain it, we shall show you only two shop methods. One uses the octagon scale on the framing square. The other uses a ruler or straightedge.

3.7.1 **TOOLS NEEDED**	*Ruler* *Framing square*	*Dividers* *Straightedge*

3.7.2
HOW TO USE THE
OCTAGON SCALE
ON THE FRAMING
SQUARE

STEP 1 / Use the octagon scale on the tongue face side of the framing
square.

STEP 2 / Lay out a perfect square as described in Section 3.3.

STEP 3 / With the dividers, take as many indicators from the octagon

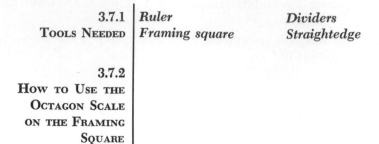

Octagon scale
on framing square

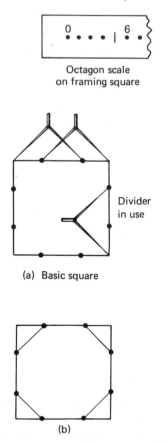

Divider
in use

(a) Basic square

(b)

FIGURE 3-13   HOW TO MAKE AN OCTAGON LAYOUT

scale as there are inches across the laid-out square. (See Figure 3-13; for 6 inches put one pointer at the "0" indicator, the other at the "6" indicator.)

STEP 4 / Place one point of the divider at the corner and make a mark with the other point along the outer edge of the layout (see Figure 3-13a).

STEP 5 / Repeat step 4 on the other three sides.

STEP 6 / Repeat steps 4 and 5, going right instead of left.

STEP 7 / Connect each marked point made by the dividers (see Figure 3-13b). The resultant angle is 45 degrees.

STEP 8 / Prove your work. With a ruler, measure the length of each of the eight sides. They must all be exactly equal.

3.7.3
HOW TO USE
A STRAIGHTEDGE

STEP 1 / Lay out a square the size of the width of the octagon.

STEP 2 / With the straightedge, *lightly* mark the center by placing one edge of the straightedge diagonally across the squared layout (see Figure 3-14).

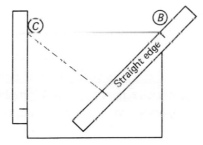

FIGURE 3-14   HOW TO MAKE AN OCTAGON, ALTERNATIVE
                     METHOD

STEP 3 / Shift the straightedge to the opposite two corners and *lightly* mark a line in the middle of the layout (Figure 3-14, callout A). (**NOTE:** *Masking tape may first be applied so that no marks are made on the board surface.*)

STEP 4 / Place one edge and the end of the straightedge from any corner along the lines drawn and mark *on the straightedge* the middle intersect point (Figure 3-14, callout B).

STEP 5 / Take the straightedge, place the end even with the corner of the laid-out square and mark a line even with the mark on the straightedge (Figure 3-14, callout C).

STEP 6 / Repeat step 5 for the other corners, then reverse the procedure, making a total of eight marks.

STEP 7 / Connect the pair of marks as shown in Figure 3-13.

STEP 8 / Prove your work. With a ruler or dividers, measure the length of each side. They must all be the same.

3.7.4
WHAT TO DO IF YOUR CHECK PROVES THAT YOU MADE AN ERROR

STEP 1 / Check your square:

  a / Is each side accurate in length?

  b / Are the diagonals of the same length?

STEP 2 / Check your dividers:

  a / Have you placed the dividers' points at position zero and the inch indicator correctly?

  b / Have the dividers moved?

  c / Have you placed the dividers accurately on each corner?

  d / Have you made all eight points correctly?

  e / Have you drawn connecting lines accurately?

STEP 3 / Check your center point and straightedge mark:

  a / Have you determined the exact center?

  b / Have you accurately marked your straightedge?

  c / Have you made your eight marks correctly from the four corners?

3.8
HOW TO MAKE A CIRCLE

The making of a circle is shown by two methods, with a piece of string and with a pair of dividers.

3.8.1	*String and brad*	*Dividers*
TOOLS NEEDED	*Ruler*	

3.8.2
HOW TO USE
A STRING

CAUTION

This method is not 100 percent accurate, but it does work.

STEP 1 / Mark the center of the layout and drive a brad partway in.

STEP 2 / Tie one end of the string around the brad.

STEP 3 / Tie the other end of the string around a pencil. Make the tie so that the pencil when held straight up equals the radius of the circle desired.

STEP 4 / Make a circle with the pencil; be sure to keep the line tight (see Figure 3-15).

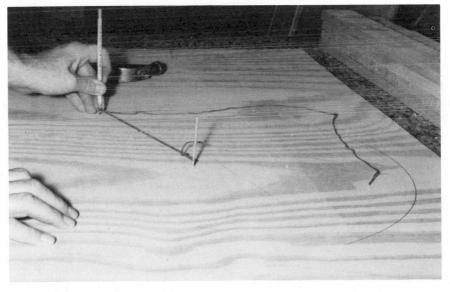

FIGURE 3-15   HOW TO MAKE A CIRCLE LAYOUT WITH STRING

3.8.3
How to Use
a Pair of Dividers

STEP 1 / Mark the center of a layout.

STEP 2 / Set and lock the dividers to a distance equal to the radius
of the circle desired.

STEP 3 / Place one point of the divider on the center mark.

STEP 4 / Use the other point to scribe a circle.

3.9
HOW TO
MAKE A
HEXAGON
LAYOUT

Three shop methods for making a hexagon are explained in this section:
making a layout with a circle, with a framing square, and with a piece
of string. Also provided for you is a check to determine your accuracy.

3.9.1
Tools Needed

Ruler   *Dividers or string*
Framing square

3.9.2
How to Use
a Circle

STEP 1 / Determine the width of the layout.

STEP 2 / Divide the width by 2; the result is the radius.

STEP 3 / Starting at the center, scribe a circle with dividers using
the radius previously determined.

STEP 4 / With the dividers unchanged, place one point on any part
of the circle (see Figure 3-16).

STEP 5 / With the other end of the divider, make a mark at both
points where the divider intersects the circle (Figure 3-16,
callout A).

STEP 6 / Move the divider and place one point at either mark made
in step 5.

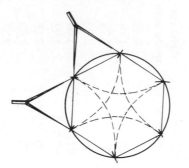

FIGURE 3-16   HOW TO MAKE A HEXAGON LAYOUT

STEP 7 / With the other point, make a mark that intersects the circle. Continue until all six marks are made.

STEP 8 / Connect each mark to its adjacent mark with a line.

3.9.3
HOW TO USE
A FRAMING SQUARE

STEP 1 / From Table 3-1 (p. 78) determine that a 60-degree angle requires using the 7-inch mark on the body and the 4-inch mark on the tongue of the square.

STEP 2 / Determine what length each side of the hexagon is to be.

STEP 3 / Using a straight side on the piece being laid out, place the body with the 7-inch mark (*a*) parallel to the edge as shown in Figure 3-17.

STEP 4 / Make a mark (*b*) on the piece at the 4-inch mark of the tongue.

STEP 5 / Draw a line with square or straightedge between the two points at 7 inches (*a*) and 4 inches (*b*). Make the line as long as the desired length of one side of the layout [labeled end point (*c*)].

STEP 6 / Reverse the square and repeat steps 3, 4, and 5 to make a second side. [Start again at point (*a*). Label the end of the line (*d*).]

STEP 7 / With the square placed along the edge of the board at points *c* and *d*, make a line along the tongue equal in length to sides *ab* or *ad*. Label the ends *e* and *f*, respectively.

STEP 8 / Once again lay the square parallel to each line just drawn

TABLE 3-1
PROPERTIES OF POLYGONS *

Name	No. sides	Setting (square inches)	Exterior angle	Interior angle	Miter angle	Area for unity side
Triangle	3	7 4	120	60	30	0.433
Square	4	12 12	90	90	45	1
Pentagon	5	13¾ 10	72	108	54	1.72
Hexagon	6	4 7	60	120	60	2.6
Heptagon	7	12½ 6	51.43	128.57	64.29	3.63
Octagon	8	18 7½	45	135	67.5	4.82
Nonagon	9	22½ 9	40	140	70	6.18
Decagon	10	9½ 3	36	144	72	7.69
Undecagon	11	10¾ 3	32.7	147.3	73.65	9.37
Duodecagon	12	11¼ 3	30	150	75	11.2

* Courtesy of Howard W. Sams & Co., Inc.

in step 7 with the blade measurement of 7 inches at the end of the line, first point *e*, then point *f*.

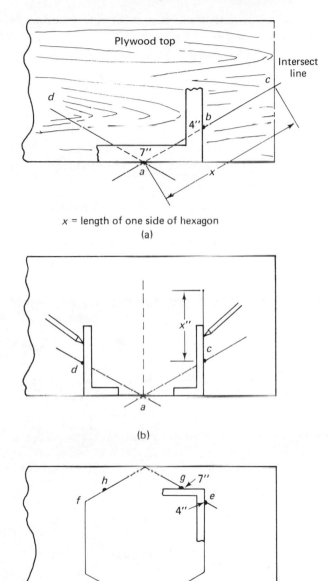

x = length of one side of hexagon

(a)

(b)

(c)

FIGURE 3-17   HOW TO MAKE A HEXAGON WITH A SQUARE

Step 9 / Mark a point on the layout equal to 4 inches along the tongue (labeled g and h).

Step 10 / Draw a line that connects points e and g and another that connects f and h.

Step 11 / Extend the lines to complete the hexagon.

3.9.4
How to Use
a String

Caution

This method is not as accurate as ones described previously.

Figure 3-18   How to make a hexagon layout with string

STEP 1 /   Determine the radius of the layout by dividing the desired diameter by 2.

STEP 2 /   Mark the center of the layout and nail a small brad partway in.

STEP 3 /   Tie a string around the brad and the other end around the pencil so that the pencil tip reaches exactly the outer edge of the radius. Scribe a circle.

STEP 4 /   Remove the brad and string and transfer the brad to any point on the edge of the circle. Stretch the line and with the pencil draw an intersecting line (see Figure 3-18).

STEP 5 /   Make five more intersectional points.

STEP 6 /   Connect the adjacent intersectional points to form the hexagon.

STEP 7 /   Place the square along the straightedge with the outer edge of the tongue at the original point (a). The tongue edge when extended must intersect at the opposite (f and g), respectively. All six lines must be of exactly the same length. With a ruler, measure the diameter of each set of opposite points; they must each be exactly the same.

3.10
HOW TO
MAKE AN
ELLIPSE

Two shop methods are presented for your use. With both there is a chance for inaccuracy, but they are both very easy to use. The first method uses a string, where a loop of string is stretched about a pencil and two brads or nails. The second method is more difficult and uses a straightedge. Two marks are made on the straightedge. One mark is always kept on the vertical line drawn on the table top. The other mark on the straightedge is kept on the horizontal line, which is also drawn on the table top. The ellipse is always marked at the same end of the straightedge.

3.10.1
TOOLS NEEDED | *Ruler*   *Straightedge*
| *String and brads*

3.10.2
How to Use
a String

Caution

This method may be inaccurate.

Step 1 / Determine the desired length and width of the ellipse.

Step 2 / Draw two lines, *AB* and *CD*, at a 90-degree angle that intersects at point *E* (see Figure 3-19).

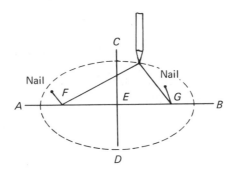

Figure 3-19   How to make an ellipse layout

Step 3 / With a ruler (or dividers), measure the distance *CE* and make two marks *F* and *G* along the axis *AB* from *E* *equal* in length to *CE*.

Step 4 / Insert pins or brads at points *F* and *G*.

Step 5 / Tie a piece of string so that it forms a loop equal in length to *AG* or *FGC*.

Step 6. / Insert a pencil top inside the looped string, pull it tight, and scribe the ellipse. *Keep the string against pins F and G at all times.*

3.10.3
How to Use
a Straightedge

Step 1 / Determine the desired length and width of the ellipse.

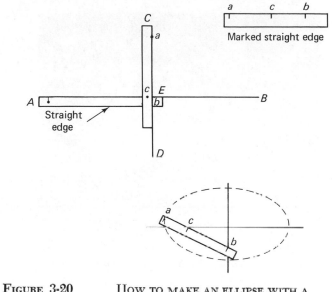

FIGURE 3-20   HOW TO MAKE AN ELLIPSE WITH A
                     STRAIGHTEDGE

STEP 2 / Draw two axes, AB and CD, that intersect at 90 degrees at point E (Figure 3-20).

STEP 3 / With the straightedge, make a set of marks *on the straight-edge* equal to AE (*ab*) and another set equal to CE (*ac*).

STEP 4 / Slide the straightedge around so that point *b* is always on axis CD and point C is always on axis AB, and make a set of marks at point *a*. Connect all points.

3.11
HOW TO
MAKE A
POLYGON

Table 3-1 provides you with the tools to make any polygon you may wish, ranging from a 3-sided triangle to a 12-sided duodecagon. The two columns of settings represent framing, one for the body and the other for the tongue. The *external angle* is the angle measured from the base line, where the base line equals 0 to 180 degrees (Figure 3-21). The *internal angle* is the remaining portion of the 180 degrees; for a pentagon that would be $180 - 72 = 108$ degrees.

FIGURE 3-21   HOW TO MAKE A POLYGON FROM TABLE
                     3-1

We have examined some of the usual furniture shapes. The methods illustrated in laying them out made use of shop tools. Geometric principles can be substituted if one has the knowledge. However, the shop method should prove adequate since material usually used to lay out cabinet tops will be plywood or particle board, and one or more edges will be *true* (straight). The shape of a piece is a design feature and often the most distinctive one. There are other features that create distinction; they are accents and are called *moldings.*

3.12
MOLDING

Moldings are made for many purposes and come in a great variety of styles and shapes, a few of which are *plant-ons, veneer strips, base moldings, crown moldings,* and *ornamental moldings.*

3.12.1
PLANT-ON
AND ITS USES

Plant-ons are by definition molded, sculptured, or carved assemblies glued to a surface to create a relief effect. They are, as a rule, made

FIGURE 3-22   PLANT-ONS

85

from wood and plastic. They can be bought finished and unfinished.
Figure 3-22 shows two examples of plant-ons. The one on the hexagonal
table adds relief to plain sides, whereas the rectangular table uses the
plant-on to add a subtle accent of Spanish styling. The plant-on is especially useful when making provincial and Mediterranean furniture.
In some cases it may also be used on Early American furniture.

To stimulate a carved door, a recess is made on the face of a
door by gluing pieces around the outer edge (Figure 3-23). Then the
plant-on is inserted into the recess, where it is glued. Or a panel door
may be made with the rails (top and bottom) and styles (side pieces)
mortised and tenoned together. Then a ¼-inch panel is inserted at the
back, and a plant-on can be glued to the ¼-inch panel. The width of
the rails and styles must be accurately figured so an exact recess in the
center can be created.

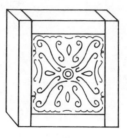

FIGURE 3-23   HOW TO INSERT A PLANT-ON IN A DOOR

Plant-ons can be used to decorate *crowns* on cabinets. They may
also provide ornament for table legs between the table top and skirt
edge.

3.12.2
VENEER STRIP
AND ITS USES

The veneer strips shown in Figure 3-24 are made from various kinds
of wood. As you can see, the designs and patterns that are created are
many. Also note the variety of sizes. These strips may (1) be glued on
as an overlay or (2) may be set in flush with the surrounding wood. To
set them in flush requires routing a groove the width of the veneer
strip to a depth equal in thickness to the veneer.

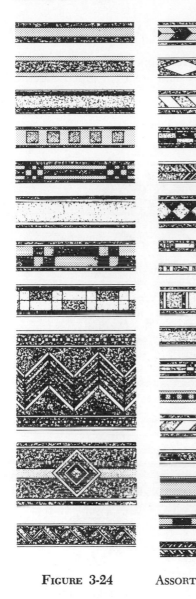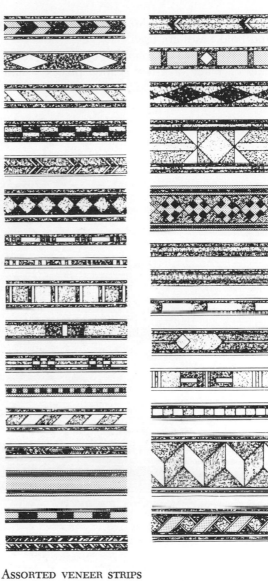

FIGURE 3-24   ASSORTED VENEER STRIPS

3.12.3
BASE MOLDING
AND ITS USES
AND STYLES

The base of a cabinet is frequently one of its distinctive features. In many styles, such as Mediterranean and Early American, rather large and bold bases are used.

A base may be molded or shaped from one piece of wood, or it may be made of a few shaped pieces which are then glued together as shown in Figure 3-25.

FIGURE 3-25   CABINET WITH BASE MADE FROM MORE THAN ONE PIECE (*Courtesy of Drexel*)

On kitchen cabinets, bathroom vanities, and certain modern cabinets the bases are straight with no shapes and are recessed. On the kitchen and bath cabinets the recessed base provides toe space for persons standing next to the cabinet. The base is usually recessed 3 inches and has a height of 3½ to 4 inches (Figure 3-26).

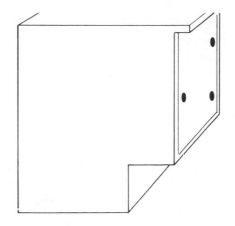

FIGURE 3-26 RECESSED BASE ON CABINET

FIGURE 3-27 CROWN MOLDING ON EARLY AMERICAN CABINET (*Courtesy of Temple Stuart*)

3.12.4
CROWN MOLDING
AND ITS USES
AND STYLES

Whether a wall cabinet reaches the ceiling or not, it usually has a crown molding. The upper part of a cabinet, like the base, aids in creating a particular style. It may be simple, as on kitchen cabinets, or it may be ornate as on French, Spanish, or Italian provincial, or Early American cabinets (Figure 3-27). More often than not, the elaborate crown on a cabinet is made from more than one piece of wood. Each piece is usually shaped separately, then the pieces are glued together.

3.12.5
ORNAMENTAL
MOLDING

Some molding can be purchased already shaped: quarter-round, half-round, cove, bed molding, and others. More often than not, though, they are made from fir or pine. On almost all cabinets, fir is unacceptable because of its color or grain. Pine, on the other hand, may be used when the remainder of the cabinet is made from light woods. It has a fault, though; it is very soft and porous. It will take stain more rapidly than hardwoods and become darker.

The best material for ornamental molding is the same stock that is used to make facings. By using the same material, you are assured of matching the color and the grain.

Most moldings can be made by a person who has normal shop tools. Table saws or radial saws can make the large cove moldings; and the router, the radial arm saw with the shaping heads, or the shaper can make the smaller moldings. Figure 3-28 shows the various molding shapes that can be made from routing and shaping bits.

QUESTIONS

1 / What is the criterion that is almost always used to describe the shape of a cabinet?

2 / What is the primary purpose of the miter square?

3 / What is the octagon scale on the framing square and where is it located?

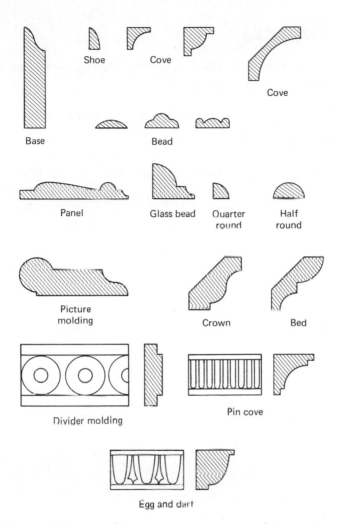

Shoe   Cove

Cove

Base   Bead

Panel   Glass bead   Quarter round   Half round

Picture molding   Crown   Bed

Divider molding   Pin cove

Egg and dart

FIGURE 3-28   SHAPES OF MOLDINGS AND THEIR NAMES

4 / What are the steps to be undertaken when laying out a square?

5 / What are the steps required to make a golden mean rectangle?

6 / How is a midpoint located when a triangle is being laid out?

7 / What ratio is needed to lay out a perfect diamond?

8 / What are the steps to be undertaken when laying out an octagon?

9 / What angle is measured from the base line where the line equals 0 to 180 degrees?

10 / What type of furniture utilizes plant-ons especially effectively?

PROJECT |

Draw a plan for an end table. Make your drawing according to the following details:

a /   Make the top equal to a "golden mean rectangle" where 1 in the formula 1 : 1.618 equals 20".

b /   Make its height just below the arm of the sofa.

c /   Design it with Early American features.

UNIT II

Unit II, which consists of a series of six chapters, examines and instructs the reader in the making of a number of cabinet joints: butt, rabbet, dado, mortise, tenon, and dowel. Each chapter details when to use the joint, why it is advantageous, and what design effects it can create. Equally important are the step-by-step procedures for making the joint with hand tools, portable shop power tools, and shop bench or floor-model tools. Each chapter is organized in this way so that you can quickly locate the method appropriate for the tools you have on hand. Discussion of each procedure is preceded by a list of tools needed, so you need simply take the book to the store or copy out the list of tools before making your purchases.

4

HOW TO
MAKE
A BUTT JOINT

This is the first in a series of chapters that will help you to understand the various joints used in woodworking. Each chapter explains techniques for making the joint as well as suggestions as to when to use the joint.

After reading about how and when to use the butt joint, three methods are provided which explain how to make the joint. The first method shows how to make the butt joint with hand tools. The second method shows and explains how to make the joint with portable power tools. The third method shows how to make the joint with bench power tools.

4.1
FUNCTIONAL
QUALITIES
AND
APPLICATIONS

As with any joint that is used in woodworking it must provide an answer to a problem of joining two boards together. The butt joint provides such a capability. When pieces that are to be joined are properly prepared and proper glues are used, the results are very good. A butt joint can be a very good joint and a very easy joint to make. Figure 4-1 shows a butt joint. The joint, as shown, provides a means for making a wide surface. Since the two boards are in *complete* contact over their entire length, the joint should have good strength once the glue dries.

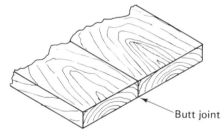

Butt joint

FIGURE 4-1   BUTT JOINT (PARALLEL BOARDS)

A right-angle butt joint is frequently used on cabinet frames, especially in kitchen cabinets. This joint has less quality than the parallel joint, as can be seen in Figure 4-2. The joint is essentially a weak one but very functional, and when it is built carefully, it is quite adequate. Our example shows (by use of the weight) the way the joint is weak. If you use a saw with many teeth—a No. 12 or No. 14 hand saw, or a planer blade with upward of 200 teeth in a power machine—when cutting the board, your joint will hold better and will be stronger. Why? Look at Figure 4-3, which shows two boards cut off. One (a) has been cut with a standard No. 8 hand saw, the other (b) has been cut with a planer saw. The No. 8 hand saw, although classified as a cross-cut saw, actually makes a very ragged cut. You can see by the figure that the edges are coarse and torn and that the interior fibers are torn also. The result is a very porous end cut. Now look again at (b). Notice how smooth the edges are and how little the inner fibers are torn.

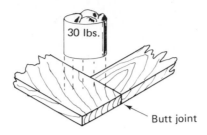

FIGURE 4-2   BUTT JOINT WITH BOARDS AT RIGHT ANGLES

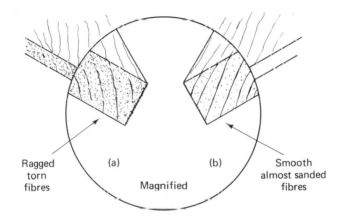

FIGURE 4-3   END CUTS FOR BUTT JOINTING

What difference does this really make? It makes a great deal of difference. For any good joint to be really bonded with strength, the glue must cover 100 percent of the surface. In Figure 4-3a the glue will seep into the torn fibers, and only those fibers that come in contact with the glue and other surface will bond. However, in Figure 4-3b, because of the smoothness of the cut (no tearing), the glue will bond almost all fibers to the other board and result in a joint of very good quality.

When large wide surfaces are needed and plywood is not to be used, the butt joint is frequently used. When picture frames are cut, their miters are usually butted together and glued. Besides its use in facing kitchen cabinets, the butt joint can be used on any occasional table or cabinet, for example, when applying edge molding, plant-ons, or base molding.

4.2
DESIGN EFFECTS CREATED BY USE OF THE BUTT JOINT

First and foremost the application of veneer to a table top makes the most dramatic and effective use of the butt joint. Selected pieces of fine, matching veneers are carefully cut on biases and butted to create designs that emanate from the natural grain of the wood. Figure 4-4 shows part of a table top in which a craftsman has butted veneer together to create a design effect.

Another design effect created with a butt joint is the inlaid chess table, wherein squares of birch and walnut are butted against each other and then a frame is butted to the outer edges of the 64-square layout. You have just been given a few examples of the butt joint as it is used to create a design effect. But can the joint be used to overcome problems?

FIGURE 4-4   DESIGN EFFECTS WITH VENEER AND THE BUTT JOINT

4.3
PROBLEMS SOLVED BY USE OF THE BUTT JOINT

The butt joint is very effective in joining two or more boards together to make a wide surface. Since most lumber that we buy is flat-cut, warping (an unwanted curving of the board) occurs. This is especially so with boards 6 to 12 inches wide. The gluing together of two or three 6-inch boards to make a flat, wide surface frequently results in an undesirable product. Figure 4-5a shows such an example. The butt joint can be used very effectively to overcome this problem. Notice in Figure 4-5b that the boards have been cut narrow (approximately 2½ inches) and have been turned to where every other board is placed same side up.

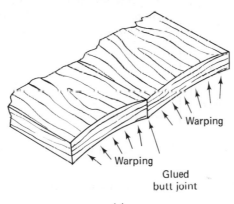

Warping

Warping

Glued
butt joint

(a)

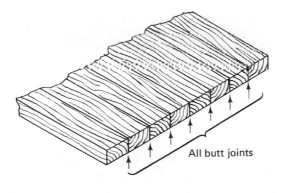

All butt joints

(b)

FIGURE 4-5   HOW TO ELIMINATE WARPING WITH BUTT
                 JOINTS

4.4
HOW TO
MAKE A
BUTT JOINT
WITH HAND
TOOLS

The first method of making a butt joint is by use of hand tools. We shall examine each of the two basic applications of the butt joint.

4.4.1
TOOLS NEEDED

Jack and surface plane   *No. 10 (or finer) hand saw*
Combination square   *Bar clamps, 2*

4.4.2
How to Butt
Two Edges
Together

STEP 1 /   Lay the surfaces that are to be butted against each other (Figure 4-6a).

STEP 2 /   Determine if they exactly touch each other for the full length.

STEP 3 /   Plane, using a surface or jack plane, the boards wherever a bulge or hollow appears (Figure 4-6b).

STEP 4 /   Repeat step 1 as often as needed. When the boards fit perfectly, apply glue and a clamp (Figure 4-6c).

4.4.3
How to Butt an
End Butt and
a Side Butt

STEP 1 /   Make sure that the side (edge) of the board is straight and 90 degrees in angle. Use the combination square (Figure 4-6d).

STEP 2 /   Cut, with a fine-toothed saw, the end of board to be joined. Be especially careful to obtain the angle desired (Figure 4-6e).

STEP 3 /   Check the cut for a 90-degree fit as in step 1 (Figure 4-6d).

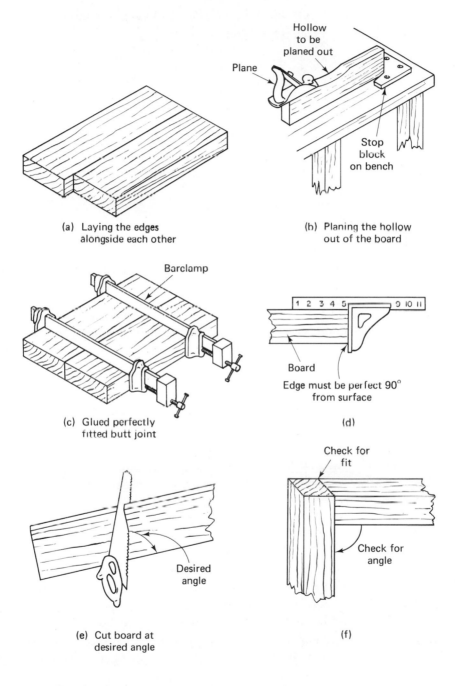

(a) Laying the edges
alongside each other

(b) Planing the hollow
out of the board

(c) Glued perfectly
fitted butt joint

(d)

(e) Cut board at
desired angle

(f)

FIGURE 4-6   HOW TO MAKE A BUTT JOINT

STEP 4 /   Lay the pieces flat and check for fit and angle (Figure 4-6f).

STEP 5 /   Glue and clamp the joint.

4.5 HOW TO MAKE A BUTT JOINT WITH PORTABLE POWER TOOLS AND HAND TOOLS

To make the butt joint with portable power tools requires exacting skill. These tools are very fast. They weigh a lot and they can easily destroy a piece of wood. One of the two types of butt joints requires use of the portable planer. The other type of butt joint requires the use of the plane and power hand saw. The two types are the butting of two edges of wood, and the butting of an edge and an end.

4.5.1 TOOLS NEEDED	*Combination square* *Portable hand saw*	*Portable planer* *Bar clamps, 2*

4.5.2 How to Butt Two Edges Together

STEP 1 /   Lay against each other the surfaces that are to be butted (Figure 4-6a).

STEP 2 /   Determine if they exactly fit against each other for their entire length.

STEP 3 /   With a portable electric planer, dress the edge of the board (both if needed) until it is straight (Figure 4-6b).

STEP 4 /   With a combination square, check the edge just planed to be sure that it is cut at 90 degrees throughout its entire length (Figure 4-6d).

STEP 5 /   If the boards fit, glue and clamp them (Figure 4-6e).

4.5.3
How to Butt
an Edge to an
End Piece

Step 1 / Make sure that the edge of the board to receive the end butt is straight and at 90 degrees (Figure 4-6d).

Step 2 / Cut the board that is to have the end cut with a portable electric saw (Figure 4-7). *Use a planer saw blade.*

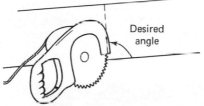
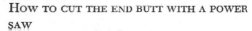

Desired angle

Figure 4-7   How to cut the end butt with a power saw

Step 3 / Check the end cut for the accurate angle desired and 90-degree cut (Figure 4-6d).

Step 4 / Lay both pieces to be joined flat on a bench and check the joint (Figure 4-6f).

Step 5 / Glue and clamp.

4.6
HOW TO
MAKE A
BUTT JOINT
WITH BENCH
POWER TOOLS

By far the easiest method of making the butt joint is with bench tools. The jointer will easily plane the edge of a board straight and at 90 degrees with the surface in one operation. A radial arm saw will easily cut an end of the board to make an end and a side butt joint. If a radial arm saw is not available but a table saw is, the cutoff guide set at 0 degrees can be used. This guide, when used properly, can guide the board through the saw blade, and an accurate end cut can be made.

4.6.1 TOOLS NEEDED	*Radial arm saw or table saw* *Jointer, 6 inch, or equivalent*	*Clamps*

4.6.2 HOW TO BUTT TWO EDGES TOGETHER

STEP 1 / Dress the two pieces to be glued together on the jointer (Figure 4-8).

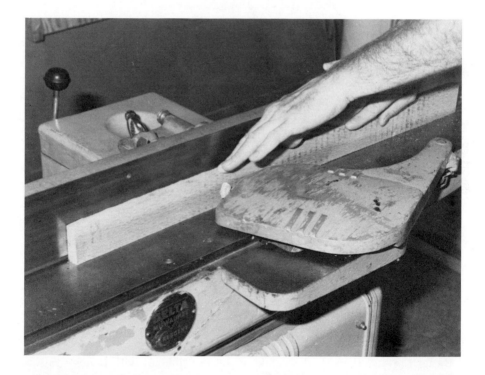

FIGURE 4-8   HOW TO JOIN THE EDGE OF A BOARD

STEP 2 / Lay the dressed edges against each other and check for total contact. Redo either piece on the jointer as necessary.

STEP 3 / Glue and clamp.

4.6.3
How to Butt
an End to an
Edge Piece

Step 1 / Dress the edge of the piece if necessary (Figure 4-8).

Step 2 / Place the other piece (the one that is to have the end cut) against the guide on the radial arm saw. With a fine-toothed blade (200 teeth per blade), draw the saw through the board (Figure 4-9).

Figure 4-9   How to cut the end of a board with a radial arm saw

Step 3 / Lay the pieces on a flat table and check the fit. All surfaces that are to be glued must touch.

Step 4 / Recut as necessary.

Step 5 / Glue and clamp.

QUESTIONS |

1 / What does the butt joint provide a means of making?

2 / What steps must be taken to make the butt joint functionally stronger?

3 / What makes a most dramatic and effective use of veneer in its application of veneer to a table top?

4 / What problem can the butt joint be very effectively used to overcome?

5 / What are the steps needed in butting an end butt to a butt side?

6 / What are some characteristics to be careful of when making butt joints with portable power tools?

7 / What degree of an angle is needed to make a butt joint?

8 / What machine easily planes the edge of a board straight and at 90 degrees?

9 / A radial arm saw will easily cut the end of a board to make what degree?

10 / What is the most important thing to remember when gluing butt joints?

PROJECT |

Take some maple and make a meat cutting board, joining all the pieces together using the butt joint. When the pieces fit properly, glue them together with waterproof glue, and clamp them. Cut and sand the board to be 18″ wide by 24″ long by 2″ thick.

5

HOW TO
MAKE
A RABBET JOINT

The rabbet joint, which has been in use for hundreds of years, was identified briefly in Chapter 1. This joint can be made relatively easy with a specially designed hand plane called a *side rabbet plane* (see Figure 5-1). It can also be made with a hand saw and a chisel, as we shall see in this chapter.

The joint can also be made with a router, using a dado or rabbet bit, and it can also be made with a table saw, radial arm, and jointer.

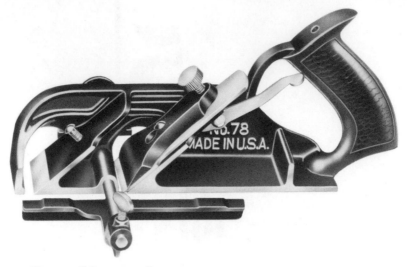

FIGURE 5-1   RABBET PLANE WITH ADJUSTABLE GUIDE
                (*Courtesy of Stanley Tools*)

**5.1
FUNCTIONAL
QUALITIES
AND
APPLICATIONS**

Figure 5-2 shows a rabbet joint. Notice how an L-shaped cut is made
into the piece of wood across the end and along the side. This cut is
never made arbitrarily. It always conforms in its size to the dimension
of the piece it will join. For example, if a rabbet joint is used to join

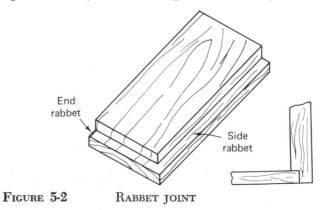

FIGURE 5-2   RABBET JOINT

the sides of a box made from ¾-inch stock lumber, one dimension of the rabbet will be ¾ inch. The other will be a selected depth. Refer to Figure 5-3 and note how the dimensions are cut to allow for an exact fit of an end piece.

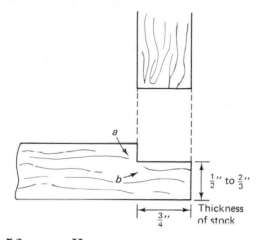

FIGURE 5-3   HOW TO MAKE A RABBET JOINT CONFORM

A joint made with a rabbet is functionally stronger than a butt joint. In the first place, there are two gluing surfaces, compared with one in the butt joint. Figure 5-3 shows these as *a* and *b*. Second, if nails and screws can be used, they can be driven from both sides (Figure 5-4).

Another quality feature of the rabbet joint is that it is easier to make a square corner. After the rabbet is cut across the end of a board and the second piece used in the joint is tightly glued or butted to

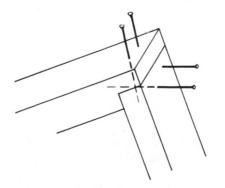

FIGURE 5-4   HOW TO NAIL A RABBET JOINT

surfaces *a* and *b* (Figure 5-3), a square joint results. Another quality feature of the joint is that the piece being fit into the rabbet cut will not have an end showing, and the piece with the rabbet cut will only have approximately half its end thickness showing.

The rabbet joint is used extensively. Wooden windows have rabbets where the glass fits; so do picture frames. When cabinet backs are hidden from side view, a rabbet is made into the side pieces and top piece. Box fronts and backs and certain cabinets have all four sides rabbeted.

5.2
PROBLEMS
SOLVED BY
USE OF THE
RABBET JOINT

Squaring a corner is always a problem and the use of a rabbet aids in making the corner square. When the two pieces of the butt joint were glued or nailed, the end cut had to be rigidly held even with the outside of the other piece. Using the rabbet makes the job easier. The piece with no cut is securely held against surface *a* as shown in Figure 5-3. It is straight and square.

Correcting for a twist in either piece being used can easily be done with a rabbet joint. Stock sometimes has a slight twist in it. This means that when the board is laid flat, three of the four corners on either flat side touch the surface and the fourth does not. Using a rabbet joint correctly can eliminate the twist.

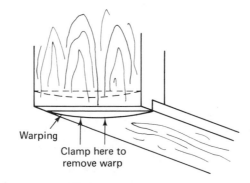

Warping

Clamp here to
remove warp

FIGURE 5-5   HOW TO STRAIGHTEN A WARP WITH A
                    RABBET JOINT

Warping can be eliminated by use of the rabbet joint. For instance, if a side of a cabinet or bookcase is warped, the warp can be eliminated by clamping the warped section tightly into the rabbet (see Figure 5-5). Removing a bow in the length of a side of a bookcase can be done easily with the use of the rabbet joint. By manually pulling the sides in (or pushing them out) or by clamping the sides, a bow can be eliminated. Once straightened, the joint can be nailed or glued and left to dry (see Figure 5-6).

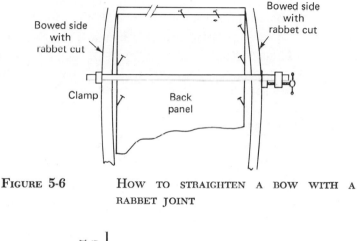

FIGURE 5-6   HOW TO STRAIGHTEN A BOW WITH A RABBET JOINT

5.3
HOW TO MAKE A RABBET JOINT WITH HAND TOOLS

There are quite a few possible tools to use to make a rabbet joint. The length of the rabbet usually will dictate which tools best fit the job. Another factor that determines the best tool to use is the grain of the wood. Planes are usually used when the rabbet runs parallel to the grain. However, a saw is a better tool to use when cutting across the grain.

	Cross-cut hand saw	*Chisel*
5.3.1	*Side rabbet plane*	*Combination square*
TOOLS NEEDED	*with adjustable*	
	attachment	

5.3.2
How to Cut
a Rabbet Joint
Across the Grain
with Hand Saw
and Chisel

STEP 1 /   Mark a line on the surface where the cut is to be made. The position of the line should be equal to the thickness of the board fitting into the rabbet (Figure 5-7a).

STEP 2 /   Reset the combination square and mark the depth of the cut (Figure 5-7a).

STEP 3 /   With a fine-toothed (No. 10) hand saw, cut along the top (flat surface) line. The line should still be seen when the cut is complete. Make the cut equal to the depth of the desired rabbet (Figure 5-7b).

STEP 4 /   With sharpened chisel and mallet, chip along the end line, removing stock and making a rabbet (Figure 5-7c).

STEP 5 /   Smooth the chiseled edge with a chisel.

STEP 6 /   Sandpaper the joint lightly. *Do not round* the surfaces or an improper fit will result.

5.3.3
How to Plane
a Rabbet Joint
with the Grain
Along the Side
of the Stock

STEP 1 /   Mark the width and depth of the rabbet with a combination square according to steps 1 and 2 in Section 5.3.2 (Figure 5-7a and b).

STEP 2 /   Set the adjustable guide on the side rabbet plane so that the edge of the blade is even with either line. The plane can be used either on the edge or on the flat surface. The direction of the grain in the wood and side of the plane that has the guide will dictate how the plane is used (Figure 5-7d).

STEP 3 /   Make successive cuts with the plane. Be sure to hold the guide against the wood surface.

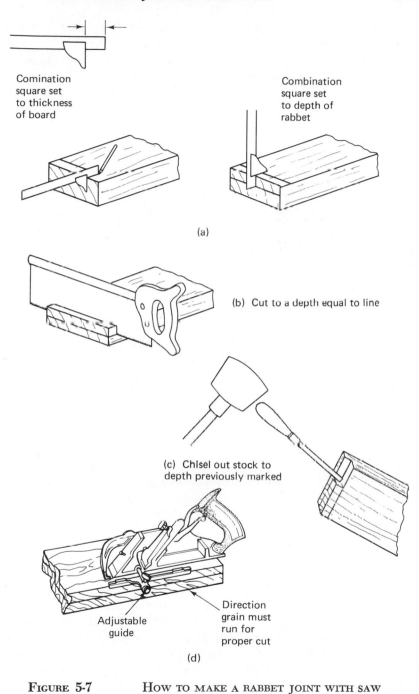

Comination square set to thickness of board

Combination square set to depth of rabbet

(a)

(b) Cut to a depth equal to line

(c) Chisel out stock to depth previously marked

Adjustable guide

Direction grain must run for proper cut

(d)

FIGURE 5-7   HOW TO MAKE A RABBET JOINT WITH SAW
AND CHISEL

STEP 4 / Stop planing when the cut touches the entire length of the line.

STEP 5 / Try to fit the other piece into the rabbet cut. Dress any parts of the cut that are out of square.

5.4
HOW TO MAKE A RABBET JOINT WITH PORTABLE ELECTRIC TOOLS

Either the router or portable power saw can be used to make a rabbet. Of the two machines, the router makes a finer cut and does it in one operation. The power saw requires two separate cuts. The router is limited because of the sizes of bits that it uses. For instance, if the rabbet were to be 1 inch deep by ¾ inch wide, a saw would probably be used. Most router rabbet bits are limited to ½-inch-deep cuts and none are 1 inch across.

5.4.1
TOOLS NEEDED

Portable router with rabbet bits   *Straightedge*
Portable power saw   *Clamps*
   Combination square

5.4.2
HOW TO CUT A RABBET JOINT WITH A ROUTER AND RABBET BIT

Two types of router blades, shown in Figure 5-8, may be used to make a rabbet. Figure 5-8a shows a typical rabbet bit. Notice that the lower part of the bit is in the form of a guide pin. When using this bit, the pin portion is held against the stock as the router is moved along the piece. These bits are made to cut rabbets of ⅛ to ¾ inch. The most common bits are the ¼ inch and ⅜ inch.

The second bit shown in Figure 5-8b is actually a dado bit. We

(a) Rabbet bit with guide tip

(b) Dado bit used to make
a rabbet joint

FIGURE 5-8   BITS USED TO MAKE RABBETS

have not discussed the dado yet, but it is a type of joint. The dado bit
can also be used to make a rabbet. However, the guide attachment
must be used on the router since there is no guide pin on the bit. To use
a dado bit to cut a rabbet you must not only adjust the depth of the
cut but set the guide attachment for the desired width of the rabbet.

STEP 1 / Install the router bit into the router and secure it firmly.

STEP 2 / Adjust the router base for the desired *depth* of the rabbet.

STEP 3 / When using a dado bit, adjust the guide for the desired width of the rabbet.

STEP 4 / Try the router on a scrap piece of stock.

CAUTION

Do not use any stock less than 18 inches long because control of both piece and router cannot be handled without the chance of cutting your hands or fingers. Clamp the piece to the work bench.

TIP

Use of the router when making a rabbet cut:

1 / To avoid splitting and splintering, firmly hold the router and gently feed it part of the width into the stock, moving the router in the direction opposite to the one in which the blade is spinning. It will cut, but only in small pieces. Follow this cut with a regular cut at full width.

2 / To make an end rabbet on a narrow piece of stock, make a jig as shown in Figure 5-9. Clamp the stock firmly.

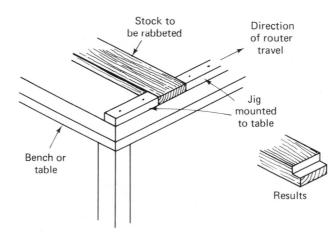

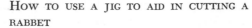

FIGURE 5-9   HOW TO USE A JIG TO AID IN CUTTING A RABBET

5.4.3
How to Cut
a Rabbet Joint
with a Portable
Power Saw

STEP 1 / Lay out the width and depth of the rabbet with a combination square in the same way you would if you were using the hand-saw method.

STEP 2 / Set the saw blade for the desired depth of the rabbet by adjusting the base on the saw.

STEP 3 / Install the adjustable guide on the saw.

STEP 4 / Set the guide for the width of the desired rabbet.

STEP 5 / Try the saw on a scrap piece of stock. If correct, proceed to make the first rabbet cut.

STEP 6 / Reset both the depth and width adjustments for the other cut (the edge cut). Clamp the board to the upright position.

STEP 7 / Holding the saw very straight, make the second cut (Figure 5-10).

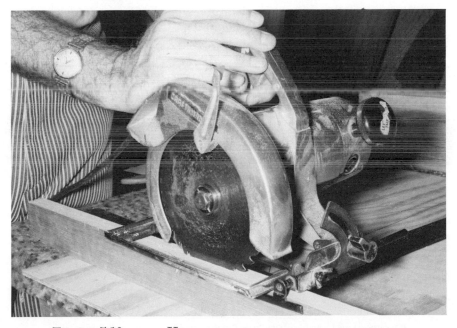

FIGURE 5-10   How to make an edge cut with a power saw

NOTE: The second cut can only be made on the *long* side of a piece of stock. It *cannot* be made *safely* on the end of a piece of stock.

TIP

Use of the power saw when making a rabbet cut:

1 / Never make an edge cut with the saw. Use a chisel to chip out the stock after making the width cut.

2 / If no guide is available for the saw, use two C clamps and a straight piece of stock. Measure from the edge of the blade to the outer edge of the saw base as shown in Figure 5-11. Clamp the straight edge to the stock to be cut at the distance measured from saw blade to base edge. Set the blade of the saw for the proper depth and make the cut by holding the edge of the saw base *against* the straight edge. This method can be used for both cross-cut and ripping directions.

3 / If the width cut is deeper than ¾ inch from the outer edge, use the saw free-hand and make a series of cuts about ⅜ to ½ inch apart between the exact width cut and the edge or end of the board (Figure 5-12). After the cuts have been made, chisel out the stock to complete the rabbet cut.

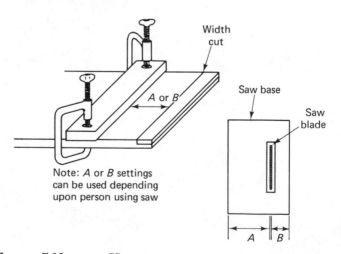

Note: *A* or *B* settings can be used depending upon person using saw

FIGURE 5-11   HOW TO USE A CLAMP STRAIGHTEDGE IN-
                      STEAD OF A SAW-GUIDE ATTACHMENT

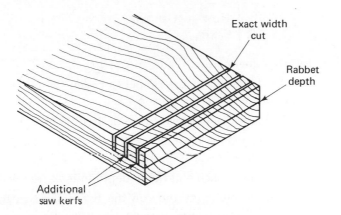

Exact width
cut

Rabbet
depth

Additional
saw kerfs

FIGURE 5-12   HOW TO MAKE CUTS FOR EASIER CHIPPING

5.5 HOW TO MAKE A RABBET JOINT WITH BENCH POWER TOOLS

Four shop power tools can be used to make a rabbet cut: the table saw, the radial arm saw, the jointer, and the shaper. The following instructions for making the joint are parallel to those for hand power tools, but in using these machines the boards are generally passed through the machine.

5.5.1 How to Cut a Rabbet Joint with Table Saw and Fine-Toothed Blade

Both the *end* and *side rabbet cuts* can be made easily with a table saw. To make a side rabbet cut requires use of the fence on the saw. To make an end cut requires using the T or angle guide and/or the fence. Both types can be made with a single blade or with dado blades installed.

How to Use the
Fence

Step 1 / Install a fine-toothed blade and secure it.

Step 2 / Set the depth cut of the rabbet between the fence and the *inside* of the blade (Figure 5-13a).

Step 3 / Set the blade height equal to the desired width of the rabbet.

Step 4 / Turn the machine on and run the stock through. Both end and side may be cut (Figure 5-13b).

Step 5 / Reset the saw fence and blade depth to make the width cut.

Step 6 / Turn the machine on and run the board through with the *flat* surface on the table surface (Figure 5-13c).

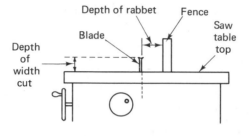

(a)

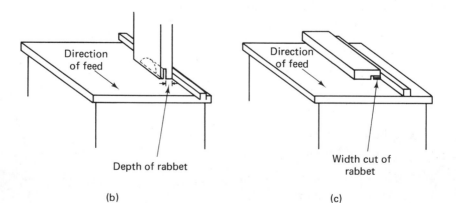

(b)   (c)

Figure 5-13   How to make a rabbet cut with a
                        table saw

How to Use the
Miter Gauge

Step 1 / Repeat steps 1, 2, 3, and 4.

Step 2 / With the miter gauge set at zero degrees ("0"), hold the stock against the gauge and against the fence. Push the gauge past the saw blade.

CAUTION

The small piece that is cut free will be between the saw blade and the fence. It will fly to the rear past you or hit you if you happen to stand directly behind the blade.

TIP

If you use the miter gauge to hold the stock but do not wish the scrap piece to fly to the rear, you may use the method shown in Figure 5-14. Notice that a block of wood is clamped to the fence. The width of the rabbet is set from the outer surface of the block of wood and outer teeth of the blade. When the stock is pushed through the saw, the scrap piece will not be wedged between the blade and fence as before.

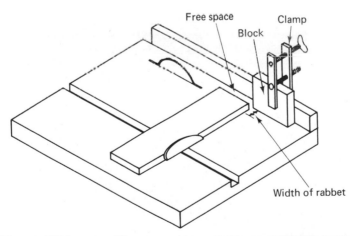

Free space   Clamp
          Block
          Width of rabbet

Figure 5-14   How to use a block to prevent feed-back

How to Use Dado
Blades to Make a
Depth Cut

Step 1 /   Install the dado blades for a cutting width slightly wider
than the required depth of the rabbet, as detailed on your
plan.

Step 2 /   Set the fence for a cut equal to the thickness of the stock
minus the depth of the rabbet; for example, ⅜-inch rabbet
in ¾-inch stock indicates a fence-to-blade setting of ⅜ inch.

Step 3 /   Turn the saw on and guide the stock through the machine,
making sure that the stock is held firmly against the fence.
The miter gauge may be used to guide the piece past the
saw blade.

How to Use Dado
Blades to Make a
Width Cut

Step 1 /   Install dado blades for a cutting width slightly wider than
the desired rabbet, as detailed on your plan.

Step 2 /   Set the height of the blades for the depth of rabbet.

Step 3 /   Using a scrap piece of stock ¾ by 2½ by 24 inches set the
fence for a setting of ¾ inch or slightly less. Run the scrap

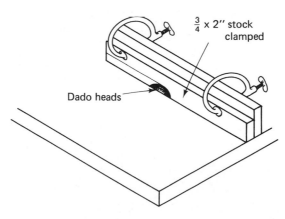

$\frac{3}{4}$ x 2″ stock
clamped

Dado heads

FIGURE 5-15   HOW TO USE A BLOCK WITH DADO HEADS TO
MAKE A WIDTH RABBET CUT

stock through partway and while still holding the stock, turn the machine off (Figure 5-15).

Step 4 / Clamp the scrap stock before and after the blade. *Do not* put the clamps to *low*.

Step 5 / Run the stock through flat surface down. Both end and side cuts can be made this way.

5.5.2
How to Cut a Rabbet Joint with a Radial Arm Saw

The simplest method of cutting a rabbet into a piece of stock with a radial arm is to use dado heads on the saw. For most jobs one pass with the saw completes the cut. However, if a set of dados is not available, a standard fine-toothed blade can be used for cross-cut work and a combination blade can be used for side cuts (ripping).

How to Use Dado Blades to Make a Cross-Cut Rabbet Cut

Step 1 / Install dado blades to a width slightly greater than the *width* of the rabbet. *Do not exceed ¾ inch* because insufficient shaft length will be left to secure the nut.

Step 2 / Set the depth of the cut with the crank on the radial arm. This may be done as shown in Figure 5-16. Roll the saw partway out with the *power off*, then adjust the saw depth so that the *lowest* tooth just touches the line previously drawn.

Step 3 / Clamp a block at either end of the stock being rabbetted, after positioning the stock that is to be cut. This block, when clamped, allows you to make exact cuts in as many boards as you need. (See block clamped in Figure 5-16.)

Step 4 / Turn on the saw and draw the saw through the stock while holding the piece firmly against the table, the fence, and the clamped block.

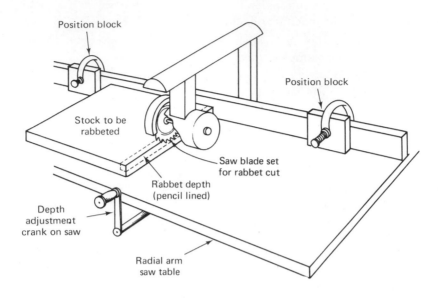

FIGURE 5-16   HOW TO SET THE DEPTH FOR A RABBET CUT

> HOW TO USE DADO
> HEADS TO MAKE A
> SIDE RABBET CUT

STEP 1 / Install the dado blades for a slightly wider cut than the width of the rabbet (Figure 5-17).

STEP 2 / Turn the radial arm saw for ripping.

STEP 3 / Adjust the blade for the proper depth. (See Figure 5-16; the same method can be used.)

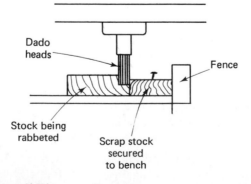

FIGURE 5-17   SAFE WAY TO MAKE A SIDE RABBET CUT

STEP 4 / Secure a scrap piece of stock, *which must be parallel* and not less than 24 inches long against the saw table fence.

STEP 5 / Move the dado heads to a position against the scrap piece. Lock the saw.

STEP 6 / Turn the machine on and try running a scrap piece through the setup. Check your results.

TIP

The method described allows the entire piece of stock to be outside the saw blade as opposed to using the fence as the guide. This is a safe way to make side rabbet cuts.

HOW TO USE A
STANDARD BLADE TO
MAKE A RABBET
CUT WITH A RADIAL
ARM SAW

STEP 1 / Set the depth of the cut as shown in Figure 5-16.

STEP 2 / Set the width of the cut by clamping a block against the end of the board that is to be rabbetted.

STEP 3 / Turn on the saw and make successive cuts with the blade. Move the stock that is being rabbetted farther away from the clamped block with each succeeding pass of the saw.

NOTE: This same method can be used when making a side rabbet cut. Use the procedures for setting up the saw given in "How to Use Dado Heads to Make a Side Rabbet Cut."

HOW TO USE A
ROUTER RABBET OR
DADO BIT IN A
RADIAL ARM SAW TO
MAKE A RABBET CUT

STEP 1 / Remove the saw blade.

STEP 2 / At the opposite end of the motor shaft, install the drill chuck and router bit.

STEP 3 / Rotate the motor shaft 90 degrees so that the router bit is facing *down*.

STEP 4 / Set the depth and width of the cuts as listed above, using blocks and guides as necessary.

STEP 5 / Turn the machine on. Pull the machine slowly through for a cross cut; push the material through for a side rabbet cut.

5.5.3
HOW TO CUT
A RABBET WITH
A JOINTER

CAUTION

When rabbet cuts are made on a jointer, the safety guard is usually removed. Therefore, a safety hazard exists. *Be especially careful* not to place your hands or body near the blades (Fig. 5-18).

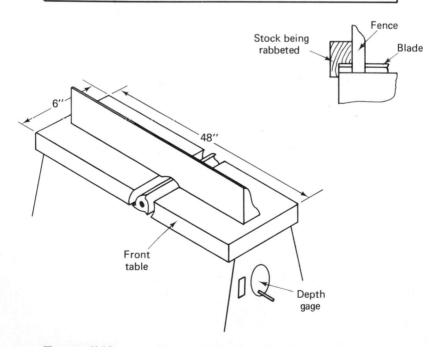

FIGURE 5-18   HOW TO MAKE A RABBET ON A JOINTER

STEP 1 /   Remove the blade guard from the jointer.

STEP 2 /   Set the fence to a position that allows for the depth or width cut of the rabbet.

STEP 3 /   Lower the rear table to take about a ⅛-inch cut on the first pass.

STEP 4 /   Lower the rear table ⅛ inch for each succeeding pass until the rabbet is completely cut.

NOTE: Successively even cuts result in an accurate job. Deep cuts may cause splitting, splintering, and uneven work.

| 5.5.4 |
| How to Cut |
| a Rabbet Joint |
| with a Shaper |

A shaper is very much like a router except that the shaper motor is mounted below a table. The shaft sticks through the center of the table, and blades are installed on the shaft.

STEP 1 /   Install a rabbet blade on the shaper shaft. *Secure it.*

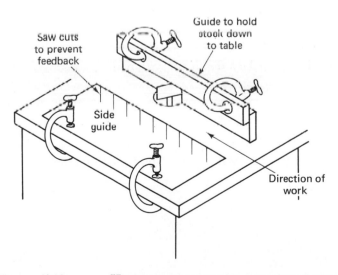

FIGURE 5-19   HOW TO USE GUIDES TO HOLD STOCK WHEN USING A SHAPER

STEP 2 / Set the guides (fences) so that the width of the rabbet can be cut.

STEP 3 / Set the depth of the rabbet by adjusting the motor position.

STEP 4 / Try a piece of scrap stock *not less than 24 inches long* to avoid any chance of placing hands close to blade.

STEP 5 / If narrow or long pieces are to be rabbetted, use blocks and clamps to hold moving stock in place as it is pushed through the shaping machine. Refer to Figure 5-19.

QUESTIONS |

1 / What is the purpose of a rabbet joint?

2 / What joint that we have studied is functionally less strong than a joint made with a rabbet?

3 / Is it easier or harder using the rabbet joint to make a square corner?

4 / Is it true that the rabbet joint can be used to eliminate warping?

5 / What tool is used when the rabbet cut runs parallel to the grain?

6 / What two portable electric tools can be used to make a rabbet cut?

7 / What four shop power tools can be used to make a rabbet cut?

8 / What are two tips to remember when using a router to make a rabbet cut?

9 / How do you cut a rabbet with a table saw and fine-toothed blade?

10 / How do you make a depth cut with dado blades?

PROJECT |

Take some pine and make a picture frame. In the back of the frame make a rabbet joint so that you can inset glass, picture, and backing.

6

HOW TO
MAKE
A DADO JOINT

The best workmanship is often accomplished when time is spent making strong joints in the wood. The time involved in machine setting or hand cutting a dado joint definitely pays off in an excellent product. In almost any cabinet you build, the use of the dado joint will play an important part in its total design and strength.

Figure 6-1 shows the two basic dado joints. The one on the left (Figure 6-1a) is a straight dado joint. Notice how the dado (cutaway stock) is made from edge to edge of the stock. In the other example (Figure 6-1b) the dado is stopped back from the face edge. The stock that will fit into the dado must have a notch cut into it to complete the joint. This method is excellent to use when no facings are to be used on the cabinet.

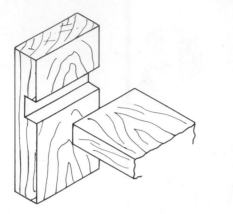

(a)   (b)

FIGURE 6-1   TWO BASIC DADO JOINTS

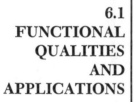

6.1 FUNCTIONAL QUALITIES AND APPLICATIONS

Of all the types of joints used in cabinetmaking, the dado joint creates the strongest joint. The principle in making the joint is to remove a section of wood from one of the pieces in the exact dimensions of the piece to fit into the dado. The stock that is dadoed is weakened by the dado, but when the other piece is inserted and glued, full strength is restored.

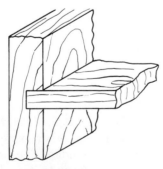
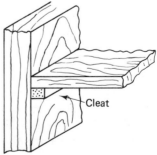

Cleat

(a) Dadoed shelf   (b) Cleating a shelf

FIGURE 6-2   QUALITY OF A DADO JOINT

From the illustration in Figure 6-1 you might have already guessed that the dado cut is usually made into a vertical section of a cabinet. This is true; usually shelves are dadoed into the side pieces. However, a dado joint can be used in horizontal pieces as well. You might also note from Figure 6-1 that no additional bracing is required to hold the shelf. To illustrate just how good this joiint is, study Figure 6-2.

Figure 6-2 illustrates the difference between cleating a shelf and dadoing a shelf. As shown in Figure 6-2a, the shelf is actually inserted into the vertical side piece. Because the shelf stock replaces the original stock that was removed to make the dado, total strength is restored. In addition to the functional quality, the clean lines created by the joint and its inherent squaring ability are advantages.

The *cleating method* is a poor substitute for the dado. In Figure 6-2b note that a cleat has been fastened to the vertical side piece. Then the shelf is laid on top and glued or nailed/screwed and glued. Actually a butt joint is created. An inherent weakness exists: (1) the cleat is the main support and it is held in place by screws and glue, and (2) the only bond the shelf has with the side of the cabinet is the glue bond. When the shelf is loaded with books, a great strain is placed upon the joint and separation can and often does occur.

If no facings are to be used on the cabinet, or if narrow facings are to be used, the cleat presents a problem. How can it be finished to look neat? It really cannot. Not only is the cleat unsightly, but it creates a nuisance. The book that is stored next to the side of the cabinet must be short enough to fit under the cleat. The end grain of the cleat shows when the facings are narrow.

6.2
PROBLEMS
SOLVED BY
USE OF THE
DADO JOINT

6.2.1
SQUARING

If you have tried to fasten a shelf to the side of a bookcase or kitchen cabinet, you know the problem you can have keeping it straight and square. The dado joint, by the nature of its cut, aids in providing a square guide. Hidden fastening can be used while the piece is being squared. Refer to Figure 6-3 and note the *toenailing;* this keeps the joint tight until the glue dries.

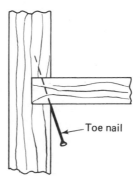

FIGURE 6-3   HOW TO TOENAIL A DADO JOINT

6.2.2 RECESSING ADJUSTABLE SHELF BRACKETS

The dado is a very effective method for recessing a metal adjustable-shelf bracket. If, for instance, this type of bracket was flush-mounted in a bookcase, the books next to the bracket would stand away from the cabinet side wall. In addition, shelf space is sacrificed. By routing a dado into the side of the bookcase and recessing the shelf bracket, books may be stacked against the wooden sides of the case.

6.2.3 TABLE LEG BRACES

Frequently tables and benches need to be stabilized. This is especially so when heavy work is to be performed. A dado made in the form of a *half-lap joint* provides such a stiffening device (Figure 6-4). (The half-lap joint will be discussed later.)

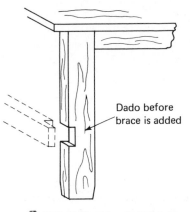

FIGURE 6-4   DADO USED AS A HALF-LAP

6.2.4
DADOING
FOR A PANEL

Inserting a panel into a frame or door where both sides are to show is easily accomplished by use of the dado. Figure 6-5 shows a rail with a dado made into it. The dado should be as wide as the thickness of the panel. The depth is variable.

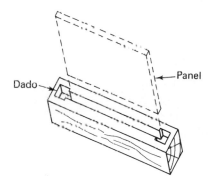

FIGURE 6-5   DADO MADE TO HOUSE A PANEL

By now it should be obvious that the major difference between a rabbet joint and a dado joint is the position of the joint in the stock. The rabbet joint has one open end and the dado has no open ends. Therefore we can expect that the methods for making a dado joint will be similar to those used in making a rabbet joint.

6.3
METHODS
THAT CAN
BE USED TO
MAKE A
DADO JOINT

The dado can be made with hand tools such as a saw and chisel. If hand tools are used, certain limitations exist. First, the length of the dado cut is restrictive. Trying to cut the sides of a dado in excess of 12 inches is extremely difficult. Cutting a perfect side cut at 90 degrees and square is very difficult. Generally a craftsman will undercut the side with his saw to make a clean fit at the surface edge.

Two hand power tools are very effective in making a dado. They are the router with dado bit, and the power saw. The router may be able to make the cut in one pass, depending upon the width and depth of the dado. The saw must be set up to make at least two passes, one for each side of the dado. Then two or three intermediate passes are usually made with the saw. These passes make it easier to chip out the stock that remains in the dado cut.

The radial arm and table saw are the two best bench power tools to use when making a dado. It is possible to install dado heads on each of these machines. One pass with the stock in each machine usually completes the dado. However, a single blade can be used to make a dado. At least two setups and passes must be made. Now let's make the joint by various means.

6.4
HOW TO
MAKE A
DADO JOINT
WITH
HAND TOOLS

The hand tools that you may have readily aavilable to make a dado joint are the hand saw, straight back saw, and chisel. One that you may not have but that is available is the dado chipper (shown in Figure 6-6). This tool makes it very easy to chip the center from the dado joint after the side cuts are made. The tool's blade is adjustable and can be resharpened as needed. If you do not plan to buy electric

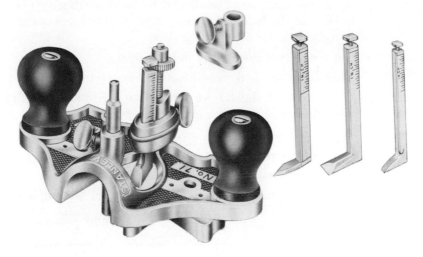

FIGURE 6-6   DADO CHIPPING TOOL (*Courtesy of Stanley Tools*)

tools and plan to do a lot of cabinetmaking, this tool could be very useful.

<table>
<tr><td>6.4.1
TOOLS NEEDED</td><td>*Hand or back saw*
Chisel
Mallet
Square, combination
   and/or framing</td><td>*Straightedge*
C clamps
Ruler</td></tr>
</table>

6.4.2
HOW TO CROSS-CUT
A DADO JOINT
FREE-HAND
WITH SAW

STEP 1 / Layout the dado with square and pencil.

   a / Make one line across the board.

   b / Measure for the width of the dado and make a mark.

   c / Draw a second line over the mark across the board.

   d / Set the combination square for the depth of the dado and mark both edges where the dado will be.

STEP 2 / Using the hand saw (be careful to *leave the line on*), cut the first of the two. Continue cutting until the saw makes a straight path the depth of the dado.

STEP 3 / Cut the second side as you did the first.

STEP 4 / Make one, two, or three more cuts between the first two.

STEP 5 / Using a chisel slightly *narrower* than the dado cut, chip away the remaining stock in the dado joint.

   a / Start at a depth about halfway.

   b / Start at both ends and work toward the center.

   c / Continue chipping until the desired depth is reached.

   d / Smooth the base of the cut with chisel, file, or sanding block.

STEP 6 / Use a chipper tool instead of a chisel if available.

TIP

Your chances of a good fit are enhanced if you *undercut* the side cuts. Refer to Figure 6-7 for a description of undercutting.

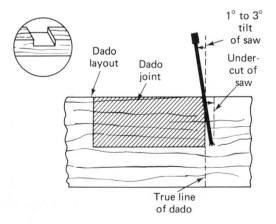

FIGURE 6-7   HOW TO UNDERCUT WITH A SAW

6.4.3
How to Cross-Cut
a Dado Joint
with Hand Saw
and Straightedge
Guide

When a cross-cut dado joint wider than 6 inches is necessary, it becomes difficult to keep the saw in line. A straightedge and C clamps are used as aids in overcoming this problem.

STEP 1 / Lay out the dado on the board.

STEP 2 / Lay the straightedge along the outside of one of the side cuts. Clamp it in place with the two C clamps (wooden clamps may be used).

STEP 3 / Place the saw against the straightedge and have *all* the teeth touch the board.

STEP 4 / Draw the saw back and forth.

STEP 5 / Tilt the saw away from the straightedge 1 to 3 degrees for an *under*cut.

STEP 6 / Continue cutting until the proper depth is reached.

STEP 7 / Repeat these steps for the second side cut.

STEP 8 / Make intermediate cuts by hand.

STEP 9 / Chip out the remaining stock.

6.5
HOW TO
MAKE A
DADO JOINT
WITH
PORTABLE
POWER TOOLS

The two best power tools that can be used to make a dado joint are the router and the power saw. The router may be used with its own guide attachment, or a straightedge may be clamped onto the board being dadoed. The power saw may be used exactly as the router. There is a difference, though; the saw will require at least two cuts, whereas one pass with the router often cuts the entire dado.

	Router with guide	*Framing square*
6.5.1	*Dado bit for router*	*Combination square*
TOOLS NEEDED	*Straightedge*	*Ruler*
	C clamps, 2	

6.5.2
HOW TO CUT
A DADO JOINT
ALONG THE GRAIN
WITH ROUTER

STEP 1 / Lay out the board to be dadoed with a framing square and/or combination square.

STEP 2 / Set the adjustable guide on the router so that the dado bit is positioned where the cut will be made. **NOTE:** *There are limits when using the guide.*

STEP 3 / Set the dado bit to the depth of dado desired by adjusting the router base.

STEP 4 / Turn the router on and with the guide *against the edge of the stock,* lower the router onto the surface.

STEP 5 / Slide the router along the stock from start to end of the desired dado.

TIP

Do not allow the router to remain stopped with the motor turned on, as the tip will burn.

6.5.3
HOW TO CUT
A DADO JOINT
ACROSS THE GRAIN
WITH ROUTER

STEP 1 / Lay out the piece of stock to be dadoed.

STEP 2 / Set the dado bit for the desired depth of the dado cut.

STEP 3 / Measure from the edge of the dado bit (flat side) to the edge of the router base (X). (See Figure 6-8.)

STEP 4 / Clamp a straightedge at a point equal to the distance measured in step 3 either to the right or to the left of the dado layout.

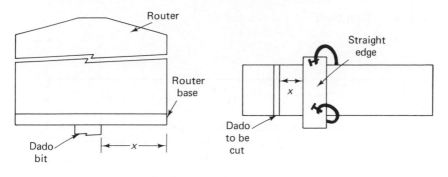

FIGURE 6-8   HOW TO USE A STRAIGHTEDGE AS A GUIDE

STEP 5 / Draw the router through the stock, keeping the router base against the straightedge.

6.5.4
HOW TO CROSS-CUT A DADO JOINT USING A JIG

STEP 1 / Make a jig as shown in Figure 6-9.

STEP 2 / Set the depth of the dado bit to pass below the router jig the desired depth of the dado.

STEP 3 / Clamp the stock to be routed against the guide (front or back) of the jig table.

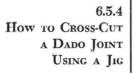

Cross sectional
view

y = width of router base

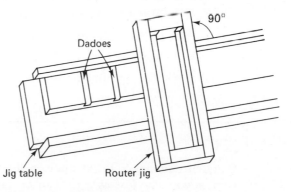

FIGURE 6-9   ROUTER JIG FOR DADOING

STEP 4 / Run the router down the jig.

TIPS

1 / Make the jig table guides slightly higher than the thickness of the stock being dadoed; for example, for ¾-inch stock, use ⅞-inch jig table guides.

2 / Spray the router jig with repeated coats of spray wax so that the router will slide more easily.

3 / Make the router jig long enough to allow the router bit to clear the table guides.

6.5.5
How to Cut
a Dado Joint
with Power Saw

STEP 1 / Set the blade on the saw for the depth of the desired dado.

STEP 2 / If cutting with the grain, set the adjustable guide for one of the side cuts of the dado. **NOTE:** *With the same setting, make this cut in every piece being dadoed.*

STEP 3 / If cutting across the grain, clamp a straightedge onto the surface. (See the instructions in Section 6.5.3.)

STEP 4 / Readjust the guide to cut the other side.

STEP 5 / In the case of cross cuts, reposition the straightedge.

STEP 6 / Make intermediate cuts between the side cuts.

STEP 7 / Chip out the remaining material.

TIP

If much dadoing is to be done, a jig can be made for your power saw just as a jig can be made for a router.

6.6
HOW TO
MAKE A
DADO JOINT
WITH BENCH
POWER TOOLS

There are two bench power tools that can be used to make a dado. They are the radial arm saw and the table saw. Both machines can be fitted with a set of dado blades.

The radial arm saw has an advantage over the table saw for the user because the dado can be seen at all times. If a blind dado is to be made, it is easy to see where to stop the travel of the blades. Dados with and against the grain can both be cut on the radial arm saw. If multiple cuts of dados are made in a series of boards, clamp a block to the table fence and cut the same in *every* piece; then move the block and cut the second dado in every piece. Repeat this process for each duplicate cut.

The table saw can be used for cutting dados, but it has a limitation. The dado is made on the bottom side of the board and cannot be seen by the craftsman. Splintering at the outer edges of the stock may occur when the stick is not exactly straight when fed through the saw.

There is one definite advantage in using the table saw to cut dados. The table saw is the most effective tool to use when a double blind with the grain dado is to be cut. Procedures for making this cut are outlined below. The really critical parts of the operation are the starting and stopping positions.

6.6.1 TOOLS NEEDED	*Radial arm saw* *Table saw*	*Framing square*

6.6.2
HOW TO CUT A
DADO JOINT WITH
RADIAL ARM SAW

STEP 1 / Install the dado blades on the saw shaft for the width of the stock to fit into the dado.

CAUTION

Make sure that the chipper blade edges fit into the spaces between the saw-blade teeth and *do not* touch the teeth. NOTE: Changing blades in a radial arm saw may cause blade travel to be in error, especially on small, inexpensive machines.

STEP 2 / Using the framing square, test the blade travel (with power off) for *square* with the table fence and *plumb* with the table surface (see Figure 6-10).

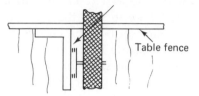

(a) Saw blade must travel
against square

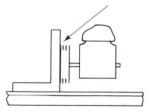

(b) Saw blade must be
plumb with square

FIGURE 6-10   MAKING SURE THAT THE BLADES RUN TRUE

STEP 3 / Set the blades for the desired depth of dado cut.

STEP 4 / Try a sample cut on a piece of scrap. The piece fitting into the cut should easily slide into the cut. If it is too tight or loose, see the tips below.

STEP 5 / Position the piece to be dadoed, which has previously been laid out, against the table fence.

STEP 6 / Clamp a block to the fence.

STEP 7 / Make a duplicate cut in each board; then reposition the clamped block.

TIPS

1 / If the cut is too narrow, cut a piece of heavy paper or 15-pound felt. Slip it over the motor shaft and in between the chipper blades.

2 / If the cut is too loose, remove one of the chippers and replace with a thinner one. If you don't have a thin one, slip a paper spacer between the blades until the exact width is obtained.

3 / Where stock being dadoed is too wide for the saw, make the cut between 60 and 70 percent on the first pass; then when all pieces have been cut, rotate the piece 180 degrees. *Reset* the block and complete the cut.

4 / When blind dados are made, separate setups must be made for right and left side pieces.

6.6.3
HOW TO CUT A DADO JOINT ALONG THE GRAIN WITH RADIAL ARM SAW

STEP 1 / Install blades and try a sample cut for width and depth (cross cut).

STEP 2 / Rotate the saw head 90 degrees. Measure the distance from the fence to blade. *Lock* in position.

STEP 3 / Push the stock to be dadoed through the saw. *Make sure that you push from the front side.*

6.6.4
HOW TO CUT A DADO JOINT ACROSS THE GRAIN WITH TABLE SAW

STEP 1 / Install the dado blades for the desired width of dado cut.

STEP 2 / Set the blades for the desired depth.

STEP 3 / With a framing square and cutoff guide attachment for the saw, make sure that the guide is set accurately.

STEP 4 / Try a scrap for cut size and fit.

STEP 5 / Position the fence with the spacer block clamped for the first dado cut (see Figure 6-11). NOTE: *A piece of lumber has been screwed to the miter gauge. This piece makes it easier to guide your stock through the saw.*

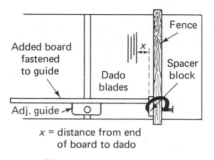

x = distance from end of board to dado

FIGURE 6-11   HOW TO USE A GAUGE AND SPACER BLOCK

STEP 6 / Cut all pieces that are the same; then change settings of gauges and fence.

6.6.5
HOW TO CUT A
BLIND DADO JOINT
ALONG THE GRAIN
WITH TABLE SAW

STEP 1 / Install the blades and set for depth.

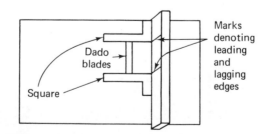

FIGURE 6-12   HOW TO MARK LEADING AND LAGGING
                      EDGES ON THE FENCE

STEP 2 / Set the fence for the proper position of the dado.

STEP 3 / Make a line on the fence where the blade comes through the table (see Figure 6-12) and mark the leading and lagging edges. There are two methods available for making the cut:

a / Make a line on the outside of the stock to be dadoed, indicating where the dado will start and stop (see Figure 6-13).

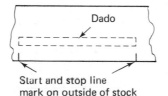

FIGURE 6-13   IIOW TO MARK THE OUTSIDE OF THE STOCK

b / If the stock is to be dadoed within 3 to 6 inches of the ends, make two additional lines on the fence, one for the start of the operation and one for the stop (see Figure 6-14).

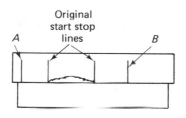

FIGURE 6-14   STOCK START AND STOP LINES

STEP 4 / Turn the saw on and using method 1 or 2 as a guide, *lower* the stock onto the table while sliding it down the surface of the fence.

STEP 5 / Once on the table, push it to the stop point, then *lift* it off.

QUESTIONS |

1 / In what part of cabinetmaking does the dado joint play an important part?

2 / What is the leading principle to be followed in making the dado joint?

3 / What is the difference between making a dado joint for shelving and the cleating method?

4 / The dado provides a stiffening device in the form of what joint?

5 / What two hand power tools are very effective in making a dado?

6 / What is a dado chipping tool and how is it used?

7 / How is the dado made with hand tools?

8 / What is one definite advantage of using the table saw to cut dadoes?

9 / What is the advantage of a table saw over a radial arm saw when making a dado?

10 / Can you describe two methods that can be used to make a dado?

PROJECT |

Using mahogany, make a small bookcase. When making and installing the shelves, use your hand tools to make the dado joints in the first two shelves. Use your portable power tools to make the dado joints in the rest of the end pieces. Then compare the quality of the dado joints.

7

HOW TO MAKE A MORTISE

Making a mortise goes hand in hand with making a tenon. The two pieces fit together to make a very strong cabinet joint. However, a mortise can be used by itself with a mortise lock.

Some texts discuss the mortise and tenon as one subject. However, there is a particular series of steps that must be performed when making the mortise. Since this book is devoted to providing step-by-step instructions on how to make joints, the mortise is examined in this chapter and the tenon in Chapter 8.

So that we are sure what the subject is, look at Figure 7-1. It shows the two basic types of mortises: Figure 7-1a a *closed* mortise and Figure 7-1b an *open* mortise. There are other variations of the mortise, but they all fall in these two categories.

Some of the variations of the mortise, along with their tenons, are shown in Figure 7-2. Figure 7-2a shows a haunched mortise and tenon

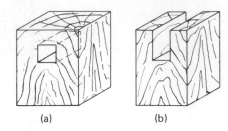

(a)   (b)

FIGURE 7-1   CLOSED AND OPEN MORTISES

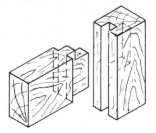

(a) Haunched mortise and tenon joint

(c) Rounded mortise and tenon joint

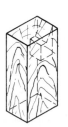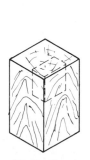

(b) Mortise and tenon joint
     concealed haunch

(d) Barefaced mortise and tenon joint

FIGURE 7-2   VARIATIONS OF MORTISE AND TENON
                      JOINTS

joint. You should recognize that this is a dado in the mortised piece of stock. For the tenon to fit snugly, a piece of its stock (the haunch) is left. When the two pieces are clamped together, the haunch replaces the dadoed section.

Figure 7-2b shows a concealed haunch mortise and tenon joint. This joint is more difficult to make because of the angle of the haunch. The effect that is obtained when using this joint is that the full end of the mortised piece is intact.

Figure 7-2c shows a standard blind mortise but one made with auger or router bits. Note the rounded corners. The tenon must also have its corners rounded.

Figure 7-2d illustrates a bareface mortise and tenon joint. This joint is frequently used in table manufacturing. One side of the tenon is flush with the outside of the stock, but the mortise is usually centered in its stock.

7.1
FUNCTIONAL QUALITIES AND APPLICATIONS

The mortise and tenon combine to make one of the strongest joints used in woodworking. With no glue at all and exceptionally well-fitted pieces, the joint is self-sustaining. However, with the addition of glue, the joint is almost indestructible.

Cabinet facings are frequently joined at the corners with the joint. The vertical pieces, called *styles*, usually, but not always, have the mortise. The horizontal pieces, called *rails*, usually have the tenons. Doors made by the *frame and panel* method usually are made using the mortise and tenon. And this is where the *haunched* style is found.

Tables and chairs are made from stock materials as a rule. Their pieces must be made rigid and there are very few pieces to work with. Therefore, the mortise and tenon joint is frequently used. Notice, as shown in Figure 7-3, how the table rail just below the table top fits into the table leg. The mortise and tenon can be found in every style of furniture from Early American to Spanish Mediterranean.

To show you how wide the application of the mortise is, take a look at a door in your home, which has styles and rails. This door is made rigid by the use of the mortise and tenon. Have you ever seen

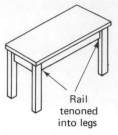

Rail
tenoned
into legs

FIGURE 7-3   TABLE WITH RAIL TENONED INTO THE LEG

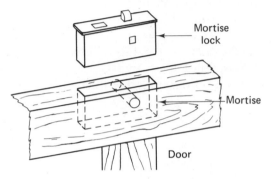

Mortise
lock

Mortise

Door

FIGURE 7-4   MORTISE FOR LOCK

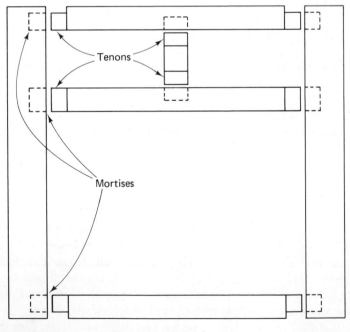

Tenons

Mortises

FIGURE 7-5   CABINET FRONT

a wooden screen door? Its styles and rails are joined by the mortise and tenon.

Door locks are being made and used today which require mortising so that the main portion of the lock can be inserted into the door. Figure 7-4 shows an example of such a lock.

The open-shelf type of bookcase, in which the ends are made to resemble a ladder, provides an excellent opportunity for the use of the mortise and tenon. The rails in this case provide the shelf supports.

Another common application of the mortise is in the framing of kitchen cabinets and other cabinets that can be built for the home, shop, or office. In these cases there may be occasion for putting a mortise in either the rails or the styles. The design of the front will dictate which part of the joint is used where. Look at the blowout of a cabinet front shown in Figure 7-5.

7.2
PROBLEMS SOLVED BY USE OF THE MORTISE AND TENON JOINT

The most significant problem that is overcome by the use of the mortise and tenon in combination is that of instability. In the case of the table rail joining the leg and the chair rail joining the leg, a real weakness would be present if such a joint were not used. A butt joint would be very unsatisfactory in every case. No weight could be applied to the rail sections.

A frame for a cabinet or panel can be made and kept square and rigid with the mortise and tenon joint. This use overcomes a weakness that a butt-jointed frame would have. Repeated opening and closing of a frame door would subject the butt joint to pressures it could not stand. But the mortise and tenon can effectively stand the pressure.

Ease of assembly is another problem that can be overcome by use of the mortise and tenon. Whether you are making one or one hundred units makes no difference. By using the joint as often as necessary, a minimum number of clamps will hold all the pieces together. Looking at Figure 7-5 as an example, you can see that two bar clamps will actually hold the frame. If the vertical center divider is properly made, no clamps may be necessary. However, a small bar clamp may be used.

7.3
METHODS
THAT CAN
BE USED TO
MAKE THE
MORTISE
JOINT

Hand tools, such as the brace and auger, can be used, or, if a portable electrical drill or router is available, it can be used in place of the hand brace. The table drill press or mortise machine are the shop tools that can make the mortise.

Since all three general classes of tools can be used, the procedure section will describe how to make the joint by all three methods.

7.4
HOW TO
MAKE A
MORTISE
JOINT WITH
HAND TOOLS

The brace and auger (often called a *bit*) are used to drill holes into the stock and then a chisel (very sharp) is used to clean out the stock remaining between holes. Finally, the mortise is made rectangular by correcting the corners to 90 degrees with a chisel.

7.4.1
TOOLS NEEDED

Brace
Augers (¼ inch, No. 4; 5/16 inch, No. 5; ⅜ inch, No. 6; ½ inch, No. 8)
Chisel (¼, ⅜, ½, and either 1 or 1¼ inch for parallel cleaning)

Hammer
Combination square
Dividers/scribe

7.4.2
How to Cut a
Mortise Joint
with Brace and
Auger, and Chisel

STEP 1 / Lay out the mortise to be cut on the piece of stock (see Figure 7-6a and the tip below on centering). NOTE: *If more than one piece will be duplicated, lay out all pieces at the same time (see Figure 7-6b).*

a / Draw a center line.

b / Measure half the width of the mortise on each side of the center line.

c / Set the combination square to this outer line and tighten the square screw (Figure 7-6c).

STEP 2 / Select the size auger that will cut a hole the width of the mortise and install it in the brace.

STEP 3 / Drill a series of holes from each end of the mortise layout to the center, along the center line (see Figure 7-7). NOTE: *The best position to drill from is the end as shown in Figure 7-7a. It is very critical that you drill straight down with reference to sides of the piece of stock. It is not as critical to drill straight down with reference to the length of the mortise (see Figure 7-7b).*

STEP 4 / Chisel out the stock between the holes.

STEP 5 / Square the corners using a chisel slightly smaller in width than the width of the mortise.

TIP

To properly find the center of a board, see Figure 7-8. When you wish to find the center of any board, take a ruler and place it so that the total width of the board is shown in full inches. The selection of inches should be such that easy division using whole numbers is obtained. For example, to divide a board in half: use 2 inches or multiples of 2 inches (i.e., 2, 4, 6, 10 inches); thirds: use 3 inches or multiples of 3 inches (i.e., 3, 6, 9, 12 inches); quarters: use 4 inches or multiples of 4 inches (i.e., 4, 8, 12, 16 inches).

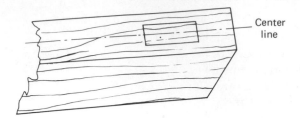

(a) Mortise laid out

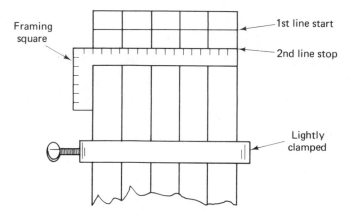

(b) Gang layout

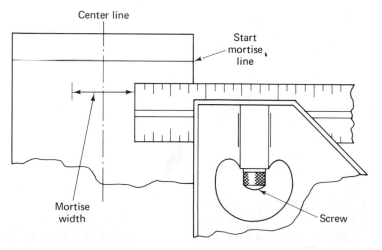

(c) Setting combination square

FIGURE 7-6   HOW TO MAKE A MORTISE LAYOUT

154

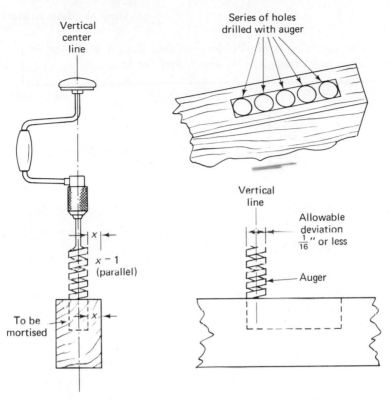

(a) End view, critical alignment   (b) Side view, not critical alignment

Figure 7-7   How to drill the mortise

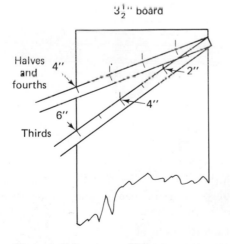
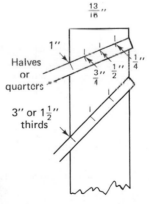

Figure 7-8   How to find the center of a board and divide a board into equal parts

> For dimensions of divisions of less than 1 inch, for ½ inch, use 1 inch; for ¼, use 1; and for ⅓ use 3.

**7.5
HOW TO
MAKE A
MORTISE
JOINT WITH
PORTABLE
POWER TOOLS**

Two basic portable power tools can be used to make a mortise: the drill and the router. These tools make mortises with rounded corners. Therefore, it is necessary to square the corners with a chisel. If you leave the mortise with round edges, you will have to round the corners on a tenon.

**7.5.1
TOOLS NEEDED**

Power drill
*Set of wood bits for
 ¼-inch power drill
 (sizes ¼, 5/16, ⅜
 and ½ inch, espe-
 cially)*

Chisel
Hammer
Combination square
*Router with mortise
 bit*

**7.5.2
HOW TO CUT A
MORTISE JOINT
WITH POWER DRILL**

STEP 1 / Lay out the mortise as shown in Figure 7-6.

STEP 2 / Drill a series of holes along the center line from one end of the mortise layout to the other.

STEP 3 / Clean out the mortise with a chisel.

STEP 4 / Square the corners with a chisel slightly *smaller* than the width of the mortise.

7.5.3
How to Cut a
Mortise Joint
with Router
and Mortise Bit

Step 1 / Lay out the mortise as per Figure 7-6.

Step 2 / Clamp a board to one side of the board with the layout. Make sure that the second board (2 by 4 inches or equivalent) is *flush* with the top of the first board (see Figure 7-9).

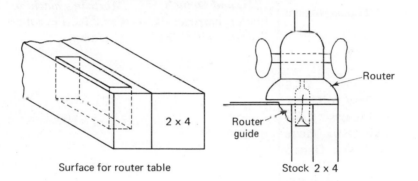

2 x 4

Surface for router table

Router

Router guide

Stock 2 x 4

Figure 7-9   How to make a table surface for the
                  router to rest on while cutting

Step 3 / Predrill a guide hole with an electric drill and wood bit (this is the safest method).

Step 4 / Insert the router bit into the hole. Turn on the machine. *Keep the router guide against the stock.*

Step 5 / Square the corners with a chisel.

7.6
HOW TO
MAKE A
MORTISE
JOINT WITH
BENCH
POWER TOOLS

For the home hobbiest and student, the probability of having a mortise machine is remote, but since it may be available to some readers, instructions for its use are included in this section. It would be quite common for the reader to have a drill press, however, so first we shall present a detailed procedure for its use in making a mortise. You will find two headings: one for using the drill press with standard twist drills or router bits, and the other for using a drill press with a mortise attachment.

7.6.1 **TOOLS NEEDED**	*Drill press* *Twist drills: ½, 5/16,* *⅜, and ¼ inch* *Router mortise: ¼,* *5/16, and ⅜ inch*	*Mortising attachment* *for drill press* *Mortising machine* *Combination square* *C clamp*

7.6.2
HOW TO CUT A
MORTISE JOINT
WITH DRILL PRESS
AND TWIST DRILLS
OR ROUTER
MORTISE BIT

STEP   1 /   Lay out the pieces to be mortised, as shown in Figure 7-6.

STEP   2 /   Install a bit into the drill and secure. (Use a bit equal in width to the mortise desired.)

STEP   3 /   Set one of the pieces to be mortised on the drill table, lower the drill to just above the wood, and lock.

STEP   4 /   Loosen the back fence and reposition so that the fence is *against* the stock and the drill bit is centered over the mortise to be made. Tighten the nuts.

STEP   5 /   Move the stock so that the drill bit can pass by the end of it.

STEP   6 /   Loosen and adjust the drill-bit depth to equal the mortise depth. Lock the adjustment nut.

STEP   7 /   Place the stock to be mortised against the fence.

STEP   8 /   Use 2 C clamps and a piece of stock lumber, e.g., 5/4 by 3 by 24 inches or 2 by 4 by 24 inches. Clamp the stock to the drill table after pushing it against the piece to be mortised (see Figure 7-10). NOTE: *The use of the wooden block creates a path for the material to be mortised*

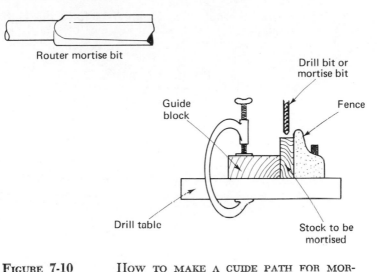

Router mortise bit

Drill bit or mortise bit

Guide block

Fence

Drill table

Stock to be mortised

FIGURE 7-10   IIow to make a guide path for mortising

to slide along. It also aids in keeping the stock straight up and down.

STEP 9 / Make a series of holes within the boundaries of the mortise layout as (if using a drill bit) in Figure 7-7.

STEP 10 / Clean out the mortise.

a / Using the drill press and drill bit, lower the bit into the mortise a small ¼ inch in depth at a time and *slowly slide the stock back and forth* with the mortise. Repeat this step until the full depth is reached.

b / Using a chisel, clean out all stock between the ends of the mortise; straighten the side wall of the mortise.

STEP 11 / Lower a router mortise bit into the mortise layout and slide to the other end of the mortise layout.

STEP 12 / Square the corners of the mortise with a chisel.

7.6.3
How to Cut a Mortise Joint with Drill Press and Mortising Attachment

STEP 1 / Install the mortise attachment following the instructions ac-

companying the unit (see Figure 7-11 for a description of
the attachment).

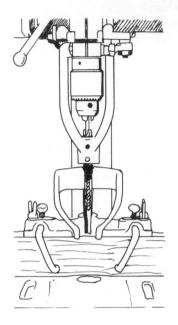

FIGURE 7-11   MORTISE ATTACHMENT FOR DRILL PRESS

STEP 2 /   Set the drill fence so that it is against the stock to be mortised and the mortise layout is centered under the mortise
bit in the drill.

STEP 3 /   Using C clamps and 24-inch stock, clamp the stock to the
table against the stock to be mortised.

STEP 4 /   Set the depth of the mortise bit and lock.

STEP 5 /   Set the stock holders (part of the fence on many models)
to rest lightly on the stock to be mortised. NOTE: *Stock
holders or some other type of restraining device* must *be
used when using the mortise attachment. The drill bit
cleans out the wood within the mortise chisel. However, the
chisel (four-sided) forces the wood into the bit and has force
against it from the outside. Therefore, removing the assembly after the downstroke has been completed is difficult.
The stock will rise with the bit and chisel unless a restraint
is used.*

STEP 6 /   Drill out the mortise until a complete mortise is made.

<table>
<tr><td>

7.6.4
HOW TO CUT A
MORTISE JOINT
WITH MORTISING
MACHINE

</td></tr>
</table>

STEP 1 / Lay out the stock to be mortised according to Figure 7-6.

STEP 2 / Select and install the mortise bit assembly into the mortise machine.

STEP 3 / Using the following hand cranks (see Figure 7-12), set the machine for operation:

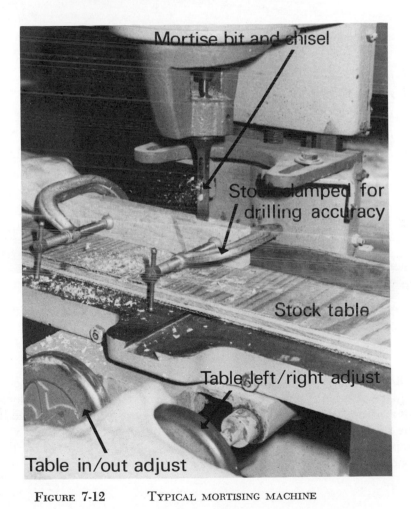

FIGURE 7-12   TYPICAL MORTISING MACHINE

a / Front-to-rear control: Center the stock under the bit assembly. (Keep the stock against the fence.)

b / Left-to-right-to-left control: Position so there is enough travel to completely cut the length of the mortise.

c / Up-down-table-position control: With the foot pedal fully depressed, adjust the control so that the depth of the mortise bit equals the desired depth of the mortise to be cut.

d / Stock holders: Position stock holders and lock: Definitely vertical or both vertical and front to rear.

STEP 4 / Turn on the machine and make a series of cuts until the mortise has been completed.

QUESTIONS |

1 / What are the two basic types of mortise?

2 / In what part of a cabinet is the mortise frequently used?

3 / What is the name of the vertical piece of a cabinet facing?

4 / What is the name of the horizontal piece of a cabinet facing?

5 / For what method is the haunch style of mortise and tenon used?

6 / What is the most significant problem that can be solved by use of the mortise and tenon in combination?

7 / What are hand tools that are used to make the mortise?

8 / When using a mortise attachment on a drill press, what is the primary type of restraining device that must be used?

9 / How is a mortise cut out with a power drill?

10 / What is the procedure used to cut a mortise with a mortising machine?

PROJECT |

Using a hammer and a set of sharpened chisels, cut a sample mortise in a piece of scrap 2″ by 4″ by 16″. Make the mortise ½″ wide by 4″ long by 2″ deep. When finished, check the accuracy of your work to see if the sides of the mortise are parallel to the outer surfaces of the 2 x 4. Repeat the above project on a piece of wood 1″ by 3″ x 16″. Make the mortise ⅜″ wide by 4″ long by 2″ deep.

8

HOW TO
MAKE
A TENON JOINT

The tenon is usually used together with the mortise. Since it is, the shop methods presented in this chapter show how to lay out a tenon from a previously made mortise. Before explaining the step-by-step procedures for cutting a tenon, an explanation is given of how to lay out the tenon.

8.1
HOW TO
LAY OUT A
TENON JOINT

If a set of plans is being used to make a project, the layout for a tenon may be shown from the side view. A top view may also be shown if,

163

for instance, a haunch will be cut. The total thickness of the stock is given on the drawing, as is the thickness of the completed tenon and whether or not the tenon is centered or offset.

For the shop method, though, laying out a tenon can be simplified if the tenon is made as long as the width of the stock that has the mortise. Figure 8-1 shows an example. Notice how the flanges of the tenon are shown equal to the inside edge of the style. The total depth of the mortise (shown as the dashed area) is less than the width of the style. Therefore, additional cuts are required on the tenon. First, the tenon length is cut to fit the depth of the mortise. Second, the top edge of the tenon is cut, thereby completing the tenon. This method results in some wasted stock, but it has a very important benefit: its use eliminates almost all chance for error.

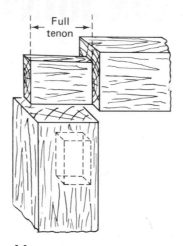

FIGURE 8-1   MAKE THE TENON AS LONG AS THE WIDTH
                    OF THE MORTISE STOCK

8.1.1
HOW TO MINIMIZE
THE CHANCE
FOR ERROR

Suppose that a panel and frame must be made as shown in Figure 8-2. The parts are labeled as follows: *a*, rails (top and bottom); *b*, styles (sides); and *c*, panel (center piece). The styles are mortised to a depth of slightly more than half the width of the style. The rails are cut the full width of the panel. After the full tenon is made, the finishing length of the tenon will equal half the width of the style. The little space re-

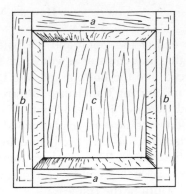

FIGURE 8-2   MORTISED AND TENONED PANEL AND FRAME

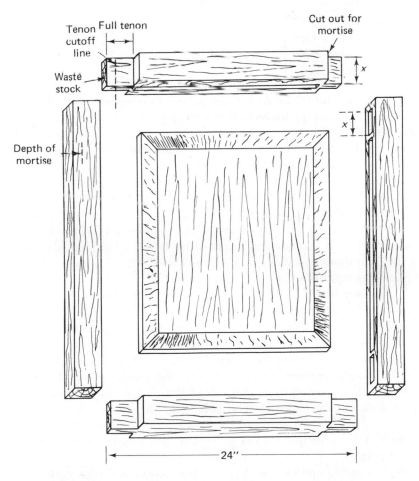

FIGURE 8-3   BLOWUP OF THE FRAME AND PANEL

maining between the end of the tenon and the bottom of the mortise is important. Excess glue and chips or sawdust are sometimes trapped by the tenon and forced into the bottom and into this small space.

Getting back to minimizing the chance for error, let's explode the view of the panel and frame of Figure 8-2 into Figure 8-3. In Figure 8-3 we made one slight modification to the actual finished pieces of the frame. We show the tenons as they are before final fitting (reaching to the outer edge of the styles). This is where the chance for error is eliminated. The frame is 24 inches wide. Therefore, the rails are precut to 24 inches (the total width of the frame).

8.1.2
How to Lay Out the Tenon Joint on the Rails

The next step would be to lay out a tenon on each end of the rails. Then cut and trim the tenon to fit the mortise. If you noticed, only once was it necessary to use a ruler during the layout. Since the tenon was made for the full width of the stock (then cut off), the completed panel and frame will be 24 inches wide.

An alternative method can be used. It is a bit more tricky. A mistake can easily be made, especially during the cutting stage. Again, use Figures 8-2 and 8-3 as examples. This method requires you to calculate the distance between the styles (total width 24 inches less the width of each side). Next you add the length of each tenon (one half the width of the style times two styles). This total plus the first figure (intermediate length) results in the exact length of the rail pieces.

You see that the method is not too difficult. However, errors are easily made while making the calculations and later while using the machines or hand tools. A cut on the wrong side of a pencil line, for instance, results in a panel that is smaller by ⅛ inch. There are occasions when this mortised piece has a width over 4 inches. The waste (using the full-length-mortise method) may be too costly, especially where many pieces are being cut. For a rule of thumb, use the following table when determining which method is best for the job:

Style 1 to 4 inches with a mortise	Use full-length-tenon method
Style 4 inches and over with a mortise	Use intermediate-length + two-tenon-length method

| Depth of mortise 1 to 4 inches stock width | 30 to 55 percent of the width of stock |
| Depth of mortise on over 4 inches stock width | 2 inches to 50 percent of the width of the stock |

Now let us review some of the functional qualities that a tenon might be used for.

8.2
FUNCTIONAL
QUALITIES
AND
APPLICATIONS

As shown in Chapter 7, the tenon is usually used with the mortise. The two pieces join to make a very strong and secure joint. The strength that the tenon gives to the joint comes from the fact that the piece having the tenon reaches almost the full width of a frame, or under the full length of the table top, or across the full width of a door. Although these examples indicate that the tenon is usually used with the rail, it is not restricted to this use. On many case fronts (cabinet facings) a vertical piece of stock is mortised and tenoned to provide the framework for drawers. In modern cabinet facings single doors are used in preference to double doors. A style will be tenoned into the center of the opening at the top and bottom, thereby making a separation for the two doors.

8.3
PROBLEMS
SOLVED BY
USE OF THE
TENON JOINT

When absolute *rigidity* is required, the tenon in combination with the mortise provides an answer. If the frame facing of a cabinet has a door attached, it will be subjected to continuous use, such as *slamming, jarring,* and the *weather.* The mortise and tenon joint is the best joint to use to prevent breaking at the joints.

Another problem that may be overcome is that of keeping the

frames and/or panels square. A well-prepared and fitted joint results in a square (90 degree) corner.

Finally, the joint provides superior strength, especially when compared with the strength of the butt joint and the dado joint.

8.4
METHODS
THAT CAN BE
USED TO
MAKE THE
TENON JOINT

Hand tools such as the hand saw and the chisel are commonly used in making the tenon. Portable power tools such as the electric saw and the router can also be used to make the joint.

Three shop power tools can be used to make the tenon. These are the radial arm saw, the table saw, and the band saw. A band saw may be used only if the craftsman can set his machine for perfect cuts.

8.5
HOW TO LAY
OUT A
TENON JOINT
BY SHOP
METHODS

STEP 1 / Place the stock to be tenoned as shown in Figure 8-4a and mark the dimensions of the tenon as shown. This is the finished thickness of the tenon and establishes its position. NOTE: *If an offset tenon is desired, place the stock as shown in Figure 8-4b.*

STEP 2 / Place the tenon at right angles to the mortised stock and the end of the piece *even* with the outer edge of the mortised stock (Figure 8-4c).

STEP 3 / Make a small pencil mark on the tenon stock. Complete the cross-cut line with the combination square.

STEP 4 / Set the combination square for the depth of the tenon mark made in step 1. Make lines on three sides of the stock—the end and both sides. (See Figure 8-4d.)

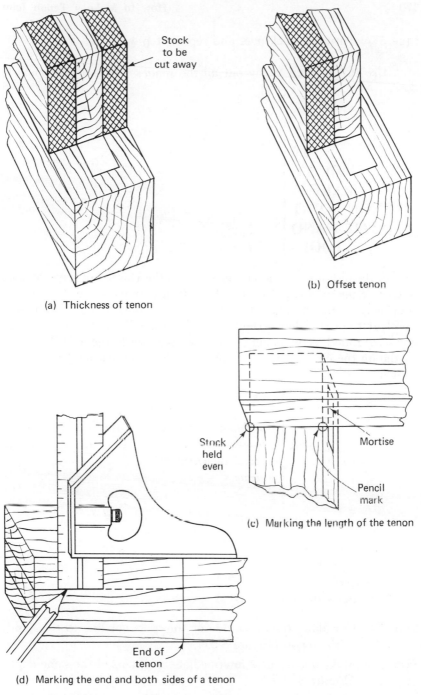

(a) Thickness of tenon

(b) Offset tenon

Stock
to be
cut away

Stock
held
even

Mortise

Pencil
mark

(c) Marking the length of the tenon

End of
tenon

(d) Marking the end and both sides of a tenon

FIGURE 8-4　　　HOW TO LAY OUT A TENON BY SHOP
METHODS

169

STEP 5 / Turn the stock over and repeat step 4.

Use this method to lay out all the tenons where a *full tenon* is used.

8.6
HOW TO MAKE A TENON JOINT WITH HAND TOOLS

Two of the oldest tools known, the saw and the chisel, are used to make a tenon. Select a sharp No. 9 or No. 10 saw or back saw for the job (the more teeth, the finer the cut). Use a hollow-ground, sharpened chisel. If the chisel has a steel end on the handle, a 12- to 14-ounce standard round claw hammer can be used with the chisel. If the handle on the chisel is wood or plastic, use a wooden mallet to strike the chisel.

8.6.1
TOOLS NEEDED

Combination square   *Cross-cut saw (No. 9*
Chisel (minimum ½   *or 10) or back saw*
to 2 inch), wood
type

8.6.2
HOW TO CUT A TENON JOINT WITH HAND SAW AND CHISEL

STEP 1 / Cut along the outer side of the cross-cut line to the depth of the tenon (Figure 8-5a).

STEP 2 / Make one or more intermediate cross cuts of the same depth (Figure 8-5b).

STEP 3 / Observe the direction of grain in the stock (along the side) (Figure 8-5c).

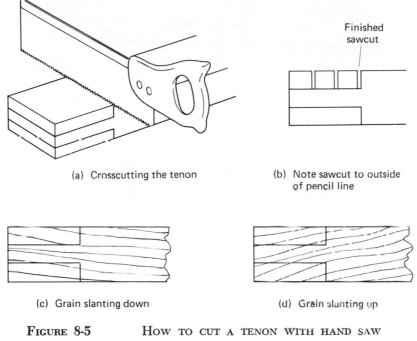

(a) Crosscutting the tenon

(b) Note sawcut to outside of pencil line

Finished sawcut

(c) Grain slanting down

(d) Grain slanting up

FIGURE 8-5   HOW TO CUT A TENON WITH HAND SAW AND CHISEL

a / If the grain is slanting down from the end of the stock past the cross cut, use chisel instructions A below (Figure 8-6).

b / If the grain is parallel or slanting upward from the end of the stock to the cross cut, use chisel instructions B below.

PROCEDURE A:
CHISELING
INSTRUCTIONS FOR
GRAIN SLANTING
DOWN

STEP 1 / Trace the grain (annual ring) back from the cross cut to the end of the stock (Figure 8-6a).

STEP 2 / Lay the chisel edge (flat side down) along that annual ring (Figure 8-6b).

STEP 3 / Strike the chisel handle, chipping out the stock.

STEP 4 / Reposition the chisel and clean out the remainder from the

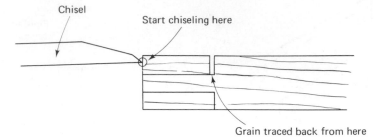

(a/b) First chisel position

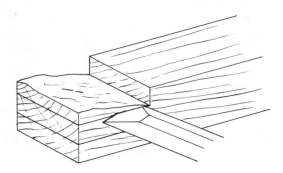

(c) Second and following
chisel positions

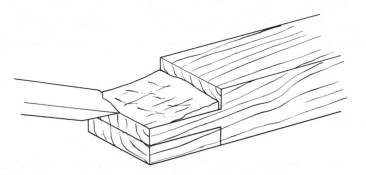

(d) Chiseling with grain
parallel or slanting up

FIGURE 8-6   HOW TO CHISEL WITH GRAIN RUNNING UP
OR DOWN

cross cut toward the end of the stock (from the sides) (Figure 8-6c).

| PROCEDURE B:
| CHISELING
| INSTRUCTIONS FOR
| PARALLEL OR
| UPWARD-SLANTING
| GRAIN

STEP 1 / Place the chisel (flat side down) even with the tenon end mark.

STEP 2 / Strike the chisel to chip the stock out.

STEP 3 / Reverse the chisel (level side down) and with short, easy strokes chip the stock until the tenon side is clean and level (see Figure 8-6d).

STEP 4 / Chisel out the stock along the previously drawn lines using either procedure A or procedure B.

STEP 5 / Check the cut by using a combination square.

a / Make sure that the flange cut is straight down or slightly undercut.

b / Make sure that the tenon surface to be chiseled is flat and smooth (sand if necessary).

STEP 6 / Turn the stock over and repeat steps 1 through 5 for the other flat cut if the tenon is other than offset to the edge.

STEP 7 / Measure the actual depth of the mortise (record your measurement).

STEP 8 / Cut the tenon 1/16 inch *shorter* than the mortise depth.

STEP 9 / If a haunch is needed, cut it now.

STEP 10 / If a blind tenon is needed with a top or bottom edge cut out, lay the tenon over the mortise and mark for the cut. Cut away the stock.

STEP 11 / Cut a 45-degree corner on each side of the tenon (Figure 8-7). This will aid in fitting, provide an escape path for chips and sawdust, allow extra space for excess glue, and prevent splitting of the mortise.

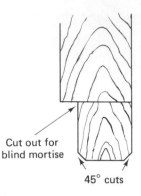

Cut out for
blind mortise

45° cuts

FIGURE 8-7   FINISHED TENON

TIP

A block of wood may be clamped along the cross-cut
line to aid in guiding the saw.

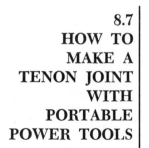

8.7
HOW TO
MAKE A
TENON JOINT
WITH
PORTABLE
POWER TOOLS

The two portable power tools most readily available for making a
tenon are the electric saw and the router. Of the two, the electric saw
approximates the hand saw in the preceding step-by-step procedures.
However, with electric power available, more cross cuts are usually
made than are made with hand saws. Using the router with a dado
bit installed requires a certain amount of skill to make an exact cut.
A fence of some sort is usually used, although the guide attachment
may be used. (This may be very unsafe in some cases, so use extreme
caution.)

The portable jig or saber saw *cannot* be used with any accuracy.

8.7.1 **TOOLS NEEDED**	*Power electric saw* *with cross-cut* *(fine-toothed)* *blade* *Router with dado* *blade*	*Straightedge (short, 4* *to 12 inches)* *C clamps, 2* *Chisel* *Combination square*

8.7.2
HOW TO CUT
A TENON JOINT
WITH PORTABLE
ELECTRIC SAW

STEP 1 / Lay out the tenon following the instructions given earlier.

STEP 2 / Set the saw on top of the stock and adjust the blade for the proper depth.

STEP 3 / Free hand, saw a cross cut to the outside of the cross-cut line drawn on the stock.

STEP 4 / With a guide, clamp a straightedge guide to the stock at a point where the outer edge of the saw base is after the blade has first been positioned (see Figure 8-8).

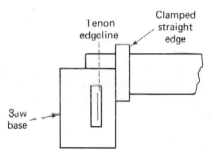

FIGURE 8-8   HOW TO USE A GUIDE

STEP 5 / *With an adjustable saw guide,* set the guide to pass along the end of the stock.

STEP 6 / Make successive cross cuts between the first cut and the end of the stock.

STEP 7 / Make one final cross cut at the end of the stock. This cut makes it easy to determine exactly where to chisel.

STEP 8 / Turn the stock over and repeat the above steps.

STEP   9 / With a sharp chisel, remove the excess stock.

STEP 10 / Trim the ends and haunches, and cut 45-degree corners.

8.7.3
HOW TO CUT
A TENON JOINT
WITH A ROUTER

STEP 1 / Install a dado bit into the router and set the depth to cut
away the stock.

STEP 2 / Make a jig to hold the stock being tenoned and set the fence

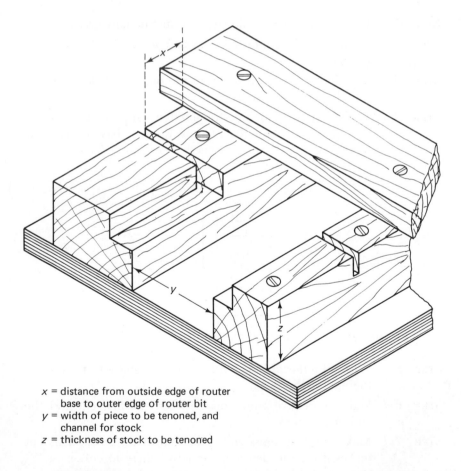

x = distance from outside edge of router
base to outer edge of router bit
y = width of piece to be tenoned, and
channel for stock
z = thickness of stock to be tenoned

FIGURE 8-9   HOW TO ROUTE A JIG TO MAKE TENONS

(straightedge) so that the first cut is made near the cross-cut line (see Figure 8-9).

STEP 3 / Cut the cross cut by hand with either a hand or an electric saw. Do not use the router. NOTE: *Chipping and splintering occurs whenever a router blade passes the end of the stock while cross-cutting. This happens because the router cutting edge is being forced into the wood, and at the edge the fibers lose their strength and tear.*

STEP 4 / Using the router, make successive passes over the area of the tenon. *Keep the router base flat and firm down on the jig and tenon stock.*

STEP 5 / *Turn the stock over, reinsert into the jig,* and repeat steps 1 through 4.

STEP 6 / Trim the ends and haunches, cut 45-degree corners, and try the tenon for fit.

8.8
HOW TO MAKE A TENON JOINT WITH BENCH POWER TOOLS

Three bench power tools can be used to make tenons in wood. They are the radial arm saw (most preferred), the table saw, and the band saw (least preferred). All three machines require exact machine set-ups. The blades must be exactly 90 degrees with the tables, and the fences must be 90 degrees with the travel of the blade (in the case of the radial arm saw) or stock (in the case of the table saw).

A variety of blades can be used. For instance, by using dado blades on the radial arm saw, one-half of the tenon can be made with a few passes of the blades. In contrast, many passes would be required to make the same tenon with a standard cross-cut blade. With the table saw a fine-toothed combination blade is generally used to make the vertical cut. Sometimes a planer blade is used to cross-cut the flat cut. The wider the blade used on a band saw, the better the chances are to make a true cut. No blades less than ½ inch wide should be used when cutting tenons.

<table>
<tr><td>8.8.1
TOOLS NEEDED</td><td>Radial arm saw
Table saw with fence
and sliding adjust-
able guide
Band saw with blade
½ inch or wider</td><td>Dado blades
Cross-cut, combina-
tion, and planer
blades
C clamps</td></tr>
</table>

8.8.2
HOW TO CUT
A TENON JOINT
WITH A RADIAL
ARM SAW

STEP 1 / Lay out the tenon according to the instructions given earlier.

STEP 2 / Install dado blades (according to the manufacturer's instructions).

STEP 3 / Set the dado blades equal to the depth top mark made in step 1.

STEP 4 / Clamp a stop (board) to the fence so that the tenon can be cut without moving the stop (Figure 8-10).

a / Make the first cut with the stock against the stop as shown in Figure 8-10.

b / Make additional passes with the dado blades after moving the stock to the left each time (see the following note).

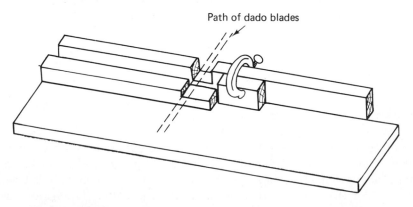

FIGURE 8-10   RADIAL ARM SAW SETUP FOR CUTTING
                 TENONS

STEP 5 / Turn the stock over and repeat steps 4a and 4b.

NOTE: *How you position the stock that is to have a tenon cut is optional, but experience will show you that the position shown in Figure 8-10 allows maximum control over both the saw and the stock. Normally the motor on the saw will pass over the tenon and hide the cut. If you reverse the stock and draw it to the right, the cutting is hidden from view and you must draw the saw forward with your left hand. For right-handed people this may be a problem.*

STEP 6 / Cut all tenons with the same setup.

STEP 7 / If a blind mortise is used and the tenon must fit:

    a / Reposition the depth of the dado blades to make the desired cut.

    b / Make the cuts on each piece. *Be careful to make the cut on the same side at each end.*

STEP 8 / Remove the dado blades and install a fine-toothed cross-cut blade.

STEP 9 / Mark the excess tenon material according to directions given earlier in the chapter.

STEP 10 / Move the stop (which is clamped to the fence) to a position where the saw will cut the excess of the tenon. Clamp the stop.

STEP 11 / Cut off all tenons.

STEP 12 / Trim the corners at a 45-degree angle.

8.8.3
HOW TO CUT A
TENON JOINT WITH
TABLE SAW AND
CROSS-CUT BLADE

Two cuts are required to make each side of a tenon. They are a vertical cut and a flat cross cut. *For safety reasons always make the vertical cuts first.*

HOW TO MAKE THE
VERTICAL CUT

STEP 1 / Lay out the tenon as explained previously.

STEP 2 / Install a sharp cross-cut blade in the saw.

STEP 3 / Set the height of the blade equal to the length of the tenon.

STEP 4 / Position the fence so that the blade is outside the line of the marked tenon.

STEP 5 / Turn the machine on and make two passes through the saw. (After the first pass rotate the stock 180 degrees and make the second cut.)

TIP

The stock must be held very stable, so a perpendicular cut is made. Any tilting of the stock causes an uneven (slanted) tenon to be made. The two methods that aid in making this cut are shown in Figure 8-11.

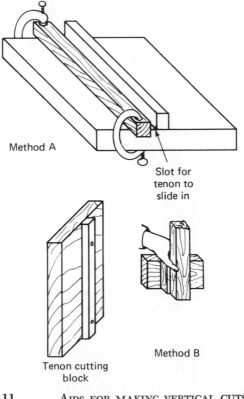

Method A

Slot for
tenon to
slide in

Tenon cutting
block

Method B

FIGURE 8-11   AIDS FOR MAKING VERTICAL CUTS ON TENONS

Method A: Using a Second Fence. Notice that a second fence has been clamped onto the table. By positioning it carefully you can create a slot for the stock to be tenoned to slide in. If you use a 2 by 4 as the second fence, it will also aid in keeping the stock perpendicular.

Method B: Using a Guide Block Free-Hand. If you make a block as shown in Figure 8-11, it is held in your left hand and the stock is held in your right. Use your left thumb as a clamp (or a small C clamp can be used) when passing the stock through the blade. This block can be made from stock of 1¼ by 6 inches or 2 by 6 inches about 10 to 12 inches long. The small guide piece is screwed onto the back and aids in holding the stock straight up.

HOW TO MAKE THE
FLAT CROSS CUT

STEP 1 / Reset the blade for the cross cut by lowering it. (If a fine cut is desired, install a planer blade.)

STEP 2 / Reposition the fence so that when the stock is butted against it, it has the saw blade to the outside (toward the end of the stock) of the layout (see Figure 8-12).

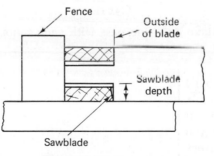

FIGURE 8-12   HOW TO MAKE A CROSS CUT ON A TENON

STEP 3 / Turn the saw on. Make a pass through the saw, then turn the stock over and make a second pass.

STEP 4 / Get out the adjustable guide and insert it (put it in the slot).

STEP 5 / Clamp a piece of stock to the fence behind the blade. You will butt the tenon against the clamped stock, then slide it out past it and through the blade, thereby cutting off the excess tenon.

Step 6 / Position the fence so that you can cut off the excess tenon (see Figure 8-13).

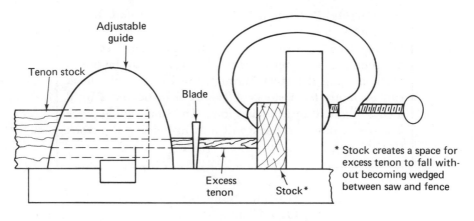

Adjustable guide

Tenon stock

Blade

Excess tenon

Stock*

* Stock creates a space for excess tenon to fall without becoming wedged between saw and fence

Figure 8-13   How to cut off excess tenon

Step 7 / Raise the blade high enough to cut off the stock. Turn the saw on and cut the excess stock from all tenons.

Caution

Make only one pass with each tenon.

8.8.4
How to Cut a Tenon Joint with Table Saw and Dado Blades

Step 1 / Install dado blades (up to ¾ inch wide).

Step 2 / Set the fence according to Figure 8-12.

Step 3 / Set the dado blades for the proper depth (Figure 8-12).

Step 4 / Using the adjustable guide, slide the stock through the saw after turning the saw on.

STEP 5 / Move the stock either in or out (depending on where you made your first cut) and repeat cutting until all stock is removed.

STEP 6 / Turn the stock over and repeat step 4.

STEP 7 / Remove the dados and install a cross-cut blade.

STEP 8 / Set the fence with a stop for cutting off excess tenon (see Figure 8-13).

STEP 9 / Cut off the excess stock.

8.8.5
How to Cut a Tenon Joint with a Band Saw

Two adjustments on the band saw must be set very accurately. One is the table tilt, set at 0 degrees. Make sure that this is accurate by using a combination square against the saw blade. The other adjustment is blade tension. The blade must be tightened properly so that no side-to-side motion exists. Properly adjusted top and bottom guides also help the blade travel.

STEP 1 / Lay out the tenon as shown in Figure 8-4.

STEP 2 / Install a wide blade (as wide as possible).

STEP 3 / Adjust the table tilt for 0 degrees.

STEP 4 / Adjust the blade tension properly.

STEP 5 / Adjust the top and bottom blade guides for minimum clearance.

STEP 6 / Set the fence to a position that will allow cutting of the tenon laterally (with the grain). See Figure 8-14 and note 1 below.

STEP 7 / Clamp a small block onto the fence at a point that allows the making of a lateral cut but stops it at its proper point.

STEP 8 / Make one cut, then turn the stock over and make the other cut.

STEP 9 / Readjust the fence so that the cross cut can be made.

STEP 10 / Cut each cross cut, keeping the end of the stock against the fence (Figure 8-14).

STEP 11 / Mark the tenon for the excess that is to be cut off. If necessary, mark for a blind mortise.

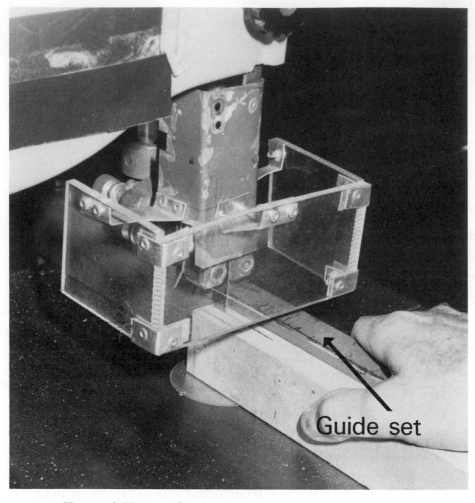

Guide set

FIGURE 8-14   SETUPS ON A BAND SAW FOR CUTTING A
                     TENON

STEP 12 / Cut off the excess free-hand or by resetting the fence (see
           Note 2).

NOTES:

   1 / If your band saw does not have a fence, use a straightedge
        and two C clamps.
   2 / If a band saw is available, it is ideal for cutting excess
        tenon material and making the small 45-degree corner cuts.

QUESTIONS |

1 / If a set of plans are being used to make a project, what view of the tenon will be shown?

2 / What are the three parts in completing a panel and frame?

3 / What is the alternative method of laying out a tenon on the rails?

4 / When is the tenon not the rail?

5 / What is the result of a well-prepared and fitted joint?

6 / When compared with the strength of the butt and dado joints, what does the tenon provide?

7 / What portable power tools can be used to make a tenon?

8 / How is a tenon made with hand tools?

9 / How is a tenon cut with the radial arm saw?

10 / Over what two items will positioning permit maximum control?

PROJECT |

Make two different tenons. Make the first one to fit into the mortise cut in the project in Chapter 7. Use another 16″ piece of 2 x 4. For the second project, make a tenon with handsaw, chisel, and hammer from a piece of 5/4″ by 2½″ by 16″ stock. Make the tenon ⅜″ thick, 2″ back, and cut a notch from it as though fitting a blind mortise.

9

HOW TO
MAKE
A DOWEL JOINT

You will recall from Chapter 1 that the dowel has been used in woodworking for a very long time. Present-day economics have caused many manufacturers of cabinets and furniture to stop using the mortise and tenon and to substitute the dowel.

9.1
HOW TO
SUBSTITUTE
THE DOWEL
JOINT FOR
THE MORTISE
AND
TENON JOINT

The doweled joint is simpler for a manufacturer to make. He can have all the pieces to be joined treated as if they were butt joints. He can have double-doweling drill presses manufactured that will drill two holes at one time. By using this machine alone a man can prepare both pieces for the dowel. The process is simple and cheap, but what strength and other properties are lost, if any?

9.2
FUNCTIONAL QUALITIES AND APPLICATIONS

The functional quality of two boards reinforced with dowels is much greater than in the simple butt joint. More than just the bond of glue is added to the joint when dowels (usually made of hardwood) are inserted across the grain. If a series of dowels is used in joining the two parallel sides of boards, it would require breaking the dowels to break the joint.

The dowel is an alternative for the tenon that basically provides the same characteristics. When two or more dowels are used rather than a single mortise and tenon, a reasonable substitution is accomplished, but inherent weakness does result. The dowel must be inserted into the end grain of one of the two pieces being joined. Even though glue has strength, it is not quite the same as having a tenon from the same piece. Another limiting factor is that the amount of wood in a dowel does not equal the amount of wood normally found in a tenon. Therefore, there has to be a slight decrease in the quality of the joint as compared to the mortise and tenon joint.

There are, of course, some applications for which it is more desirable to use the dowel than to use a mortise and tenon or a simple butt joint. We have already mentioned the ease with which the dowel joint can be made in the factory. More important, though, are situations in which two or more boards are joined at a common point, as they are when a chair is being made—such a situation is the joining of the rails of a chair to the styles. If two tenons were inserted into two mortises cut in the style,, the style would be very weak at that point. By using doweling and by offsetting the dowels, very little material is removed from the style.

We have already mentioned that doweling is fairly easy. Later the procedure section illustrates some of the techniques and devices that make the job simple. One of these devices is the dowel centering pin (Figure 9-1). It acts like a pilot, letting you know exactly where

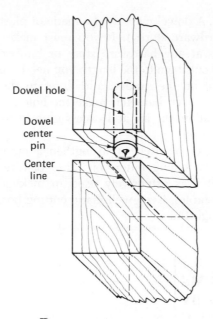

Dowel hole

Dowel
center
pin

Center
line

FIGURE 9-1   DOWEL CENTERING PIN

to center the drill bit. The other device shown in this chapter is the dowel centering tool. It is more complex but very easy to use. You merely clamp it to the stock to be doweled, adjust the scale according to its instructions, and drill through the pilot sleeve.

Several materials may be used for dowels. The best is shown in Figure 9-2. Pins such as this one can be purchased in different thicknesses and lengths. Some of the more common thicknesses are ¼, 5/16, ⅜, and ½ inch. Some of the common lengths are 1, 1½, 1¾, 2, and 2½ inches. The pin shown in Figure 9-2 has a few characteristics that are important. First notice the scoring that goes around the pin. This is designed to allow air and glue to escape from the hole the dowel is being inserted into. Another feature is the rounding off of the edges (normally square) on each end of the dowel.

A dowel may be made from maple, birch, oak, or any other wood

FIGURE 9-2   MACHINE DOWEL PIN

of great strength. A dowel may also be made of plastic (they are available in some hardware stores). If you must make your own dowels, buy dowel sticks at any hardware store or lumber yard. Take them to your shop and cut them to the length you need. Round the ends with a pocket knife or on the sander; add flutes to the dowel. Since the dowel already has a set diameter, make the hole in your stock slightly larger. This will allow the air and excess glue to come up around the outsides of the dowel.

Doweling may be used to strengthen a miter joint. It is especially useful when joining miters on large picture frames. We have already said that it is extensively used in making chairs. It is also useful in making tables. Even well-made cutting boards have doweling all the way through them.

9.3
PROBLEMS
SOLVED BY
USE OF THE
DOWEL JOINT

The doweled joint overcomes primarily the same problems of structural weakness that were solved by use of the mortise and tenon. These were stresses wherein ends of one board were supports for weight as in the case of cabinet or chair rails. The dowel joint also can be used to strengthen the inherent weakness of a butt joint. This is especially true where boards are glued on parallel sides. Another problem that can be overcome is one of end splitting. By inserting a dowel through the stock near its end, no splitting will result. From these examples you can begin to understand that joints such as the butt, miter, tongue and groove, and others can be strengthened easily and quickly by use of the dowel.

9.4
METHODS
THAT CAN
BE USED TO
MAKE THE
DOWEL JOINT

The three classifications of tools previously used will be used again in discussing the dowel joint. Hand tools and portable and bench power tools can all be used to make a dowel. In all three cases, two dowel center guide tools can be used. They are dowel centering pins (Figure 9-3) and the dowel centering attachment tool (Figure 9-4).

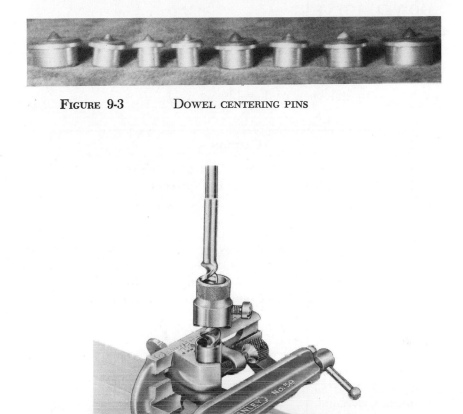

FIGURE 9-3   DOWEL CENTERING PINS

FIGURE 9-4   DOWEL CENTERING ATTACHMENT TOOL
(Courtesy of Stanley Tools)

In the following section it is assumed that the pieces to be joined are accurately cut and fit and ready for doweling. (If they are not, make them ready before following the instructions.)

9.5
HOW TO
MAKE A
DOWEL JOINT
WITH HAND
TOOLS

Once again the brace and auger are used. The selection of auger depends upon the thickness of dowel being used.

CAUTION

For the two surfaces to remain flat, the holes you drill *must* be parallel to the outer flat surfaces.

| 9.5.1 TOOLS NEEDED | Set of centering pins
Dowel centering
 attachment tool
Combination square
Dowel pins
Brace | Auger bits (No. 4 for
¼ inch; No. 5 for
5/16 inch; No. 6
for ⅜ inch; No. 8
for ½ inch) |

9.5.2
How to Drill and Dowel Using Dowel Centering Pins

NOTE: *The principal steps are the same, regardless of the angle of the pieces to be doweled.*

STEP 1 / Lay two pieces to be doweled against each other.

STEP 2 / Using a combination square, make cross-cut lines where dowels are to be installed (Figure 9-5a).

STEP 3 / Separate the pieces.

STEP 4 / Adjust the combination square for one-half the thickness of the stock.

STEP 5 / Mark the center of each cross-cut line using a square and a pencil (Figure 9-5b).

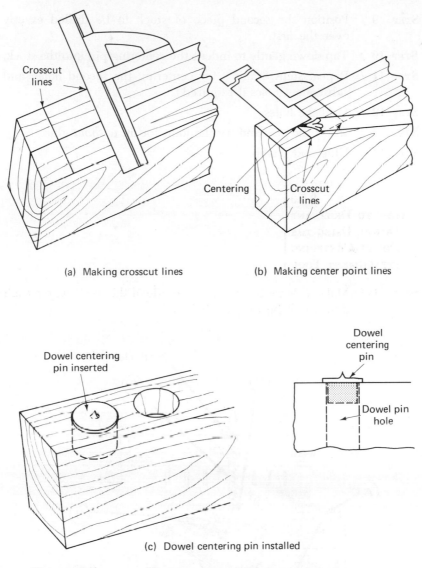

(a) Making crosscut lines   (b) Making center point lines

(c) Dowel centering pin installed

FIGURE 9-5   HOW TO USE THE DOWEL CENTERING PIN

STEP 6 / Select an auger and insert it into the brace.

STEP 7 / Drill both holes to the desired depth. (Remember to drill straight down; one way to do this would be to use a square for visual alignment.)

STEP 8 / Insert a dowel centering pin that is the same size as your dowel pin (big end down, point up) (Figure 9-5c).

STEP 9 / Position the second piece of stock to be drilled exactly over the first.

STEP 10 / Tap down gently to indent the centering pin into the stock.

STEP 11 / Repeat steps 8 and 9 for centering the second hole (and subsequent holes if required).

STEP 12 / Drill the holes.

STEP 13 / Insert the pins and try the joint for fit, *without* glue.

STEP 14 / Glue and clamp.

9.5.3
HOW TO DRILL AND DOWEL USING THE DOWEL CENTERING ATTACHMENT TOOL

STEP 1 / Make a center line on the face side of the wood where each dowel will be (Figure 9-6a).

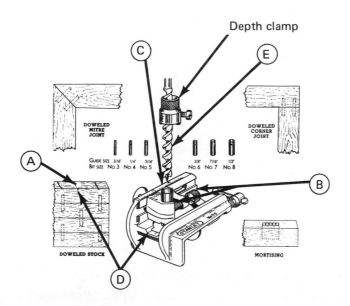

Both mark in-line

FIGURE 9-6   HOW TO USE THE DOWEL CENTERING ATTACHMENT (*Courtesy of Stanley Tools*)

STEP 2 / Select a dowel pin of suitable size and a sleeve of the same size for the guide.

STEP 3 / Secure the guide (level end up) in the slide with the bottom of the guide practically flush with the underside of the guide (Figure 9-6b).

STEP 4 / Adjust the index guide to a position equal to the thickness of the dowel. You will have to convert fractions of inches to auger-size numbers (e.g., ⅜ inch = No. 6, ½ inch = No. 8) (Figure 9-6c).

STEP 5 / Set the guide for one-half the thickness of the stock being drilled.

STEP 6 / Clamp the guide to the stock while aligning the pencil mark (step 1) and center the mark on the attachment. NOTE: *Place the attachment so that the two marks can be seen (Figure 9-6d).*

STEP 7 / Place a bit of the proper size into the guide, using care not to strike the cutting edges against the guide (Figure 9-6e).

STEP 8 / Clamp the depth gauge/stop to the bit a distance up from the sleeve equal to the desired hole depth.

STEP 9 / Insert the bit/auger in a drill or brace.

STEP 10 / Drill the hole until the clamp touches the sleeve.

9.6
HOW TO MAKE A DOWEL JOINT WITH ELECTRIC DRILL

Since a variety of bits may be used for this job, a few words may save some grief. First and probably most important, select bits that have equal and opposite cutting edges. This type of bit will eliminate the pulling tendency, minimizing the chance for offset drilling. Second, observe any instructions regarding speed of operation that come with the bits. With augers especially, a slow speed is required.

Two devices can be used to regulate the speed (revolutions per minute) of the portable electric drill. One is included in the drill switch. This drill is identified as a *variable-speed drill*. By varying the pressure on the switch you can vary the rotational speed of the drill. The second device is a *motor control unit*. This box of electronic parts sells for approximately $10.00 and works on the same principle as a switch. A speed-control knob (potentiometer) is used to regulate the rotational speed of the drill. In most cases these devices reduce the voltage but not the current; therefore you still have all the torque your drill can produce.

9.6.1
TOOLS NEEDED

Portable electric drill
Motor control unit
(optional, as
required)
Dowel centering pins

Dowel centering
attachment
Combination square
Bits and augers

9.6.2
HOW TO DRILL
AND DOWEL USING
THE DOWEL
CENTERING PINS
AND ELECTRIC DRILL

STEP 1 / Use Figure 9-5 and substitute the type of drill bit you use if you don't use an auger.

STEP 2 / Lay the two pieces to be doweled against each other.

STEP 3 / Using the combination square, make cross-cut lines where the dowels are to be installed (Figure 9-5a).

STEP 4 / Separate the pieces.

STEP 5 / Adjust the combination square for one-half the thickness of the stock.

STEP 6 / Mark the center of each cross-cut line using a square and a pencil (Figure 9-5b).

STEP 7 / Select the bit according to the thickness of the dowel pin and insert it into the electric drill.

STEP 8 / Drill both holes to the desired depth. (Remember to drill straight down.)

STEP 9 / Insert a dowel centering pin that is the same size as your dowel pin (big end down, point up) (Figure 9-5c).

STEP 10 / Position the second piece of stock to be drilled over the first.

STEP 11 / Tap down gently to indent the centering pin into the stock.

STEP 12 / Repeat steps 8 and 9 for centering the second hole (and subsequent holes if required).

STEP 13 / Drill the holes.

STEP 14 / Insert the pins and try the joint for fit, *without* glue.

STEP 15 / Glue and clamp.

9.6.3
HOW TO DRILL AND DOWEL USING THE DOWEL CENTERING ATTACHMENT AND ELECTRIC DRILL

STEP 1 / Use Figure 9-6 and substitute the type of drill bit you use if you don't use an auger.

STEP 2 / Make a center line on the face side of the wood where each dowel will be (Figure 9-6a).

STEP 3 / Select a dowel pin of suitable size and a sleeve of the same size and a sleeve of the same size for the guide.

STEP 4 / Secure the guide (level end up) in the slide with the bottom of the guide practically flush with the underside of the guide (Figure 9-6b).

STEP 5 / Adjust the index guide to a position equal to the thickness of the dowel. You will have to convert fractions of inches to auger-size numbers (e.g., ⅜ inch = No. 6, ½ inch = No. 8) (Figure 9-6c).

STEP 6 / Set the guide for one-half the thickness of the stock being drilled.

STEP 7 / Clamp the guide to the stock while aligning the pencil mark (step 1) and center mark on the attachment. **NOTE:** *Place the attachment so that the two marks can be seen (Figure 9-6d).*

STEP 8 / Place a bit of the proper size into the guide, using care not to strike the cutting edges against the guide (Figure 9-6e).

STEP 9 / Clamp the depth gauge/stop to the bit a distance up from the sleeve equal to the desired hole depth.

STEP 10 /   Insert the bit into the electric drill.

STEP 11 /   Drill the hole until the clamp touches the sleeve.

9.7
HOW TO
MAKE A
DOWEL JOINT
WITH BENCH
POWER TOOLS

The best bench tool that can be used to make a doweled joint is the drill press. It is especially good because fences and guides can be set up on the drill table. Where many pieces (all the same) have to be drilled, much time can be saved because the need for an individual layout is eliminated. There is one other bench power tool that has this capability, the radial arm saw with a drilling attachment (chuck) installed. Both of these machines make the actual task of doweling easier, and the products frequently are superior. However, the limited application (number of pieces to join) may not warrant the time required to set up the machines.

With the average shop equipment you can expect to take approximately 30 minutes to accurately set up your machines. The task involves making and securing fences and stops. Where dowels are used in one joint, two setups must be made. In the case of a frame (panel and frame), where the end of a rail is doweled, the machine must be set up several times. The considerations noted here are not given to convince you to use only hand or portable power tools but to acquaint you with the fact that the machines have limitations.

One primary limitation of the drill press may be its use in drilling the end holes for dowels. If the machine is mounted on a bench and it cannot be rotated to swing past the side of the bench, then, for example, very short rail pieces can be drilled but long ones probably 18 inches and longer cannot. In this case the drill press can be used to drill the holes in the styles and then either a portable electric drill or a brace and auger used to drill holes in the rails.

If you intend to use the radial arm saw with a chuck attached for drilling, sometimes you will fix the piece to be drilled and pull the saw into the piece. Other times you will lock the saw and force the piece into the drill bit. It depends upon such factors as the direction of feed, the length of the stock, and the angle at which you will be drilling.

Do not allow these limitations to influence you not to use machines if they are available. If you take the time to make jigs that can be used over and over, you can reduce your "make-ready" time to 5 minutes or less. You will find that a well-made jig with adjustable fences and stops can become as valuable as the power tool itself.

9.7.1 TOOLS NEEDED	*Bench or floor-model electric drill* *Assorted bits* *C clamp and fences and stops*	*Radial arm saw with drilling attachment* *Jig for drilling holes for dowels*

9.7.2 How to Drill and Dowel Using the Bench or Floor-model Electric Drill

STEP 1 / Use Figure 9-5 to help lay out the pieces to be joined.

STEP 2 / Install a bit in the drill chuck.

STEP 3 / Install a fence on the drill table.

STEP 4 / Place the stock (previously marked) against the fence and position both so that the drill bit is centered over the marking. Tighten the fence clamps.

STEP 5 / Move the stock so that the drill can be lowered along the side of the end of the stock.

STEP 6 / Set the drill-depth gage on the drill press after lowering the drill to the desired depth.

STEP 7 / Turn on the drill motor and drill the required holes.

STEP 8 / Repeat the procedure for all pieces.

STEP 9 / Dowel and glue, then clamp the joint.

TIPS

1 / Where identical multiple pieces are to be drilled, screw or bolt a strip of wood to the metal fence. Make a pencil mark on the stock at the center of the drill bit. Next make a mark left and right of the center mark a distance equal to the spacing of the dowels. Finally, make a mark left and right of the center mark a distance equal to the end of the stock to be drilled and the center of the first hole. This method will eliminate the need to perform the multiple layout on the bench.

2 / If your drill press does not have a fence, make one out of a 2-inch piece of oak or other hardwood. Carefully mark and drill a series of holes so that you can pass carriage bolts through the table (from the bottom) and through the 2-inch fence material. Secure the fence by using a large washer and wing nut on each carriage bolt.

3 / Extend the table and fence of your drill press using straight-grained oak, fir, or birch. Cut two pieces about 3 feet long. Make one for a base and one for the fence. Figure 9-7 shows you an example. Glue and screw the two pieces together. *(Make sure that your inside corner is exactly 90 degrees.)* Drill three sets of holes in the fence which will be used along with carriage bolts to hold it to the drill table. Drill one set on each end of the jig, and drill one set in the center. The sets of holes on the ends will become useful when you have to turn your drill table 90 degrees for drilling and stock. The jig will not interfere.

9.7.3
How to Drill and Dowel the End of Stock Using Drill Press

STEP 1 / Mark the pieces to be drilled using Figure 9-5a and b as an example.

STEP 2 / Set up the drill press

    a / If bench type, swing the table and drill head 90 degrees and rotate the table until it is 90 degrees with the floor.

    b / If floor type, rotate the table until it is 90 degrees with the floor.

STEP 3 / Install a fence or jig, position for drilling, and tighten. See the tip below.

STEP 4 / Lower the bit past the stock to the desired depth of the hole. Lock and set the depth gage.

STEP 5 / Using C clamps, clamp the stock to be drilled to the fence or jig.

STEP 6 / Drill the hole, rotate the stock, and drill the second hole.

STEP 7 / Fit the dowel and glue and clamp the joint.

TIP

A problem of keeping the stock lined up usually occurs when using the drill press this way. Therefore, you should take some precautions. Either extend the length of your fence by attaching an extra piece of stock or use a jig as shown in Figure 9-7. Make sure that the fence extension or jig does not interfere with the drill head.

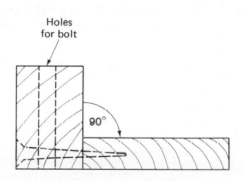

Holes
for bolt

90°

FIGURE 9-7   JIG FOR DRILL PRESS

9.7.4
HOW TO END-DRILL AND DOWEL WITH RADIAL ARM SAW AND CHUCK ATTACHMENT

STEP 1 / Remove the blade from the saw.

STEP 2 / Install a chuck on the opposite end of the motor shaft from the saw.

STEP 3 / Install a bit into the chuck and tighten.

STEP 4 / Lay out the stock to be drilled. Use Figure 9-5 a and b for guidance. NOTE: *The normal table surface is usually too low to use when drilling. If you plan to do much drilling using this machine, you may find that the time spent to make a special jig will be worth your while. The balance of steps listed in this task description assume that some method or jig will be used to complete the job. (See Figure 9-9 for a sample jig.)*

STEP 5 / Build up the table surface or installed jig.

STEP 6 / Place a previously marked piece of stock on the built-up surface (or jig) and adjust the saw to position the drill in the marked area.

STEP 7 / Nail or clamp fences on the built-up area so that feeding the stock into the turning drill results in a straight hole (see Figure 9-8a).

STEP 8 / Feed the stock into the drill.

STEP 9 / Turn the stock over and drill a second hole (if required).

9.7.5
HOW TO SIDE-DRILL AND DOWEL WITH RADIAL ARM SAW AND CHUCK ATTACHMENT

STEP 1 / Remove the blade from the saw.

STEP 2 / Install a chuck and bit on the saw (opposite end of the motor shaft).

STEP 3 / Rotate the motor 90 degrees so that the drill is pointing toward you.

STEP 4 / Build up the table surface or install the jig.

STEP 5 / Place a previously marked piece of stock on the built-up surface and adjust the saw to position the drill in the marked area.

STEP 6 / Nail or clamp fences on the built-up area so that the holes drilled will be true.

STEP 7 / Make marks (pencil) on the fence where the drill center will travel.

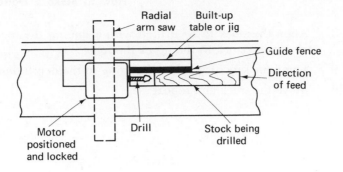

(a) End drilling for dowels

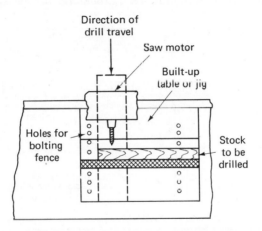

(b) Side drilling for dowels

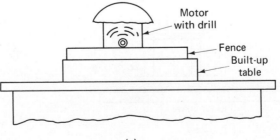

(c)

FIGURE 9-8   HOW TO DRILL WITH A RADIAL ARM SAW

STEP 8 / Align the stock to be drilled with a line on the fence and
clamp the stock to the jig of the fence.

STEP 9 / Draw the saw forward as if cutting to the depth desired.

STEP 10 / Move the stock and repeat.

**9.8
JIG FOR
DRILLING
WITH RADIAL
ARM SAW**

As mentioned earlier, sometimes a homemade device speeds up use

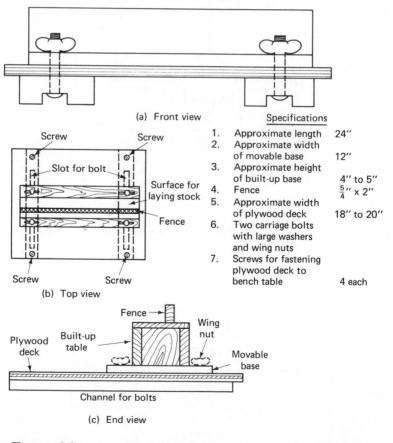

(a) Front view

Screw   Screw

Slot for bolt

Surface for
laying stock

Fence

Screw   Screw

(b) Top view

Specifications

1. Approximate length   24″
2. Approximate width
   of movable base   12″
3. Approximate height
   of built-up base   4″ to 5″
4. Fence $\frac{5}{4}$″ x 2″
5. Approximate width
   of plywood deck   18″ to 20″
6. Two carriage bolts
   with large washers
   and wing nuts
7. Screws for fastening
   plywood deck to
   bench table   4 each

Fence   Wing
                        nut
Plywood   Built-up
deck   table   Movable
                                base

Channel for bolts

(c) End view

FIGURE 9-9   JIG FOR DRILLING WITH A RADIAL ARM SAW

of the machine. It also makes it easier to get an accurate job every time. The jig shown in Figure 9-9 is one such device.

QUESTIONS |

1 / What joint has, for reasons of economics, replaced the mortise and tenon?

2 / What two factors show how the dowel joint is weaker than the mortise and tenon?

3 / What application of the dowel illustrates its usefulness?

4 / What are two important characteristics about the machine dowel pin?

5 / What is the most important problem that can be solved by use of the dowel joint?

6 / What caution must be used when using the brace and auger to make a hole for a dowel?

7 / What is the best bench tool for making a doweled joint?

8 / What are three tips to use when making a dowel with bench tools?

9 / What method can be used for end-drilling dowels using a radial arm saw?

10 / What are some of the advantages of using a jig?

PROJECT |

Make the jig for drilling with a radial arm saw if you have such a saw.

ALTERNATE PROJECT |

Make a small utility table 20″ wide by 30″ long by 28″ high. Buy four 28″ legs with square upper portions. Cut two upper bands 2½″ by 25″ by ¾″, and two more 2½″ by 15″ by ¾″. Dowel the ends of the four band pieces to the upper part of the legs. Glue and clamp. Tack nail a cross brace across one corner after squaring the frame with a square. Pre-drill four dowel holes in the long band pieces, about 2″ from each end. Drill matching holes in the underside of the 20″ by 30″ top. Insert glue and dowels, and install top.

UNIT III

Unit III consists of three short chapters. Many of the whys, wheres, and hows of joinery were answered in Unit II. Now we shall discuss certain applications of the principles that we have learned. We have selected what we believe to be the most representative uses of joints in common cabinet projects. To aid in applying these concepts, full-page instructions in large lettering, accompanied by detail drawings, are provided, all emphasizing step-by-step procedures. You can place the book down, open it to the page being consulted, and be able to read and follow the detail at a distance of 3 feet or more.

No attempt is made to provide instructions regarding the individual selection or set up of equipment, but references are provided within the text of each chapter to pertinent procedures contained in the chapters of Unit II.

10

HOW TO MAKE A FRAME AND PANEL

The frame and panel is the first in a series of types of woodworking joinery that combines basic joints to create another joint or product. A number of basic joints can be used to make the frame and panel: some are the mortise, the tenon, and the dado. In this chapter we shall discuss procedures used to make the panel and frame. Tasks such as making a dado or rabbet, for instance, are not detailed. However, references are given to chapters in Unit II in case you need to refresh your memory about how to make the joint.

10.1
FUNCTIONAL
USE AND
APPLICATIONS

The frame and panel provides a cabinetmaker with a lightweight, sturdy, decorative assembly that has many uses. The lightweight feature is understood when comparison is made with a panel of the same size made from solid wood of the same kind and thickness. Usually the panel in the frame is quite a bit thinner than the usual stock lumber.

Because several pieces are used to make a frame and panel, well-fitted joints must be made in well-seasoned lumber. If these conditions are met, the strength usually needed when frame and panel are used approaches the strength of a solid panel of equal thickness.

A great variety of design can be incorporated into a frame and panel without the skill of a woodcarver. When solid panels were used, woodcarvers might spend many weeks carving one panel. Today, lumberyards and hardware stores provide a variety of moldings and plantons that can be incorporated into frame-and-panel construction.

Some of the most frequent uses for the frame and panel are the end panels on cabinets, dust covers between drawers in chests and dressers, and as doors on any and all varieties of cabinets. Within the styles of furniture examined earlier, almost every style, at one time or another, used some version of the frame and panel.

Finally, but not last in usage, the frame and panel became a boon to cabinetmaking because it minimized the chance for splitting, which often occurred when solid wood panels were used. (Do you remember from the discussion in Chapter 1 how solid panels caused problems and limited the overall sizes of cabinets?)

10.2
METHODS
THAT CAN
BE USED TO
MAKE THE
FRAME AND
PANEL

Four methods are identified. Each will be examined later in the chapter, but first let's identify each one and point out its significant characteristics.

Method 1 suggests that the butt joint can be used for rails and styles. Moldings such as the shoe or quarter-round and modified bed molding are cut and fitted within the frame and encase the panel. Examples of this technique, used in the Victorian era, are shown in Figure 10-1.

Method 2 suggests that the mortise and tenon can be used to make the frame. Then the dado can be used to insert the panel. Of

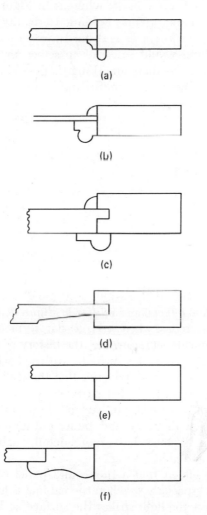

(a)

(b)

(c)

(d)

(e)

(f)

FIGURE 10-1   USE OF MOLDING TO HOLD PANELS IN FRAMES AND PANELS

course the dado could also be used with method 1. Figure 10-1c and d shows two methods in which the dado is used. Notice in Figure 10-1c that molding is used on both sides of the panel. However, the simpler design shown in Figure 10-1d is found in Early American and Colonial cabinetry.

Method 3 suggests the dowel to join the frame pieces. The dado, rabbet, or molding can be uesd to insert the panel.

Finally, method 4 suggests that a rabbet joint be used in place of the dado. Figure 10-1e and f shows two examples. In Figure 10-1e a rabbet is cut into the frame itself, whereas in Figure 10-1f the rabbet is made in the molding. (This molding is readily available already rabbetted in many lumberyards and hardware stores.)

What conditions would cause us to select any of these methods over one of the others? Is there any thing that could be obtained from a particular selection besides strength and light weight? What about design effect, that is, appearance?

10.3 DESIGN EFFECTS CREATED BY USE OF THE FRAME AND PANEL

The three design effects that a frame and panel create are *relief from flat surfaces, shadow effects,* and *effects of different wood textures.*

There are occasions when a large flat surface is desirable as a design feature on a cabinet. However, the history of fine furniture indicates a certain feeling that flat surfaces are used with simple furnishings for simple people. It also indicates that the use of frame and panel sections as a relief from these flat surfaces is a sign of affluence. Examples of furnishings of royalty in Europe show both kinds of surfaces, but those cabinets with frame and panel outnumber the other kind. These cabinets also seem to have more detail, such as carving, wood molding, gilding, and gold leafing.

The shadow effects that a frame and panel can create are very appealing. This is especially so when the cabinet is given a satin (semi-gloss) finish. Where the light strikes the surface, a deep penetration of the finish results. The grain and color of the wood reflect the beauty. These reflections melt into the shadows, which take in different hues and contrasts. Because natural light continually changes in intensity, the shadows are constantly changing. Each time the cabinet is looked at, its beauty is seen in a slightly different way.

The grain of the wood, which is what gives it is texture, is very dramatically displayed in the frame and panel. The panel may (usually does) have a large flat grain. The rails and styles of the frame may have a close grain, especially where oak is used and quarter-sawed, or the frame may have a flat grain. The moldings, if used, probably have little grain because of the way they are made. Beautiful textures result from various combinations of grain patterns. Highlights are brought out by polishing and by use of varnishes. Certain parts of the grain stain more darkly than others. Panels that are beveled at the edges have their bias-cut end grain showing. These ends take stain easily and are often darker than the adjacent flat surfaces. This creates a definite contrast in texture. If veneers are used, and matching veneers are selected, the panel's frame may lose its contrast because the focal point is the veneered surface. In these cases straight-grained wood is usually selected for the frame. Some molding may be used but it, too, will be selected so that it does not detract from the veneer, which is the focal point. There is no doubt that the frame and panel adds beauty to a cabinet, but what other features do these units have that aids in construction?

10.4
PROBLEMS SOLVED BY USE OF THE FRAME AND PANEL

First and most significant, the weight of the unit is reduced. This is easily understood because most panels range from ⅛ to ½ inch in thickness. Most of the frames have styles and rails with widths ranging up to 2½ inches, in which case the panels account for most of the area. These characteristics are in contrast with a solid panel (flat surface), which is usually ¾ inch thick.

Unless special care is taken in curing lumber, the problem of splitting and checking is always present. If this happens during the construction of a cabinet, the piece may be lost. The frame and panel overcomes this problem; because of its construction, no splitting or checking results. The frame is made from small pieces that can be easily dried, and the panel is glued into the frame, which aids in preventing splitting and checking.

A third problem that use of stock lumber has is *warping*. It doesn't matter if the warp is a bow, crook, twist, or bend; the result is the same. The problem may not be solvable. Usually large flat surfaces can be made straight by cutting the boards into narrow strips 2 to 3 inches wide, then gluing them. This is a compromise, of course, and the effect that a flat grain had is lost forever. By use of the frame and panel, warping is eliminated. The panel is held securely in the frame. It is thinner and more easily dried, and the effect of having flat-cut grain is not lost. Now let's study some methods that can be used to make a frame and panel.

10.5
HOW TO MAKE
A FRAME

Illustrations and discussions are provided for making the frame using three techniques and a combination of joints. These are the butt, dowel, and mortise and tenon, used in combination with the dado and rabbet joints. Detailed steps are provided for the sequence to use in making the joint.

The following pages provide visual examples of the methods for making a frame. Within the outline of each illustration you will see a section titled "Preferred Sequence." If you follow these steps you should have no problems in making your frame.

A few basics must be identified before you start your job. These are the selection of method of joinery and the sizing of the materials to be used for the frame.

1 / Review the illustrations and select the method of joinery you will use in making the frame. It may pay to refer to Unit II to determine if you have the tools needed to make the joints required for the frame.

2 / If one or a group of frames are to be made, precut, trim, and smooth all the pieces you will need for all the frames. It is suggested that styles and rails be cut to equal the *total* outside dimensions of the finished product. As pointed out earlier, this may cause a few inches of waste material but may save you considerable grief. Suppose that you were to select a butt joint but find that it is not satisfactory. If you have the excess material that we

lel plane with the table surface. Then tilt the front edge of the blade *up* 15 degrees. Set and lock the travel arm so that 1½ inches of the blade extends beyond the fence. Adjust the depth of the blade. Cut all four edges.

The table saw can be set up with a blade tilt of 15 degrees and blade height of 1½ inches. Position the fence so that the blade is tilted away from the fence. Cut all four edges the same way.

A shaper can be used. Install a 3- to 3½-inch saw blade on the shaper shaft, set and clamp a small piece of stock against the fence. This stock will tilt the material being cut and result in a finished bevel. Adjust the shaft height and fence depth. Cut all four edges.

In the case of Figure 10-1e, a simple rabbet is made either before or after the frame is assembled and a panel is tailored into the opening. This assembly is useful for dust covers and end panels on cabinets because of the flat surface created on the inside.

In the case of Figure 10-1f, a molding is installed within the completed frame. Forty-five-degree joints are used in the corners and a simple rabbet holds the panel in place. If a flat surface is needed, the molding can be set so that the back surface is flush with the interior.

See Figures 10-2 through 10-9 for illustrations of the use of various joints in the construction of both frames and panels.

recommend, you are free to alter your plans and us‹
a mortise and tenon.

3 / The *callouts* (circled numbers) on the illustrations ic
of special interest. These numbers correspond to the
structions under the title "Preferred Sequence."

4 / For your reference, use Chapter 4 for the butt joint, C
and 8 for the mortise and tenon, Chapter 9 for doweling,
6 for dadoing, and Chapter 5 for rabbetting.

10.6
HOW TO MAKE
A PANEL

Refer again to Figure 10-1. Shown on the figure is a cross section
each type of panel arrangement. The illustrations that follow are
ganized similar to the ones for the frame. Since there are only thr‹
basic approaches to inserting the panel, one illustration shows ho\
Figure 10-1a and b would be prepared. Another shows how to prepar‹
a panel for Figure 10-1c, d, and e. A third illustration shows how a
panel is prepared for Figure 10-1f.

In the cases of Figures 10-1a, b, and f, no dadoing or rabbetting
is used. Therefore, the frame you would make could be simple. You
could use the mortise and tenon, dowel, or butt joints. You will need
moldings of different shapes and sizes, and you will need an *accurate*
miter box and a sharp saw. Also observe in these cases that the panels
are *flat*. This makes your job easier. However, the thickness of the
panel must be taken into consideration when you are planning the
sizes of your moldings.

In the cases of Figure 10-1c and d a dado joint must be incorporated into the frame. The frame cannot be glued together until the
panel has been fitted and inserted. Notice that molding is used on both
sides of Figure 10-1c. The outside molding is useful in covering the
joint between the frame and panel in cases where you misjudge the
exact size of the opening. This panel must be fairly thick (⅜ to ½ inch)
so that a rabbet can be cut on the edges.

Figure 10-1d shows a beveled raised panel. Although shown as a
one-sided raised panel, you could make both sides beveled, thereby
having a raised panel on both sides. A variety of machines can be
used to cut the bevel.

The radial arm saw can be used. Install a smaller blade (8 inches
or less) on the saw and set the machine so that the blade is on a paral-

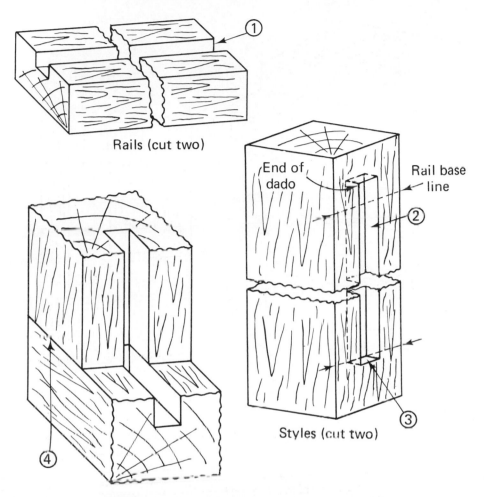

Rails (cut two)

Joint

PREFERRED SEQUENCE

① Dado rails

② Dado (blind) styles

③ Clean corners of styles with chisel

④ Glue joint with panel inserted and clamp

FIGURE 10-2   FRAME (BUTT JOINT WITH DADO)

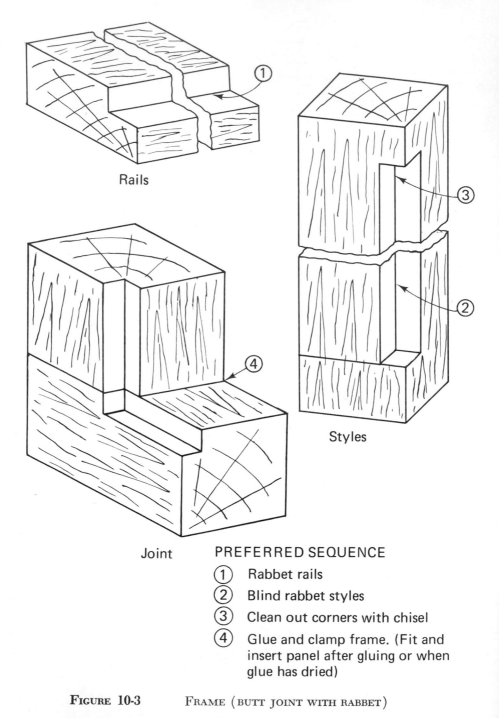

Rails

Styles

Joint

PREFERRED SEQUENCE

① Rabbet rails

② Blind rabbet styles

③ Clean out corners with chisel

④ Glue and clamp frame. (Fit and insert panel after gluing or when glue has dried)

FIGURE 10-3   FRAME (BUTT JOINT WITH RABBET)

PREFERRED SEQUENCE

① Cut two styles with dado

② Cut two rails with haunch
   at each end to fit dado in style

③ Dado rails

④ Glue joints with panel
   inserted clamp

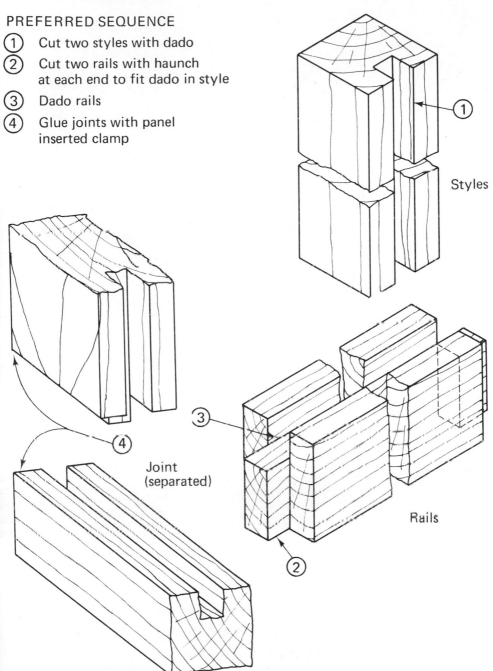

Styles

Joint
(separated)

Rails

FIGURE 10-4   FRAME (HAUNCH WITH DADO)

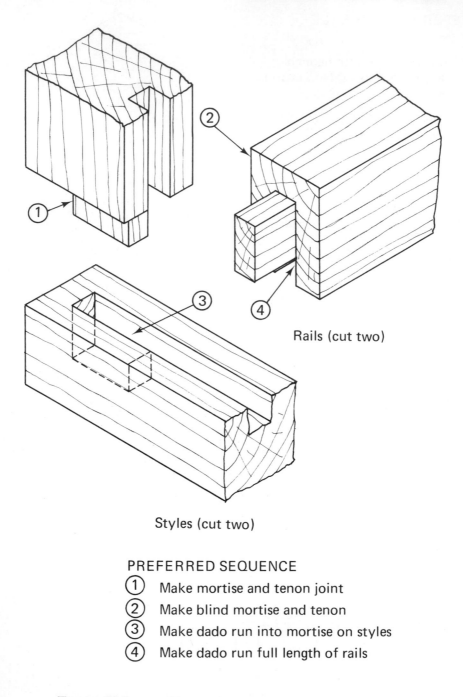

Rails (cut two)

Styles (cut two)

PREFERRED SEQUENCE
① Make mortise and tenon joint
② Make blind mortise and tenon
③ Make dado run into mortise on styles
④ Make dado run full length of rails

FIGURE 10-5   FRAME (MORTISE AND TENON AND DADO)

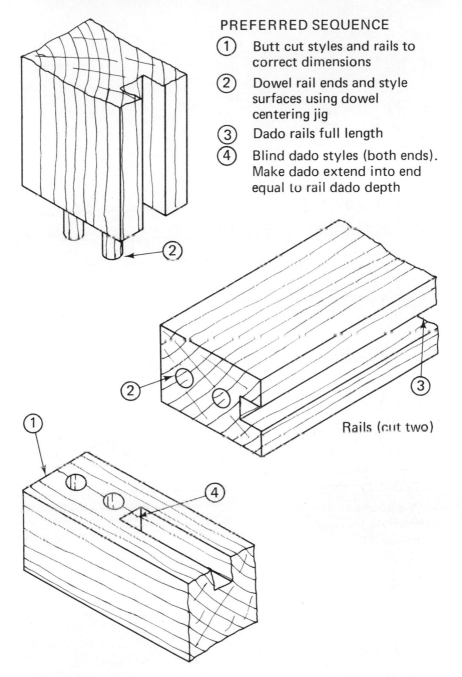

PREFERRED SEQUENCE

① Butt cut styles and rails to correct dimensions

② Dowel rail ends and style surfaces using dowel centering jig

③ Dado rails full length

④ Blind dado styles (both ends). Make dado extend into end equal to rail dado depth

Rails (cut two)

FIGURE 10-6   FRAME (DOWEL AND DADO)

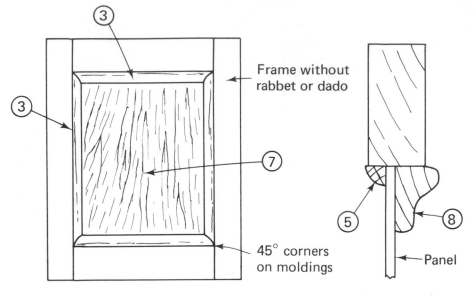

Frame without rabbet or dado

45° corners on moldings

Panel

Cut away view

PREFERRED SEQUENCE

1   Make frame using any joint desired; glue; let dry

2   Sand both sides of frame

(3) Precut molding 1 inch longer than needed

(4) Precut one end of each piece of molding on a 45° angle

(5) Measure and cut the other end of each piece of molding (back pieces first)

6   Install back pieces

(7) Cut and install panel (have grain run as shown)

(8) Install face molding

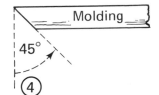

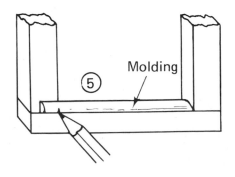

FIGURE 10-7   PANEL (WITH MOLDING)

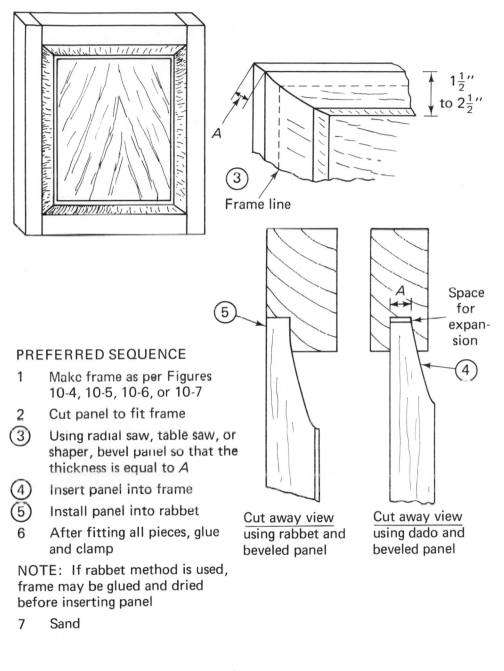

Frame line

$1\frac{1}{2}''$ to $2\frac{1}{2}''$

Space for expansion

PREFERRED SEQUENCE

1   Make frame as per Figures 10-4, 10-5, 10-6, or 10-7

2   Cut panel to fit frame

③   Using radial saw, table saw, or shaper, bevel panel so that the thickness is equal to A

④   Insert panel into frame

⑤   Install panel into rabbet

6   After fitting all pieces, glue and clamp

NOTE: If rabbet method is used, frame may be glued and dried before inserting panel

7   Sand

Cut away view using rabbet and beveled panel

Cut away view using dado and beveled panel

FIGURE 10-8   PANEL (RABBET OR DADO AND BEVELED PANEL)

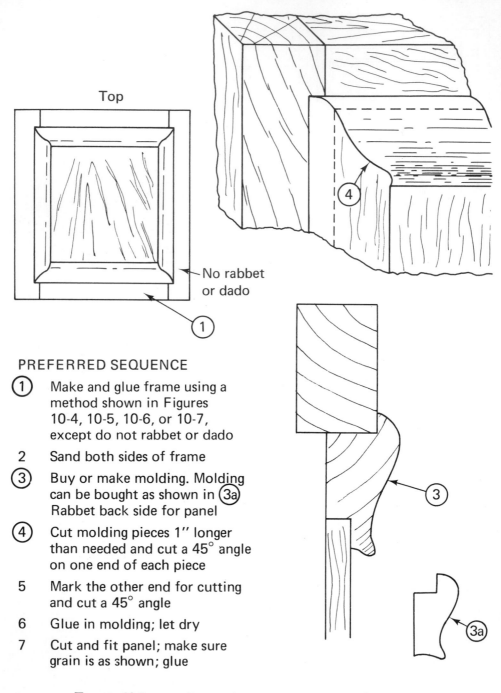

Top

No rabbet or dado

①

PREFERRED SEQUENCE

①   Make and glue frame using a method shown in Figures 10-4, 10-5, 10-6, or 10-7, except do not rabbet or dado

2   Sand both sides of frame

③   Buy or make molding. Molding can be bought as shown in ③a Rabbet back side for panel

④   Cut molding pieces 1″ longer than needed and cut a 45° angle on one end of each piece

5   Mark the other end for cutting and cut a 45° angle

6   Glue in molding; let dry

7   Cut and fit panel; make sure grain is as shown; glue

FIGURE 10-9   PANEL (MOLDING AND RABBET)

QUESTIONS |

1 / What are three places where a panel and frame may be used on a cabinet?

2 / How can the use of a panel and frame minimize the splitting that often occurs in solid panels?

3 / Of the four methods that can be used to make frames, which are desirable for a cabinet end?

4 / Can quarter-round molding be used in making a panel and frame?

5 / What is the "shadow effect"?

6 / Can the textures of wood be used on rails and styles of a panel and frame?

7 / How is warping controlled by using the panel and frame?

8 / What are the three methods of securing a panel in a frame (Figure 10-1), and how do they differ?

9 / Can you explain in detail how to make a frame with a haunch and dado?

10 / What machines are frequently used to make a beveled panel for a panel and frame?

PROJECT |

If you build the cabinet described in Chapter 13, substitute a frame and panel door for the one shown in the plan—especially if your furniture is of a European style.

ALTERNATE PROJECT |

Make a period piece of furniture for an entrance hallway. Make the ends using the frame and panel method. Install a base and one shelf plus the top, all made from ¾" plywood. Dress the plywood edges with molding, stain, and varnish.

11

HOW TO
MAKE
LAP JOINTS

The lap joint has been used extensively in construction for centuries. Because of its variety, it is also used in the manufacture of furniture and in cabinetry. As in Chapter 10, the last part of this chapter is made up of a series of full-page illustrations with a preferred sequence of steps included in each illustration. But, first, let's find out what a lap joint is.

11.1
FUNCTIONAL
USE AND
APPLICATIONS

By definition, a lap joint is a type of joint wherein one member of wood laps over the other. Figure 11-1 shows an end lap. This is probably the

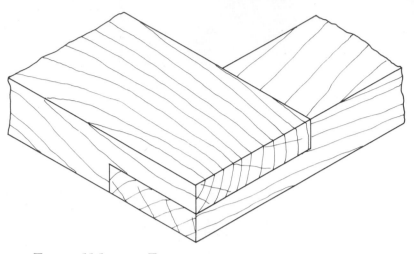

FIGURE 11-1   END LAP JOINT

simplest of all lap joints to make. Notice how the definition accurately describes the joint.

The lap joint falls within the unit of combining joints to make a new structure. It does so because the dado, rabbet, tenon, dovetail, scarf, key, and tongue and groove can be used to make lap joints. Each type of joint is shown in combination with another in the second half of this chapter.

The lap joint provides many opportunities for use in cabinet-making. Where supports are needed for open shelving, the lap joint is made from the dado and rabbet or dado and half-tenon (Figure 11-2). If a strengthened corner joint is needed where a butt joint would prove weak, the lap joint shown in Figure 11-1 would provide the added strength needed.

In instances in which a restriction of thickness is a requirement, the lap joint can be used. This might be when a dust cover is needed or in some cases in which a frame for a frame and panel is made. Because each member has one-half of its stock removed, the resultant joint retains the same thickness as the original member.

Not all lap joints are made on the plane as shown in Figure 11-1. They are made on edge, a description of which is provided later in the chapter. However, the edge lap joint is used many times in cases where a band is installed around a table. It is also used when making work benches, shop tables, and stools. Many pieces of lawn furniture, such as chaise lounges, tables, and rolling serving carts, use the edge lap joint. What are some of the methods that can be used to make the joint?

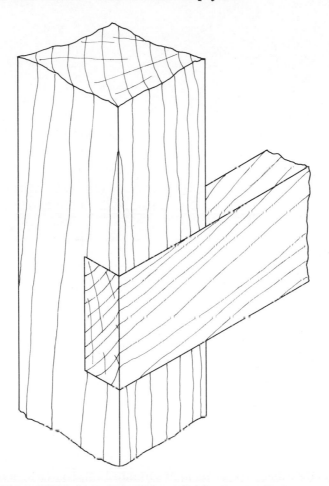

FIGURE 11-2   SHELF SUPPORTING LAP JOINT

11.2
METHODS
THAT CAN
BE USED
TO MAKE
LAP JOINTS

Figures 11-1 and 11-2 show two of the methods used to make the lap joint. They are the *end lap joint,* made with two rabbetted or half-tenon (offset tenon) pieces, and the *center lap or T lap joint,* made from a

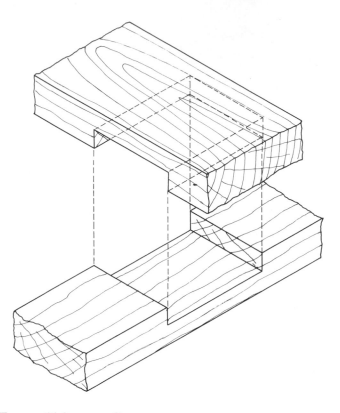

FIGURE 11-3   CROSS LAP JOINT

dado in combination with a half-tenon. A similar one is made from two dadoes and is called a *cross lap joint* (Figure 11-3). By using a dovetail in combination with a dado, another lap joint, called the *wedge lap joint,* is made (see Figure 11-4).

Another lap joint not used too frequently but very successful is the *scarf lap joint* and its companion joint called the *keyed scarf joint*. These, shown in Figure 11-5, are made so that the boards are jammed end to end. These joints may be made with straight half-tenons or rabbets, or with beveled tenons or rabbets, and on occasion a dovetail may be needed.

We said earlier that all lap joints are not made on the plane, but that some are made on edge. One of the latter is the *edge cross lap joint*. In this instance the two members are rabbeted across the stock so that the one fits into the other. Figure 11-6 shows such an example. Another is the *dovetail lap joint*. This joint, shown in Figure 11-7, requires the use of a dovetail attachment for use on a router.

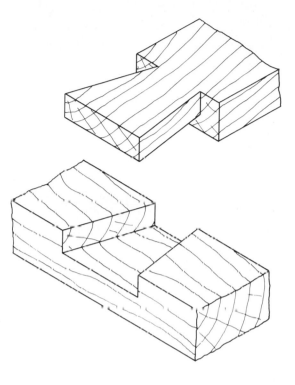

FIGURE 11-4   WEDGE LAP JOINT

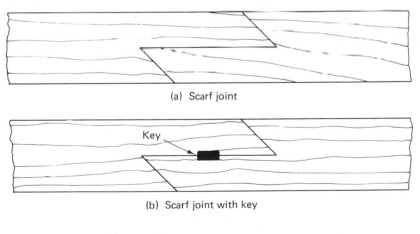

(a) Scarf joint

(b) Scarf joint with key

FIGURE 11-5   SCARF LAP JOINT

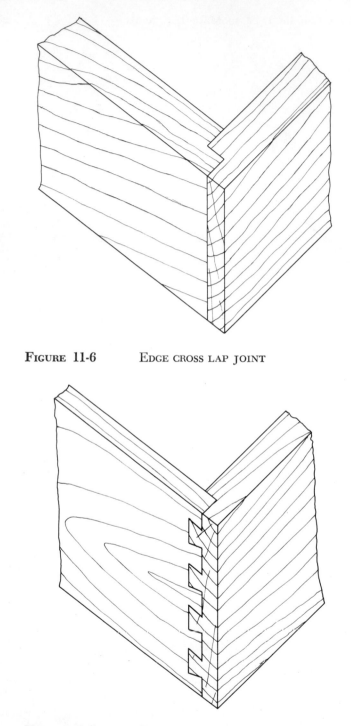

FIGURE 11-6   EDGE CROSS LAP JOINT

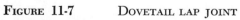

FIGURE 11-7   DOVETAIL LAP JOINT

Finally, the tongue and groove is a type of lap joint. It has many uses, some of which are shown in Figure 11-8.

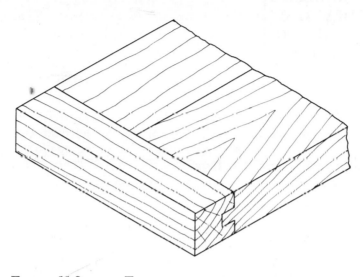

FIGURE 11-8   TONGUE AND GROOVE LAP JOINT

11.3
DESIGN
EFFECTS
CREATED BY
USE OF THE
LAP JOINT

Of the many joints and combinations of joints, the lap joint is the only one that can create a band effect. This effect is created by having the grain on the lap piece run in band-like fashion around or over a cabinet. If you can imagine that you continue the band shown in Figure 11-2 all the way around a table or cabinet, you can visualize the banding effect that would be created.

Another pattern that can be created with a lap joint is a cross or basket-weave pattern. The effect can be used on table tops, wine-bottle storage cabinets, and outdoor plant tables. In each of these instances the bands are separated slightly. Figure 11-9 shows a partial example.

11.4
PROBLEMS
SOLVED BY
USE OF THE
LAP JOINT

Using the lap joint in any of its applications provides strength in a cabinet where a butt joint would or could be used. It is not possible to substitute the lap joint for a butt joint in every case. However, as in the case shown in Figure 11-2, it is easy to understand how pull strength is increased because of the wedge. And probably the strongest lap joint created is the dovetail, shown in Figure 11-7. This joint, shown in only one application, is extremely strong and durable.

11.5
WAYS TO
MAKE THE
LAP JOINT

The full-page working illustrations depict the principal steps required to make each type of lap joint. Inserted in each page of illustrations is a preferred sequence of steps that can be used to make the joint.

In the paragraphs that follow a brief description is included to make you aware of the machines or tools that can be used to make each joint. Match the title of each paragraph with the full-page illustrations that follow.

11.5.1
CROSS LAP JOINT

The cross lap joint is best made with a radial arm saw. However, a router, table saw, or portable power saw can be used. A hand saw, chisel, hammer, or hand chipper can be used also. Refer to Chapter 6 if you need guidance in making the joint.

11.5.2
EDGE CROSS
LAP JOINT

The edge cross lap joint is made from two rabbet joints. The joint can

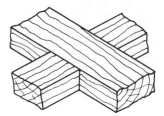

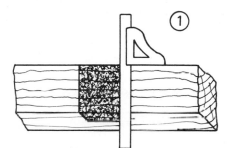

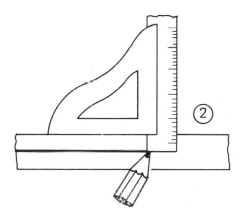

PREFERRED SEQUENCE

① Lay out both members of the joint

② Mark depth line using adjustable square

3 Cut both members

4 Stay within pencil lines

5 Clean the joint—fit

6 Glue and clamp

FIGURE 11-9   CROSS-PATTERN LAP JOINT
(A) CROSS LAP JOINT

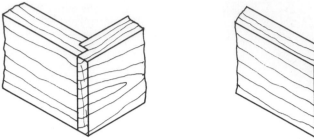
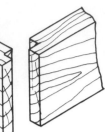

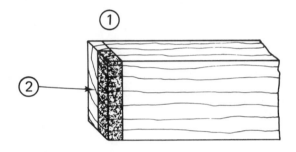

PREFERRED SEQUENCE

① Lay out rabbet on each member

② Make depth cut line equal to $\frac{1}{2}$ thickness of stock

3 Cut both pieces

4 Fit—trim, if necessary

5 Glue—clamp

FIGURE 11-9   (CONTINUED)
                   (B) EDGE CROSS LAP JOINT

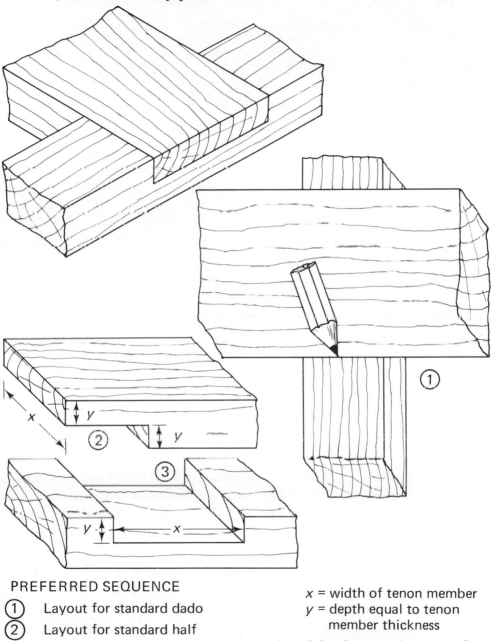

PREFERRED SEQUENCE

① Layout for standard dado
② Layout for standard half tenon
③ Cut out dado with:

x = width of tenon member
y = depth equal to tenon member thickness

4 Join pieces to determine fit
5 Glue and clamp

FIGURE 11-9   (CONTINUED)
(c) CENTER LAP OR T LAP JOINT

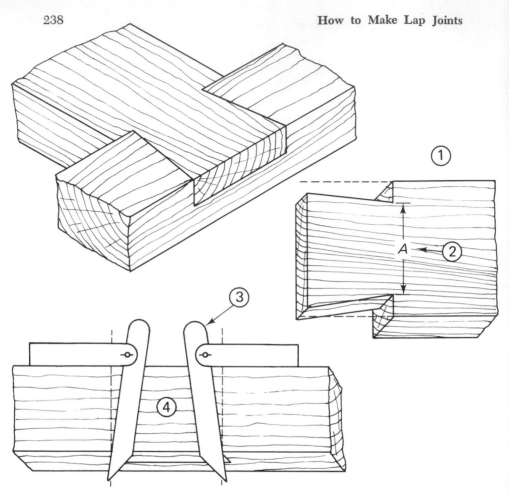

PREFERRED SEQUENCE
1   Lay out modified half tenon
2   Make narrow end of wedge equal to 75% (*A*) of the total width of tenon
3   Set "bevel square" for bias (angle)
4   Lay out modified dado
5   Cut both tenon and dado
6   Fit—trim if necessary
7   Glue and clamp

FIGURE 11-9   (CONTINUED)
                     (D) WEDGE OR DOVETAIL LAP JOINT

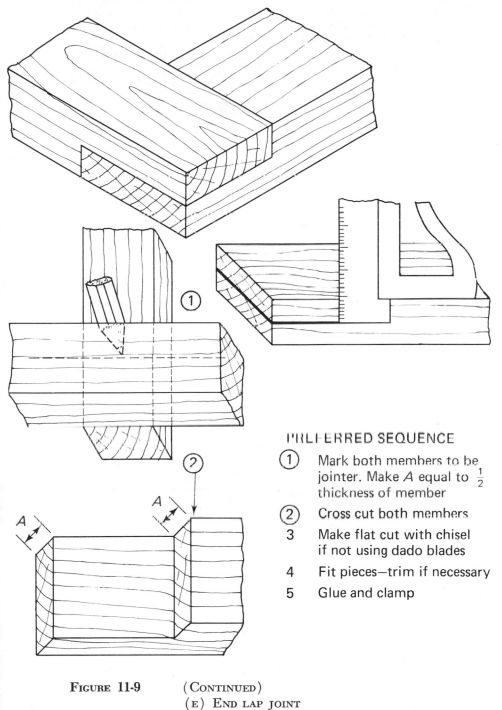

PREFERRED SEQUENCE

1. Mark both members to be jointer. Make A equal to $\frac{1}{2}$ thickness of member

2. Cross cut both members

3. Make flat cut with chisel if not using dado blades

4. Fit pieces—trim if necessary

5. Glue and clamp

FIGURE 11-9   (CONTINUED)
(E) END LAP JOINT

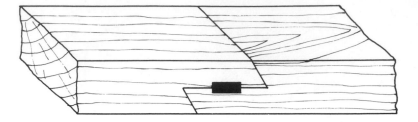

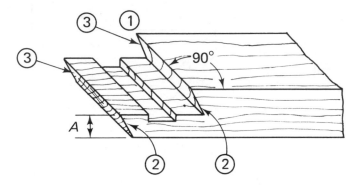

PREFERRED SEQUENCE

① Lay out both members

② Use bevel square for marking *all* bevels

③ Cut bias crosscut

4 Make flatcut

5 Lay out key dado, if used

6 Fit members

7 Make key

8 Glue—clamp

FIGURE 11-9   (CONTINUED)
(F) SCARF LAP JOINT (WITH OPTIONAL KEY)

NOTE: Use this sequence *only* if you have
       a dovetail attachment for your router

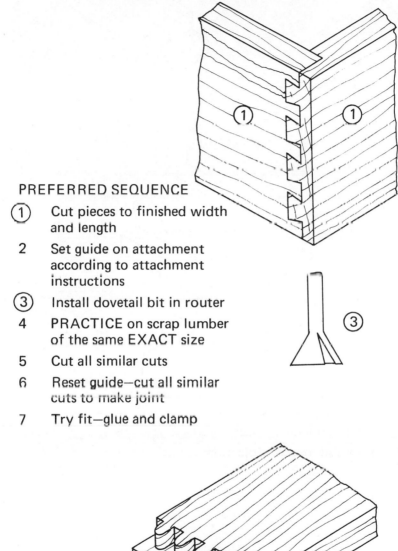

PREFERRED SEQUENCE

① Cut pieces to finished width
    and length

2 Set guide on attachment
   according to attachment
   instructions

③ Install dovetail bit in router

4 PRACTICE on scrap lumber
   of the same EXACT size

5 Cut all similar cuts

6 Reset guide—cut all similar
   cuts to make joint

7 Try fit—glue and clamp

FIGURE 11-9   (CONTINUED)
                (G) DOVETAIL LAP JOINT

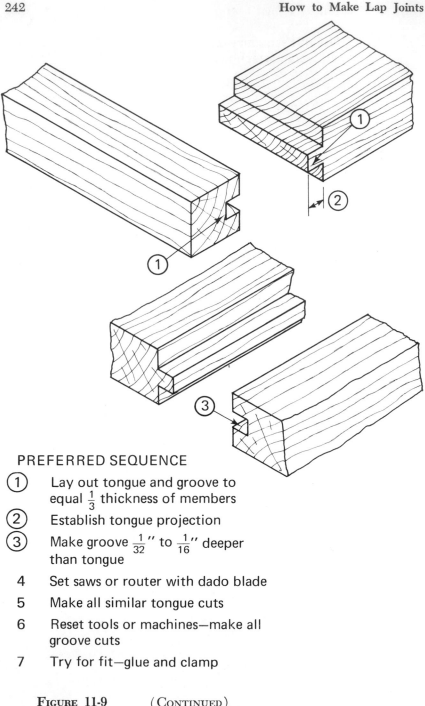

PREFERRED SEQUENCE

1. Lay out tongue and groove to equal $\frac{1}{3}$ thickness of members
2. Establish tongue projection
3. Make groove $\frac{1}{32}$ " to $\frac{1}{16}$ " deeper than tongue
4. Set saws or router with dado blade
5. Make all similar tongue cuts
6. Reset tools or machines—make all groove cuts
7. Try for fit—glue and clamp

FIGURE 11-9   (CONTINUED)
                   (H) TONGUE AND GROOVE LAP JOINT

be made with dado heads on the radial arm saw or on table saw. It can be made with standard cross-cut blades used on the two saws just mentioned and a portable power saw. It can be made with a router or shaper and with hand tools. Refer to Chapter 5 if you need guidance.

11.5.3
CENTER LAP
OR T LAP JOINT

This joint can be made with the radial arm, table saw, portable power saw, or router. It is a combination of a dado (used on one member) and a half-tenon or rabbet (used on the other member). It can be made with hand tools: the saw, the chisel, and/or the hand dado tool. Refer to Chapters 5, 6, and 8 if you need guidance.

11.5.4
WEDGE OR
DOVETAIL
LAP JOINT

This joint can be made with the radial arm saw, table saw, or portable power saw. Since the one member is a dado but with its sides on an angle, each angle cut must be made with a separate setup on the saws. When making the other member, a half-tenon is made first. Then the sides are tapered to fit the dadoed member. The hand saw, chisel, and dado chipper can be used to make both parts of the joint. Refer to Chapters 6 and 8 if you need guidance.

11.5.5
END LAP JOINT

The end lap joint consists of two half-tenons. All the power saws and the router can be used to make these pieces. Hand tools such as the saw and chisel can be used to make the half-tenons needed for the joint. Refer to Chapter 8 if you need guidance.

11.5.6
SCARF LAP JOINT

The scarf lap joint can be made most easily with a band saw. It can be made with a portable saber or jig saw, and it can be made with a table saw or portable power saw. The joint can be made very easily with a hand saw. However, extreme caution should be used when cutting vertically.

11.5.7
KEYED SCARF
LAP JOINT

Proceed to make the standard scarf lap joint using any of the tools listed in the paragraph above. Then cut a key in each piece by making a dado.

11.5.8
DOVETAIL
LAP JOINT

The only tool suggested for use is the router with its dovetail bit and dovetail jig. Follow the directions that come with the jig. If you set your router bit too low, the joint will be loose. If you set your bit too high, the pieces will not go together. Practice until the machine is set accurately.

11.5.9
TONGUE AND
GROOVE LAP JOINT

The tongue and groove lap joint consists of one member that has a dado lengthwise along one edge and another piece or pieces that has two rabbets of equal size on opposite sides, leaving a tongue in the center. The table saw is the best machine to use to make this joint. However, the radial arm saw can be used to make the tongue portion, and the router can be used to make the dado. The tongue can be made easily with a rabbet attachment on a rabbet plane. The dado can be made with a specially designed grooving hard plane. Refer to Chapter 5 for guidance.

QUESTIONS

1 / By definition, what is a lap joint?

2 / Where supports are needed for open shelving, which two joints are combined?

3 / What is the edge lap joint primarily used for?

4 / How are the end lap joint and the center lap joint made?

5 / By using a dovetail in combination with a dado, what lap joint is made?

6 / What two lap joints are not used frequently but are very successful?

7 / What is the name of the lap joint made on edge, and how is it cut?

8 / What is the strongest lap joint that can be made?

9 / What is the tongue and groove lap joint, and how is it made?

PROJECT |

Make a new workbench or picnic table using lap joints wherever two members cross each other. Make the picnic table 30″ wide by 6′ long by 30″ high. Make each seating bench (if not attached) 15″ high by 12″ wide by 6′ long. Use 2 x 4 stock everywhere except the top. For the top, use 2 x 6 stock. Stain with redwood stain.

12

HOW TO
MAKE
THE MITER AND
OTHER CUTS

The most universal of all cabinet joints is the miter. It has the most variety of application of all the joints. It is often used in the basic construction of a cabinet. The ends, tops, sides, and front are frequently mitered at 45-degree angles to make a cabinet joint. The miter is used in doors when mitered corners are desired for effect. It is used consistently when moldings are installed on cabinets: a band around the top of the cabinet, decorative trim on the face of a cabinet door, or base molding on a cabinet.

12.1
FUNCTIONAL
USE AND
APPLICATIONS

In addition to the uses stated above, the miter is used in combination with other joints, such as the lap joint, dowel, and of course the butt joint, since the miter joint is a variation of the butt joint.

Used by itself, the miter has as much or little (depending upon one's point of view) strength as a butt joint. If, for instance, the two mitered pieces are 45 degrees and joined, the relative strength is greater than two miters of 30 or 22½ degrees because of the slant of the cuts. The 30- and 22½-degree cuts have more end fibrous material than the 45-degree cut and hence less holding strength.

When the miter is used in combination with the dowel, however, it takes on the strength of a doweled joint. The same is true when the lap joint is combined with the miter. How can the miter be used in combination with the lap joint? It can be used with the end lap or tongue and groove. These methods will be illustrated later in the chapter.

Functionally the miter is very effective as a means for joining two members of the same width and thickness and of varying widths

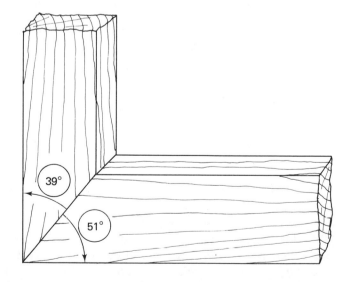

FIGURE 12-1   MITERED CORNERS WITH MEMBERS OF
VARYING WIDTHS

and the same thickness. For instance, as shown in Figure 12-1, two members of unequal width are to be joined to effectively make a right angle. Notice that to make the corner, each piece is cut at a different angle. This is not difficult to figure out or cut.

A simple shop method is shown in Figure 12-2. Notice how the one member is laid on top of the lower member and a mark made. Connecting the mark with a line to the adjacent corner results in making a miter layout. Reverse the members' positions and a miter layout can be made on the narrow member as in Figure 12-2.

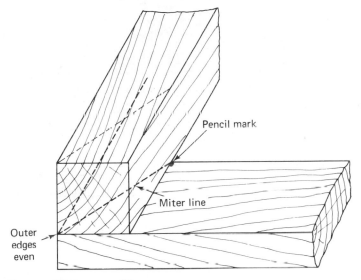

FIGURE 12-2   HOW TO MARK TO DETERMINE THE MITER
                     TO CUT

12.2
METHODS THAT CAN BE USED TO MAKE THE MITER JOINT

The simplest method to use to make the miter joint is the butt joint technique in combination with a miter box. Figure 12-3 shows a precision miter box that can be purchased in hardware stores. This tool comes with a straight back saw (also shown in Figure 12-3). The saw's

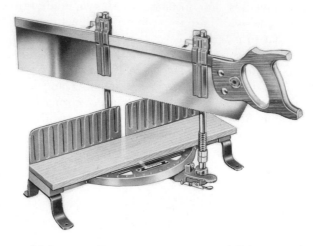

FIGURE 12-3   PRECISION MITER BOX (*Courtesy of Stanley Tools*)

position is adjustable left and right from center so that left- and right-hand miters may be cut. Wooden miter boxes, which can also be purchased in local hardware stores, are cheaper but wear out more easily and quickly loose their accuracy. In every case the miter box has limitations, in that only small pieces of stock can be cut to miters.

The miter and spline make a good reinforced joint. A basic butt type of miter is cut in both pieces, then a dado or groove is made into the miter as shown in Figure 12-4. A spline piece is cut and forced into

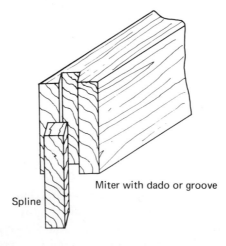

Miter with dado or groove

Spline

FIGURE 12-4   MITER AND SPLINE

the dado along with glue. Because the spline is cut across the grain, it adds considerable strength to the joint.

Another method that can be used when making a miter joint is a variation of the open mortise and tenon. In this joint, shown in Figure 12-5, the tenon and mortise members both have mitered shoulders. One disadvantage may be that the end stock shows.

A half-tenon and miter may be combined to make a joint where

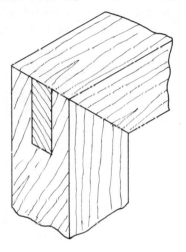

FIGURE 12-5   MITER AND MORTISE AND TENON

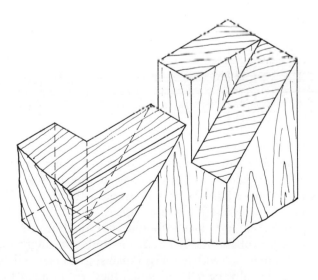

FIGURE 12-6   HALF-TENON AND MITER

a miter is needed for effect. The front side, as shown in Figure 12-6, has a miter; the back side has a straight tenon cut.

A method for joining the sides of a cabinet incorporates the miter with a rabbet or haunch. Figure 12-7 shows an end view. This method is explained later in the chapter. The advantage that this joint provides is in the assembly of the cabinet. Because of the two 90-degree corners (one inside, one outside), clamping and squaring are done easily. This mitering technique is very useful in the manufacture of contemporary and modern furniture. In using this method one also creates a design effect.

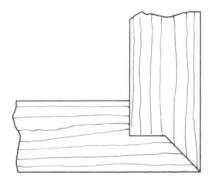

FIGURE 12-7   MITER WITH RABBET OR HAUNCH

12.3 DESIGN EFFECTS CREATED BY USE OF THE MITER

The most desirable effect created by the miter is joining two members so that no end fiber (grain) shows. End grain is objectionable to most people who appreciate beautiful cabinets. If the sides are made from soild stock and must join the top or front without use of moldings, then the miter is the best method to use.

If a paneled cabinet door is to add additional beauty, the corners of its frame will probably be mitered. The mitering might incorporate a mortise and tenon, but with good workmanship no one will ever know.

Moldings are always mitered when they are applied to cabinets, tables, or other furniture. The moldings may be flat against the surface or raised on an angle. Moldings that form part of a cabinet crown usually are cut to bevel or lean outward. Although not a part of a cabinet, moldings are also used to make picture frames. A relief effect can and often is desired, which requires a compound miter to be cut in one operation. Table 12-1 provides the angle settings for a compound miter. This table can be used to make compound miters on both table saws and radial arm saws. As shown by the dotted line, to make a corner with a 25-degree tilt requires settings of 23 and 40 degrees on the saw. If you have a radial arm saw, you would set the miter degree of the arm at 23 degrees and the bevel degree of the motor at 40 degrees.

As in other chapters within this unit, full-page displays of preferred sequences in making the joints are provided. In the making of miters in combination, a variety of machines and tools can be used. To make miters by hand requires a sharp cross-cut saw (No. 10 or finer), a chisel and hammer, and possibly a dado groover chipper.

If power tools are available, the portable saw can be used as well as the router. The router can make the half-tenon or half-lap joints. Bench saws and radial arm saws are excellent choices for making miter joints and combination miter joints.

For refresher material on individual joints, refer to Chapters 4 through 9. Select the type of joint that is needed, review, restudy, and practice making the joint. Then combine the skill learned with the miter needed for the project.

12.4
WAYS TO
MAKE THE
MITER

12.4.1
MITERED PANEL

A miter panel can be cut accurately on either the table saw or the radial arm saw. Of the two the table saw is better. Either machine should have a planer blade installed for the cutting. Refer to Chapter 4 on cutting butt joints for instructions, which can be slightly modified to cut miters. When panels are to be mitered, the stock should be first precut with all edges square at slightly larger measurements than are

TABLE 12-1
COMPOUND MITER ANGLE SETTINGS
FOUR-SIDED STRUCTURES FOR POWER SAWS *

Degree of tilt	Arm position in degrees	Motor position in degrees
0	0	0
5°	4.8°	44.75°
10°	9.7°	44.2°
15°	14.2°	43.3°
20°	18.8°	42°
25°	23.1°	40°
30°	26.8°	37.8°
35°	30°	35.25°
40°	32.8°	32.8°
45°	35.25°	30°

* Settings are for radial arm saws. See note below for table saw settings.

NOTE: *For table saw:* The arm position (above) equals the number of degrees off center for the miter gauge, and the motor positions (above) represent tilt angles off vertical.

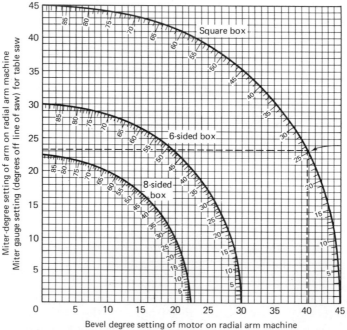

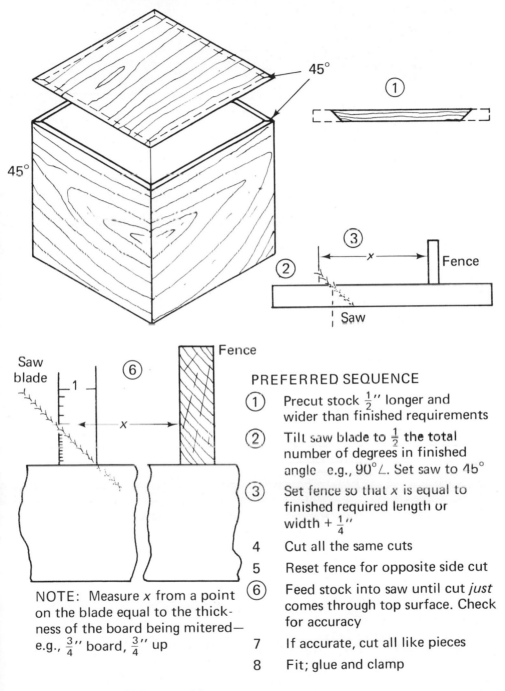

PREFERRED SEQUENCE

①   Precut stock $\frac{1}{2}''$ longer and wider than finished requirements

②   Tilt saw blade to $\frac{1}{2}$ the total number of degrees in finished angle e.g., $90°\angle$. Set saw to $45°$

③   Set fence so that x is equal to finished required length or width $+\frac{1}{4}''$

4   Cut all the same cuts

5   Reset fence for opposite side cut

⑥   Feed stock into saw until cut *just* comes through top surface. Check for accuracy

7   If accurate, cut all like pieces

8   Fit; glue and clamp

NOTE: Measure x from a point on the blade equal to the thickness of the board being mitered— e.g., $\frac{3}{4}''$ board, $\frac{3}{4}''$ up

FIGURE 12-8   MITERED PANELS

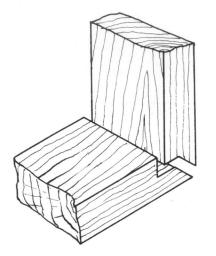

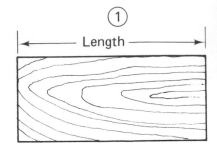

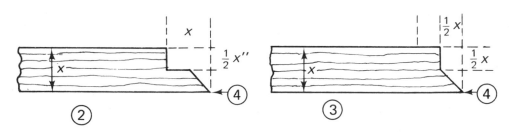

PREFERRED SEQUENCE

(1)   Precut members to the exact length required

(2)   Rabbet both ends of members $\frac{1}{2} x$ deep by x wide

(3)   Make crosscut on second member equal to $\frac{1}{2} x$ wide by $\frac{1}{2} x$ deep

(4)   Set saw blade to 45° and make miter cuts

5   Fit pieces—glue and clamp

FIGURE 12-9   MITER AND HAUNCH

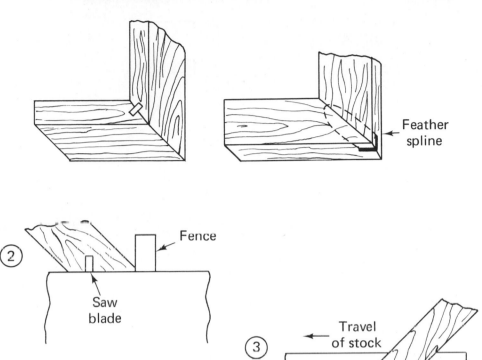

Feather spline

Fence

② Saw blade

Travel of stock

③ Saw blade

PREFERRED SEQUENCE

1 Prepare pieces as shown in Figure 12-8

② Make spline cut by making a cut 90° to direction of miter

③ Make a feather spline cut using a table saw

4 Cut spline stock

5 Shape feather to fit cut

6 Fit—glue and clamp

FIGURE 12-10   MITER AND SPLINE

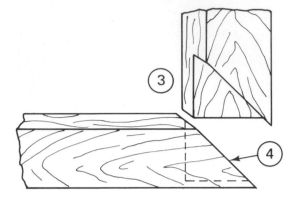

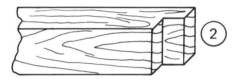

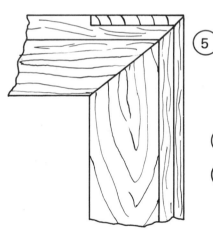

PREFERRED SEQUENCE

1   Precut members to exact length and width

2   Make full half lap on one member

3   Make beveled half lap on second member by laying out a 45° angle (other angles may be used, depending upon number of sides in the polygon)

4   Trim or cut matching miter on full half lap

5   Join members. Fit—glue and clamp

FIGURE 12-11   MITER AND HALF-TENON OR HALF LAP

required. Usually ¼ to ⅜ inch is more than sufficient. This allows for recutting should the first miters be slightly in error.

12.4.2
MITER AND HAUNCH

A miter and haunch is a modified rabbet cut. Its primary advantage is understood when assembling the joint. Because of the square rabbet corners, clamps can easily hold the joint while the glue dries. Refer to Chapter 5 if instructions are needed for machine setups. (The instructions will have to be slightly modified.)

12.4.3
MITER AND SPLINE

A miter and spline is a modification of the butt joint. Therefore, an examination of the principles of butt joints in Chapter 4 may be used should any problems arise while laying out or cutting the miter and the spline pieces. Remember that the spline should be cut so that the grain in the spline is perpendicular to the grain in the mitered pieces.

12.4.4
MITER AND HALF-TENON OR HALF-LAP

A miter and half-tenon is a modification of the lap joint. Therefore, a review of Chapter 11 should provide answers to problems that might arise. Remember that the mitered portion of the joint will be on the face side. Further, the end wood that will result as the tenon or half-lap will show. So make the joint to the point where the end wood will be at the top and bottom rather than on the sides.

QUESTIONS

1 / What joints are used in combination with the miter?

2 / How is the strength of a miter joint determined?

3 / The miter is very effective to use to join two members of what?

4 / What is the simplest method to use to make a miter joint?

5 / In the miter and spline combination, what adds considerable strength to the spline?

6 / What two other possible joints are incorporated with the miter in a method for joining the sides of a cabinet?

7 / What mitering technique is most useful when making contemporary and modern furniture?

8 / What type of hand saw is required to make a miter?

9 / What type of modified cut is the miter and haunch, and what is its primary advantage?

10 / What is the best method to use when putting molding on the tops or fronts of cabinets?

PROJECT |

Lay out and build a hexagonal commode with a diameter of 22″ and a height of 24″. Style the commode in Mediterranean or Early American. Cut and fit molding around the top edge and base by using a miter square, saw, and the butt mitered joint. Glue each piece. When all glued, sand, stain, and varnish.

UNIT IV

Thus far we have explained in detail the building blocks from which cabinets of all kinds can be built. In the discussions in Unit II of how to make individual joints by various methods and with various tools and machines, emphasis was placed upon details of setting up tools and materials. In Unit III descriptions of combining basic joints to create other useful cabinet joints were provided, accompanied by full-page illustrations. In this unit the plan of construction is carried to completion. A system is presented that can provide a step-by-step approach to building a cabinet.

Many books provide a methodology for cabinet construction. In all books that do, the author's experience and problem-solving techniques are incorporated. There is nothing wrong with this approach; in fact, it has a lot of merit. Skills and techniques that have been learned and refined are the elements by which one craftsman passes his trade to another.

The presentation in this unit provides a logical step-by-step procedure that probably differs from others you have studied. No one is best unless it is best for you. Therefore, carefully study the approach here and tailor it to fit your attitudes. A sample study is made to help explain the method employed.

13

HOW TO CONSTRUCT A CABINET

Construction of a cabinet is defined as the execution of all the tasks required to produce the cabinet. The type of undertaking will determine the depth required by the builders to satisfy the definition. For instance, if prefabricated assemblies are bought and used to build the cabinet, very limited experience and few tools are required. At the other extreme, if a builder starts with raw materials, performs all his required cutting, planing, turning, assembling, and finishing, then a significant depth of experience is required as well as a reasonable complement of tools.

This chapter and the next two are presented in flowchart fashion. This method is one whereby an overall block diagram identifies the major milestones to be achieved. Each major block is then broken into its significant task, steps, or sequences, and each is explained. Woven into the study is a project of building a small cabinet. The cabinet will require use of many types of joinery, described in Units II and III. No description is provided as to how to perform the steps in cutting the pieces to form the various joints, since these data have been given. However, an assembly sequence is provided, one that is used by many skilled cabinetmakers. The reader should study it and compare it with the method he now uses, and he may wish to modify his own method.

Figure 13-1 shows the overall block diagram flowchart for constructing and finishing a cabinet. Clearly there are three defined major areas: (1) constructing the cabinet, (2) preparing the cabinet for finish, and (3) finishing the cabinet. Of the three task areas, constructing the cabinet requires the most extensive definition. The majority of the work, in numbers of tasks, is required during the construction. Not any less important are the tasks identified in preparing and finishing the cabinet. The best-made cabinet can be destroyed by sloppy or poorly finished workmanship.

FIGURE 13-1   CABINETMAKING BLOCK DIAGRAM FLOW-CHART

Next we break the block into a four-part block diagram/flowchart. The parts are as shown in Figure 13-2: (1) sketching ideas or cutting pictures from magazines, (2) planning for acquisition of materials, (3) laying out and cutting materials, and (4) assembling the cabinet. The flowchart shows that a simple direct sequence of events occurs, starting with an idea or need for a cabinet. From the ideas, some sort of plan must be derived that will identify the materials required and the various quantities of materials. During the laying out and cutting stage of the project, parts of the job require referring to the plan for obtaining the materials, and the other part requires use of the machines

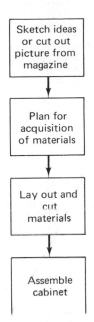

FIGURE 13-2   PRINCIPAL FACTORS IN CABINET CONSTRUC-
TION

or tools in the shop. The final step is the assembly phase, which may be accomplished in various ways. For instance, subassemblies may be made and joined, or the entire unit may be assembled in one continuous operation.

13.1
HOW TO
SKETCH IDEAS

Expanding the sketching idea block into three sub-blocks, distinct requirements are identified. Figure 13-3 shows these. They are: (1) to fit a need, (2) to show special ideas, and (3) to determine the finished appearance. The reason for sketching an idea is emphasized over cutting out a picture from a magazine in that seldom does a cutout provide exactly what is required. Usually, though, a cutout is a fair starting point from which a final decision can be made. In sketching, one does not need to be an artist. It is desirable to be able to sketch in proportion because every part of the cabinet then assumes its proper proportion. So if the cabinet is rectangular, with the height ap-

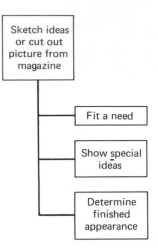

FIGURE 13-3   HOW TO SKETCH IDEAS

proximately two-thirds the length, start with a rectangle of those proportions. Remember the golden mean rectangle, studied in Chapter 3? Try using its proportions as a starting point. Along with the basic shape, continue to add personal expressions. Use both pictures and words.

13.1.1
HOW TO FIT
A NEED

To fit a need is usually the primary consideration. Considerable explanation about this subject was provided in Chapters 1 and 2. Let's use an example to show how this requirement can easily be identified. Assume that a home has an entrance hall without any useful furniture. Assume also that the family living in the home is quite normal: has kids in school, gets mail and newspapers delivered every day, and uses keys to get in and out of the home. The hall entrance is between 5 and 6 feet wide and 10 feet long. At present all the above items usually end up on the dining room table or in other rooms of the home. Sometimes confusion results because items become separated and mislaid. Clearly a need exists for a central depository for these items. A piece of furniture needs to be placed in the hall to provide a gathering place where every member of the family will make use of it. Further, because of its location and the natural tendencies of people, it will be perfectly placed; it will be the first place to get rid of items not of personal interest.

At first thought, a small table would be best. It would have a surface to collect all the items coming into the home. On second thought, a table may not be the best answer. What if some items could also be stored in the same location? A cabinet would be better. Also, a table or cabinet of rectangular proportions might not work well because the corners would project into the hall. So some special ideas must be considered.

13.1.2
How to Show
Special Ideas

Either a table or a cabinet with no outer corners projecting into the hallway becomes the first special feature. A top shape as shown in Figure 13-4 would seem to best provide what is needed. Either will eliminate a potential safety hazard. If storage space is needed, then a cabinet with a top shaped along the lines shown in Figure 13-4 would do the job. Let's sketch a credenza and see what comes out. Since the basic shape of the top is already defined, start with it. Then draw the

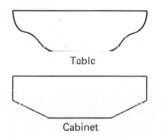

Table

Cabinet

FIGURE 13-4   TABLE OR CABINET TOP SHAPE

vertical lines representing the sides. Connect the vertical lines to form the base and add the bottom shelf. Now begin to add the special characteristics. These may be total length, height, width (from the back to front), and angles where mitered pieces will join. They may also include (see Figure 13-5) types of joints that may be required, special moldings to be made or bought, and placement of hardware and other features.

Obtaining these ideas and indicating them is not a thing that happens by chance. Remember from your studies in Chapter 2 that

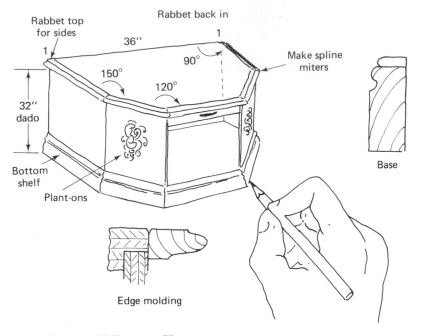

Rabbet back in

Rabbet top
for sides

36″

1

90°

Make spline
miters

1

150°

120°

32″
dado

Base

Bottom
shelf

Plant-ons

Edge molding

FIGURE 13-5   HOW TO SKETCH A CREDENZA

each style of furniture had its own characteristics. Take a walk into
the room off the hall. Review the furniture's trim, style shape, and try
to determine which method will be used in making the credenza. Will
it be an accent feature such as molding, or will it be an accent color,
harmonizing color, or a contrasting piece of furniture? Add the decision
to the sketch. If, for example, the adjoining room has cabinets with
drawers and doors, will the drawers and door on the credenza be
styled the same? Will they be the overlap or the flush type? Make a
decision and enter it into the sketch. With most of the data entered
into the sketch as the artist has shown in Figure 13-5, the final question
of finished appearance must be answered.

13.1.3
How to
Determine
Finished
Appearance

The characteristics are pretty well defined in the sketch. The color
of the cabinet can now be determined; should it be the same as the

adjoining room, or different? Will it be stained or painted? Will it be lacquered, varnished, or enameled? These questions must be answered. Assume that staining is to be done. What surface finish would stand up best over the stain and against the continuous onslaught of the variety of materials that will be dropped onto the credenza? Lacquer could be used. It is easy to spray on, and certain types can be painted on with a brush. Although it is beautiful, it is subject to damage. Repeated dampness, such as placing wet gloves or hat on it, would result in lifting and opaquing. Lacquer would not be good as a top dressing. Spar varnish would be possible, but it yellows and in a year or so the cabinet would be much darker than furniture in the adjoining room. Any synthetic varnish with polyurethane would be highly desirable. First, the finish is light and does not yellow; second, it is impervious to water as it dries to a plastic-like surface; third, it can be sprayed on, which is an excellent method for applying finishes to cabinets; and fourth, if a brush is used, very few brush marks will be seen, and most of these can be rubbed out.

So, somewhere, either on the sketch or in a note pad, enter the decision(s) reached about the finish of the cabinet. These data, plus the sketching of the cabinet with its variety of detail, should have answered the three requirements identified earlier: (1) to fit a need, (2) to show special ideas, and (3) to determine the finished appearance. With this detail not only has the cabinet been defined, but a great deal more about the elements that will go into making the cabinet has already been defined. The variety of pieces has been defined, the different types of joinery have been defined, hardware and trim requirements have been designed, and finish materials have been defined. It now becomes necessary to refine these details into specific quantities. To do this, the plan for acquisition must be made.

13.2
HOW TO
PLAN FOR
ACQUISITION
OF MATERIALS

The second milestone in constructing a cabinet is the plan for acquisition of materials. To fully define what materials will be required, a series of planning steps must first be accomplished. Figure 13-6 provides a block diagram/flowchart of how to determine the required materials. Each step in the flowchart establishes and defines a segment

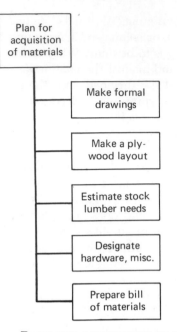

FIGURE 13-6   PLAN FOR ACQUISITION OF MATERIALS

of the plan. When all parts of the flowchart are complete, all the planning phase of the project will be complete except for the planning used in the assembly process. The steps that go into making up the plan are (1) to make formal drawings, (2) to make a plywood layout, (3) to estimate stock lumber needs, (4) to designate hardware, and (5) to prepare a bill of materials.

13.2.1
HOW TO MAKE
FORMAL DRAWINGS

Once again it may seem as though a stumbling block has been placed in the way of constructing the cabinet. The need for a formal plan may also be questioned. The stumbling block about drawing is easily overcome with the use of graph paper; and to answer the question of a need for a drawing—yes, it is needed. The reason will be evident shortly.

With the use of graph paper, which can be purchased in sizes up to 36 inches square, a scaled layout can be made very easily. From the sketch, select the longest side of the cabinet. Using the sketch of the credenza, we see that this length is 36 inches. A full-scale layout could be made on a 36- by 36-inch piece of graph paper. But, let's suppose a half-scale is selected. This means that for every segment designated on the graph, a value of 2 is used. In other words, one segment is equal to 2 inches. A one-quarter scale could also be used. This would result in a segment being equal to 4 inches. After determining the scale, decide what views are to be drawn.

First, a front view must be drawn. In the case of the credenza, a top view must also be drawn. This view will contain the miter angles and other definitions that cannot be shown on either an end or front view. Next, an end view must be drawn. Then a partial vertical view could be drawn to show the depths of dados, rabbets, braces, etc. Finally, partial views, called *breakouts* or explosions, might be drawn. These would show the detail of moldings, joints, or any significant detail that would aid later in the cutting and assembling of the cabinet. The amount of detail that should be included in each drawing is dependent upon the experience of the builder and the complexity of the cabinet. If a few basic joints are used, for instance, a dado, then just a few measuring points from a single reference point are all that may be required. If combination joints and fancy trim and moldings are to be used, more detail may be required. Details about a simple overlap door need not be drawn because its size can be verified later, and an estimated size can be listed in the bill of materials. The same information can be used for drawer fronts.

Figure 13-7 shows the formal drawing for the credenza. Notice that a top view, front view, end view and detail drawings are included. Within the top view are details including overall dimensions of the plywood, angles that must be cut, and dotted lines showing rabbet cuts that must be made to the underedge. The front view details the positioning of the bottom installation of the top and dimensions of the intermediate overall measurements. The end view shows the placement of the bottom and top and reflects how the bottom shelf is cut ½ inch narrower so that its edge matches the inside of the rabbet that is planned for on the end pieces. Detail AA defines the top trim. It includes its shape, size, and placement. Notice that because it covers part of the end piece, nailing of the ends to the top can be used during assembly. The molding outlined in the detail can be made with the router. A bed molding can be substituted if necessary. In detail BA the baseboard is drawn. Notice that it is designed to extend to the top of the dado. This allows nailing of the end panels to the bottom. The base when applied will cover the nailheads. Also note that the baseboard is made from one piece. Its upper edge is molded with a router. An alternative method can be used where the molded portion is replaced with a

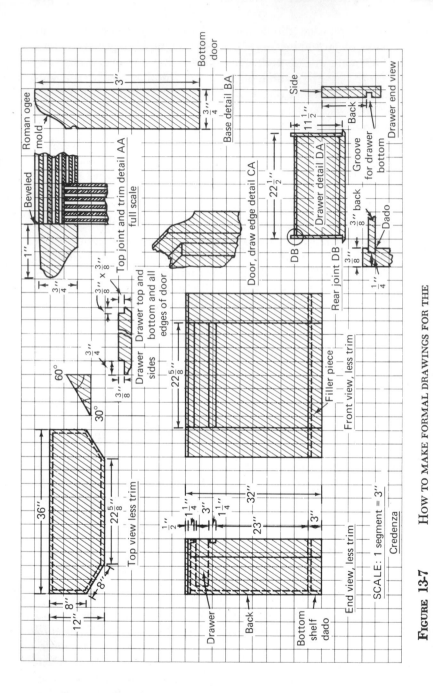

piece of quarter-round molding. Next take notice of the drawer lay-out, detail CA. The front is prepared with rabbets on all four sides, and a groove of ⅛ inch is made into the bottom for the drawer bottom. The sides are straight, grooved for the bottom, and dadoed for the back. The back is a straight piece.

Finally, a note column may be included. This column will list any and all special or unusual comments about details of the cabinet. For instance, Note 1 could be a comment about filler material between the base and bottom front edge. With the completion of the drawing the next phase can be accomplished. That is the laying out of the pieces for plywood. (Figure 13-6).

13.2.2
HOW TO MAKE
A PLYWOOD LAYOUT

Only a few basic considerations must be understood in laying out and cutting plywood. First, try to align pieces of the same width so that a straight rip can be made along the full length. This is important because it immediately provides another straight and accurate reference. It also minimizes chances for error, and it most generally results in less waste. Second, the exception to the first rule is the condition where matched grain in the doors or end panels is a requirement. In this case a cross cut would probably be made first, and rip cuts would follow. For explanation purposes a sample layout of the second method is provided in Figure 13-8.

Plywood can usually be cut to its exact required sizes because it will not shrink. Therefore, whether ripping or cross-cutting, a planer-type blade should be used. This blade does not tear the plywood and makes almost a sanded smooth cut. When laying out the pieces, *do not* forget to allow for saw-cut widths. Expect to lose ⅛ inch with each cut. For instance, if three pieces are needed, each 32 inches long, it would appear that one strip 8 feet long would do the job (3 × 32 = 96 inches = 8 feet). But two cross cuts are required, each requiring ⅛ inch, for a total waste of ¼ inch. Therefore, the last piece would be equal to 31¾ inches long. When planning measurements in cabinets, reduce the dimensions of all elements slightly to allow for saw cuttings and save a lot of material. Instead of a cabinet of 32 or 48 inches, make them 31¾ or 47¾ inches. Instead of 8 feet (96 inches), make it 1 inch less (95 inches). Instead of using a cabinet depth of 12, 16, or 24 inches, use 11⅞ or 15⅞ or 23⅞ inches. This will result in no waste. Using the formal drawing of the credenza (Figure 13-7), a plywood layout can be made.

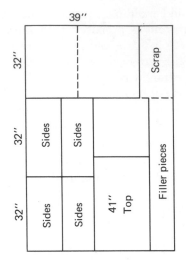

FIGURE 13-8   SAMPLE PLYWOOD LAYOUT WITH A CROSS-
CUT REQUIREMENT

If laid out properly, it should show whether one sheet of plywood
4 feet by 8 feet by ¾ inch is enough or not. Lay out the door since it is
the widest piece. Figure 13-9 shows the finished plywood layout. Notice
that there is ample material to make the cabinet pieces. Further, all
preliminary cuts may be made in ripping fashion, followed by cross-
cutting. The dimensions of the piece for the door and drawer front
have been extended from those in the drawing. They will be trimmed
later after the cabinet is assembled. With one piece of plywood being

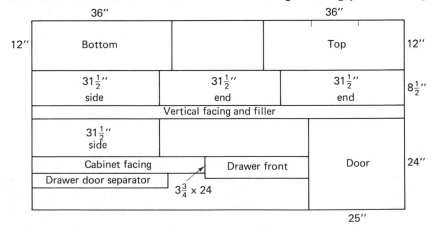

FIGURE 13-9   CREDENZA PLYWOOD LAYOUT

ample for the credenza, the next operation is that of estimating the stock lumber that is required.

13.2.3
How to Estimate
Stock Lumber
Needs

Because of the use of plywood in building most cabinets, the need for wide pieces of stock lumber is almost eliminated. This is advantageous because the narrow pieces do not as a rule warp or bow as much as the wide ones do. Further, the narrower boards are easier to handle and, most importantly, will shrink less when cut. These are very real problem areas, and consideration of them must be both understood and have allowances provided. Most stock is purchased in widths of 2, 4, 6, 8, 10, and 12 inches, and in lengths of 4 to 16 feet. The *optimum* size is 6 to 8 inches wide and 8 feet long. Although the stock is classified as, for instance, 4 inches wide, its actual measurement is 3½ inches. The other widths are comparable: 6 inches = 5½ inches (actual); 8 inches = 7½ inches (actual); 10 inches = 9½ inches (actual).

In planning for stock material, first determine the actual number of pieces that will be required. List their indiivdual dimensions, and where more than one of the same size is required, show the total quantity. Next select one of two methods for determining the size of stock lumber to buy and the total number of board feet plus 10 percent for waste. One method is to determine, from the list previously made, the widest piece that will be needed. If more than one piece is required, total their lengths until 8, 10, or 12 feet has been accumulated. Repeat the steps until all required pieces have been accounted for. With this layout complete, translate the results into the number of boards and the widths. First put the number of boards needed, then the thickness and width (in inches), and then the length (in feet): for example, 2–1″ × 8″ × 12′.

The other method is one of figuring the number of boards by laying out the required pieces as cross-cut dimensions. For instance, if six pieces 2 by 32 inches are needed, then two lengths of 1 × 8 × 32 inches are estimated. Three pieces can be cut from each 32-inch piece. After all the pieces are accounted for, accumulate the total length of all pieces with the same width. Then select a length(s) of lumber that will produce the least amount of waste.

For the credenza, stock material is needed for the top trim, drawer, and baseboard. For the top trim, one piece of 1 by 1⅛ inches by 10 feet will allow enough for cutting angles and some waste. The base is 3 inches (full) high and a corresponding approximate 10 feet long. Therefore, one piece 1 by 6 inches by 10 feet can be bought for both pieces or a piece 1 by 2 inches by 10 feet and another piece 1 by 4 inches by 10 feet can be bought. The material for the drawer that is needed is 3 inches high by ½-inch thick by approximately 4 feet long. This is established as two sides of drawer at ½ by 3 by 11½ inches, one back of drawer at ½ by 2¾ by 24 inches. Translating the drawer requirement to standard stock sizes identifies a piece of 1 by 4 inches by 4 feet. The drawer-stock requirement can be added to the other lumber previously identified or bought separately. With all the lumber identified, the other items required to build the cabinet can be designated and listed.

13.2.4
HOW TO DESIGNATE HARDWARE AND OTHER BUILDING MATERIALS

Briefly review the flowchart plan for acquisition of materials. The designating of the hardware and identification is the final decision-making block before preparing the bill of materials. Discussions made during the stage "fitting a need" can be translated into the actual selection of hardware. First, select the type of style needed: Will it be Early American wrought iron, antique brass, copper, or modern? With the style chosen, list the following requirements:

1 /   One pair of ⅜-inch inset, self-closing hinges.

2 /   Two handles or pulls (one for door and one for drawer).

3 /   Back plates for pulls.

Next list the other hardware items needed:

1 /   Nails, 4d finish, 1 pound.

2 /   Brads, 20 (for nailing back and drawn sides).

3 /   Glue, white liquid, 1 pint.

4 /   Sandpaper (see Chapter 14).

5 /   One sheet 4 by 4 feet of ⅛-inch masonite (for cabinet back and drawer bottom). **NOTE:**   *¼-inch plywood can be substituted for a finer job.*

6 / 1 pint of stain (see Chapter 15).

7 / 1 quart of varnish and thinner (see Chapter 15).

13.2.5
How to Prepare
a Bill of
Materials

With all the items needed for the cabinet, a sample listing results in a bill of materials, a sample of which is shown in Figure 13-10. When bills of materials are made, they are usually organized with the lumber (plywood and stock) listed first. The other larger pieces, such as the Masonite needed for the credenza, are listed next. Special items of wood, such as moldings, base boards, and plant-ons are listed, then hardware items. Finally, the list should include all the finishing materials. These are sandpaper, fillers, stains, paints, varnishes, and appropriate cleaner/thinners.

BILL OF MATERIALS

1 sheet plywood 4' x 8' x $\frac{3}{4}$"

10 ft. trim molding for top 1" x $1\frac{1}{4}$"

10 ft. base trim $3\frac{1}{4}$" x $\frac{3}{4}$"

4 ft. drawer sides, back $\frac{3}{4}$ x 3"

1 pair hinges 2" brass cabinet butts

2 knobs

1 pc. 4' x 4' x $\frac{1}{8}$" masonite (back)

1 bottle glue

1 lb. 4d. finish nails

1 pint stain

1 quart varnish and thinner or
   equivalent in lacquer

6 sheets sandpaper
   3 @ 150 grit
   3 @ 180 or 220 grit

1 lb. pumice

Figure 13-10   Bill of materials

When listing the various kinds and sizes of wood materials, be sure to include the type that is needed. Refer to the discussions in Unit I, if necessary, to determine which types are normally used in projects that are planned. For the credenza, which is the example case, assume the style to be Early American. The materials best suited are maple, birch, pine, and basswood. Birch plywood is readily available, so unless maple or pine are designated, use birch plywood. Stock lumber of birch, maple, or basswood can be used for the trim. If pine is selected, try to obtain pine plywood and either white or ponderosa pine for the trim. Avoid using yellow pine, which is difficult to work with, splits easily, and does not finish well.

Assuming that the materials have been identified and the local lumberyard has obtained and delivered them, the next phase in the construction of the cabinet can begin. First, though, consider the number of man-hours used thus far. The planning and estimating probably consumed from 2 to 4 hours. Obtaining the materials, including location of sources and having deliveries made, used up a day or two. From this point on, the man-hours will be directed to production, with tool preparation (e.g., sharpening chisels) as part of the production.

13.3
HOW TO CUT
MATERIALS

The first operation in the production phase is that of cutting the materials and preparing them for final use, such as planing, molding, and shaping. Figure 13-11 is a block diagram/flowchart that outlines the steps to consider and follow in cutting the materials.

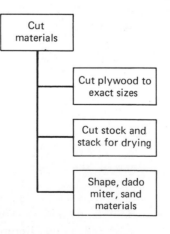

FIGURE 13-11   HOW TO CUT MATERIALS

13.3.1
How to Cut
Plywood

The first block indicates cutting materials, and the next block indicates cutting the plywood to exact sizes. As previously stated, plywood can and should be cut to the exact sizes needed. There are, of course, exceptions to this rule, two of which are identified in the sample project. They are: (1) the panels, which must be beveled; and (2) the drawer front and door. The reason that these two exceptions are made is easy to understand. Additional cuts must be made after the pieces are precut. Judge when a bit of extra stock must be left on the piece that is being cut where fitting and additional considerations not fully identified are known.

Using the plywood layout as a guide, set the machine being used to make the ripping action unless the first cut is a cross cut. Next cross-cut the pieces listed.

Tip

Mark each piece with a felt tip *along the edge*, not on the top or bottom, as it is cut. This identification is frequently useful, especially where pieces are sets or are close in size. After all the plywood pieces have been cut, stack them flat to prevent warping.

13.3.2
How to Cut,
Stack, and Dry
Stock Lumber

Next set the machines to cut the stock lumber. At this time consider these factors before cutting.

Tip

Cutting stock lumber:

1 / Cut material ⅛ inch wider than needed.
2 / Cut material ⅛ to ½ inch longer than needed.
3 / Cut extra piece or a few extra feet of each piece.

If both Tips 1 and 2 are used, a critical problem in shrinkage is allowed for. If Tip 3 is used, it might result in some waste, but if one of the pieces that is required is destroyed in some way (cut short later), the spare will be available for use.

Rip and cross-cut the stock according to the method selected in the estimating phase of the planning. Use sharp tools and use as fine a saw blade as possible, especially in the cross-cut operation. With all the materials cut, the next step is to stack the stock lumber for drying while other operations are performed. Select a dry, warm place, out of the way, where the material can lay flat. Insert spaces between levels of materials and allow air space between pieces on each row. Figure 13-12 shows a sample pile of cut pieces stacked for drying. Be sure to place the cross-pieces over each other so that no warping will occur.

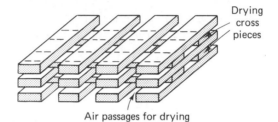

Drying cross pieces

Air passages for drying

FIGURE 13-12   HOW TO STACK AND DRY STOCK

While the lumber is drying, the basic pieces that will form the cabinet can be prepared. Details listed in the formal plan as miters, dados, and others can be made.

13.3.3
HOW TO SHAPE, DADO, MITER, AND SAND MATERIALS

Referring once again to Figure 13-11, the last step in cutting the material is that of shaping, dadoing, mitering, and sanding. Putting shaping and sanding aside for the minute, the plywood that was cut previously can be prepared by having all the required cuts made. If shelves are to be used, the dado probably will be cut into the upright pieces. If a back is to be installed, a rabbet will be needed also. Transfer the spacing of each dado from the detailed drawing to the corresponding piece of plywood. Set the machine that will be used to cut the dado with its proper pieces and try a sample cut before making the cut or cuts in the plywood panel. A good idea, though, is to make the sample cut in a piece of scrap plywood from the same sheet. After verifying that the cut is proper and accurate, set the fences or guides and make a dado in each piece that will have one in the same place. Move the guide or fence and repeat the step. After all dados are made, make the necessary rabbet cuts.

CAUTION

Be sure that the pieces that are the ends to be rabbetted are laid out where the rabbets will be opposite. An error in cutting the rabbet on the same edge in both pieces will result in a piece being wasted and the need for cutting a new piece.

If miters are to be cut on any of the edges, set the machine that will be used to make the cut for the correct angle. Mark the piece being cut, then use it to set and lock the fence. Cut all pieces to the same size and miter. Readjust the fences and make all other cuts.

After the stock lumber has dried for a few days, dress it down to its finished width and thickness by planing, then sand it with a belt sander and medium or fine paper. If any turning or shaping, such as molding edges with a router, is to be done, determine if it is best to (1) do the molding after the piece or pieces are installed on the cabinet, or (2) mold the pieces on the bench and then glue them in place.

If a selection is made to perform the molding, rout the necessary pieces; if a shaper is available, it may be used. After shaping the stock, hand-sand the piece or pieces and examine them for defects. Cut additional pieces if necessary.

If frames and panels are to be made and mortise and tenons or doweling are used, do these tasks next. Make all mortise tenons and dowel holes that are required using as few machine setups as possible. If necessary, refer to Unit II for individual equipment setups and instructions.

Examining the formal drawing of the credenza, we see that the four upright pieces require one dado each. Therefore, only one setting of the saw is needed to complete the dadoing task. Further examination shows that a rabbet ¼ by ¾ inch is needed on the *top* along every edge except the back. The back edge and end pieces require a rabbet ¼ by ⅜ inch. The side and end joints and side and front filler pieces need to be mitered. Set the machine to cut one set of joints, then the other, since both angles are different. If a spline is to be used in the miter joints, cut it after the miters are cut. With the majority of materials cut, the assembly phase can begin. There will be other cutting to do, but decisions about sizes and widths that have been left out of the drawings still have not been determined.

13.4 HOW TO ASSEMBLE A CABINET

Phase four, the assembling of the cabinet, is divided into four flow steps. These are shown in Figure 13-13 as the assembly sequence,

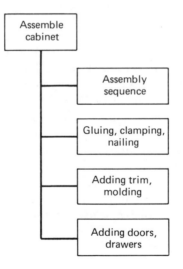

FIGURE 13-13   HOW TO ASSEMBLE A CABINET

gluing, clamping and nailing, adding trim and moldings, and adding doors and drawers. Included in these tasks are subtasks that will be required later. These include fitting the drawer sides and drawer fronts, installing drawer guides, hanging the door on its hinges, and installing handles and other hardware. There may also be tasks that require glued blocks to be installed for numerous reasons. This examination of the block diagram/flowchart will not necessarily identify each of these subtasks—only when the need for them arises.

13.4.1
ASSEMBLY
SEQUENCE

The first task in assembling the cabinet is that of determining the assembly sequence. The assembly should look something like that shown in Figure 13-14. The first subtask is that of making the subassemblies.

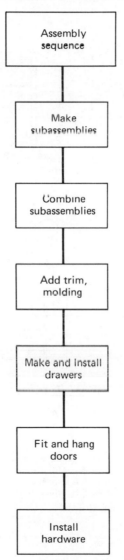

FIGURE 13-14   ASSEMBLY SEQUENCE

These may be frames and panels, dust covers (modified frame and panel used between drawers in a dresser), front of cabinet trim unit, molding combined to make a crown or base, or even simple subassemblies as basic case sections that will eventually be joined. The next subtask is that of combining the subassemblies into a whole assembly. These units should be joined so that an unbroken line in the styling results. Next add the trim by any method that seems ap-

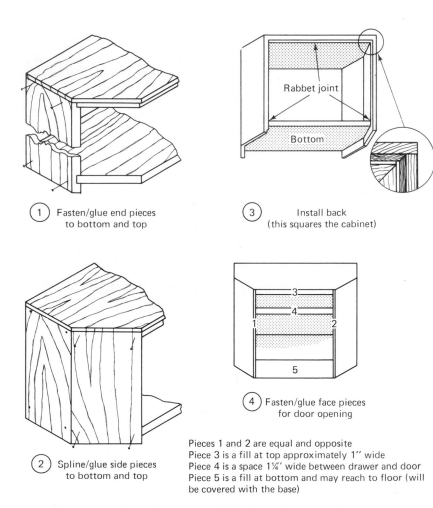

① Fasten/glue end pieces to bottom and top

③ Install back (this squares the cabinet)

② Spline/glue side pieces to bottom and top

④ Fasten/glue face pieces for door opening

Pieces 1 and 2 are equal and opposite
Piece 3 is a fill at top approximately 1" wide
Piece 4 is a space 1¼' wide between drawer and door
Piece 5 is a fill at bottom and may reach to floor (will be covered with the base)

FIGURE 13-15   HOW TO ASSEMBLE THE CREDENZA

propriate. Then make the drawers and cut, fit, and install the doors. The final step in the assembly sequence is the installation of hardware. Most packaged hardware has installation instructions printed on the back of the package. Following the instructions is a simple subtask. By applying the assembly sequence to the project of building the credenza, examination reveals that the case is the basic assembly, and the individual pieces cannot be assembled separately. So, if Figure 13-15 were to be used as a guide, blocks one and two—making and combining subassemblies—would be one subtask.

Figure 13-15 illustrates a series of steps involving the assembly of the credenza. Callout 1: Fasten and glue end pieces to bottom and top to show how the end piece fits. The bottom shelf fits into the dado in the end, and the top, with its rabbet, fits over the end. If more than

FIGURE 13-16   HOW TO ASSEMBLE A BOOKCASE

(A)   APPLYING CONTACT CEMENT

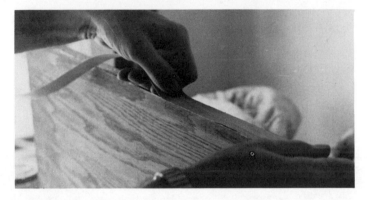

(B)   APPLYING VENEER TAPE

(C)   SANDING THE EDGES

FIGURE 13-17   HOW TO APPLY VENEER TAPE WITH CON-
                      TACT CEMENT

one shelf were dadoed into the side or end piece, when assembled they would look as shown in Figure 13-16. Notice that all the shelves have been fastened in place and the cabinet is in position to have the other end installed.

Returning to the sequence illustrated in Figure 13-15, callout 2 shows the side piece being fastened similar to the end piece. If a spline is used, it would be installed just prior to the fastening operation. After all four ends and sides have been installed, the back is installed (callout 3, Figure 13-15) and then the face pieces are installed using butt joints. For the credenza's construction the flow diagram would follow the rest of the sequence.

For a little better understanding of some of the fine points in the assembly process, let's examine the next task, as indicated in Figure 13-13, that is, the gluing, clamping, and nailing.

13.4.2
How to Glue, Clamp, and Nail

Numerous types of glue can be used in cabinet joinery. Probably the easiest and one of the best is white liquid glue, made by several manufacturers. This glue is easy to apply, washes away with water, and dries almost clear and relatively quickly. The fact that the glue washes away with water is very important because any spills on surfaces or excesses from pressure being applied can be easily and fully wiped away. If a waterproof glue is desired, the powdered glue, resin, is ideal. It is easily mixed with water and can also be wiped clean with water should it be spilled. A disadvantage, however, is that it dries to a brittle medium-brown color. One other excellent cabinet-making glue is contact cement. This is ideal to use when adding veneer tape to edges of panels or applying countertops. Figure 13-17 shows in a series of steps how the craftsman uses contact cement to apply a strip of veneer tape.

In the construction of a credenza, white liquid glue would be an excellent choice. Referring again to Figure 13-15, identify the following places as being glued:

1 / Where the end and side pieces are dadoed and where they join the top.

2 / Between the miter cuts and in the slot holding the spline (if used).

3 / Around the edge of the back and across the back edge of the bottom shelf.

4 / Each place in the front trim where two boards join.

Many types of clamps can be used in cabinet assembly, the most common being the bar or pipe clamp and the C clamp. Any of these may be purchased in local hardware stores. Because of their simplicity of operation, we add a word of caution. Steel clamps are tougher than the best wood. Therefore, use an insulator between the clamp face and the cabinet pieces. Any block of wood will usually do nicely.

In many cases nailing can be used in the assembly of a cabinet. There are restrictions, though.

1 / The nails *cannot* be placed where the heads will show when the job is finished.

2 / They must be the right size for the job.

3 / They must be the right type, such as finishing type.

Face nailing can be used if a piece of trim will cover the nails. Toenailing is usually very desirable since it allows for nailing at angles where nails seldom show. Two usual places for toenailing are under shelves into sides and at the end of the board. A chart of nail types and sizes is provided in Appendix B.

Nails, as well as glue, are used to hold pieces of the credenza together. Figure 13-16 shows that face nailing is used into the bottom shelf through the dado, and toenailing is used through the top of the end and side pieces through the rabbet and into the cabinet top. In both cases the nails will be covered by trim. The bottom nails will be covered by the base, and top nails will be covered by the edge trim, which will be glued on later. When all the pieces to the basic cabinet have been glued, nailed, and clamped in place and the glue is dry, the trim can be added.

13.4.3
How to Add
Trim and Molding

When adding trim and moldings, the miter is the joint that is required. Refer to Unit III if guides are needed on how to cut miters. Generally, though, the trim pieces are cut individually. A craftsman will usually start from the right or left and finish one corner before proceeding to the next. Using this method he can be sure that each piece fits before making the second miter cut on the other end of the trim. In the case of the credenza a craftsman would fit the end piece of base or top trim. Next he would join the miters where the end and side pieces butt; then he would cut and fit the piece across the front. Following this fit he would cut the other side piece, and finally he would cut the opposite end piece. With all the pieces cut and fitted, glue and clamp them into place. Be sure to wipe the excess glue that may spill out. While the glue is drying, work on the drawers and doors can be done.

13.4.4
How to Add Drawers and Doors

Now that the openings for drawers and doors are finally determined, measure each and proceed with cutting and assembling the pieces that make the basic drawer(s) and doors. The task is best taken in two steps. They are the cutting, fitting, and preparing of the drawer front and door, and the cutting, fitting, and assembly of the basic drawer minus the drawer front.

How to Assemble Drawer Front and Door

Since the drawer front and door of a cabinet will probably match, they may be treated in the same way. Precut the material to the proper size—length and width plus any overlap needed. If an overlap door is used, prepare a rabbet where needed. If a flush type is used, ensure that there is ⅛ to 3/16 inch total space in width and in height (e.g., opening 24 inches, door width 23 13/16 inches). On the drawer front make an additional rabbet for the drawer sides (see Figure 13-18). Then make a groove across the bottom so that the bottom of the drawer can slide into the groove.

How to Assemble Drawers

Prepare the pieces for the drawer as shown in Figure 13-18. Assemble

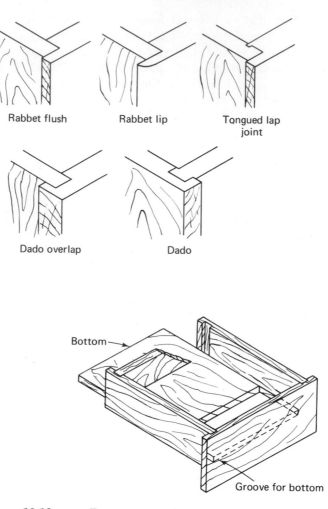

Rabbet flush   Rabbet lip   Tongued lap joint

Dado overlap   Dado

FIGURE 13-18   BASIC DRAWER PIECES

them without glue and try for fit. If good, glue and nail. Fasten drawer front to basic drawer and clamp. *Be sure* that the drawer is *square*. While the drawer is drying, the hardware can be installed on the door and in the cabinet.

HOW TO ADD HARDWARE

Install the hinges according to the directions on the hinge package.

Place the door in the door opening so that there is freedom on all four sides; fasten the hinges to the frame and try the door. Install the knob or pull. If non-self-closing hinges are used, install a magnetic or friction catch. If possible, install the knobs or pulls on the drawers. Finally, install the mechanical drawer guide into the cabinet and onto the drawer.

When these operations have been completed, cabinet construction should be complete. Stand back, review the job, and think about the job of finishing, which is about to begin.

QUESTIONS |

1 / How can a block diagram be useful to a cabinetmaker?

2 / What is usually important to include in a sketch of a cabinet?

3 / What are at least three cabinet parts or accessories that may be called special ideas?

4 / What are two ways of determining what the finished cabinet will look like?

5 / What type of drawing paper makes drawing a formal plan easier?

6 / If a scale of ¼ inch = 1 foot is used, what does this mean?

7 / What economic value can be obtained from a plywood layout?

8 / What is meant by a "plywood cross-cut" requirement?

9 / What advantage can be made by sizing a cabinet at 31¾ instead of 32 inches?

10 / What percentage of waste can be expected from the use of stock lumber?

11 / Where will stock lumber be needed on the credenza cabinet?

12 / Why should stock lumber be precut larger than necessary?

13 / Can you explain "stacking"?

14 / When can nailing be used in assembling cabinets?

15 / Why is the cutting of doors and drawer fronts often left until after the frame is installed on a cabinet?

14

HOW TO
PREPARE
A CABINET FOR
FINISHING

After constructing a cabinet, considerable effort must be spent in sanding so that the finished product will be a beautiful piece of work. An understanding of sanding and its principles is required to do the job. Before examining the principles, refer to Figure 14-1. Note that the sanding phase is the second of three phases in constructing and finishing cabinets. This block in the flowchart is the second of three operations. To better grasp the full task of preparing a cabinet for finishing, see Figure 14-2.

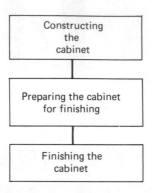

FIGURE 14-1   HOW TO PREPARE FOR THE FINISH

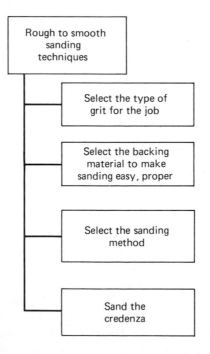

FIGURE 14-2   ROUGH-TO-SMOOTH SANDING TECHNIQUES

14.1
ROUGH-TO-SMOOTH SANDING TECHNIQUES

There are three decision blocks which when used will provide the answer of how to sand the credenza. They are:

1 / Select the type of grit for the job. This selection also provides the answer to what size of grit is required and whether the type of sandpaper should be the open-coated or closed-coated variety.

2 / The second step is selection of the weight and type of sandpaper backing material that is best for the job.

3 / The final step is to decide what type of operation should be used—hand, vibrator, belt sander, disk, drum, or all methods, but at different times for different purposes.

But before examining the properties of sandpaper, a few terms must be defined.

14.2
TERMS

hardness

Hardness is defined as the factor that determines the ability of the abrasive to penetrate the object to be ground or sanded. If the abrasive is not sufficiently hard to penetrate a surface, the only result would be heating, through friction, which would result in a burnishing or polishing operation.

toughness

If the ability of an abrasive mineral to penetrate an object is the first consideration, the second is that an abrasive mineral must have sufficient resistance toward shearing or breaking down that the initial penetration may continue through use of the product. If a mineral is hard enough to cut into the material but because of its brittleness will wear away rapidly, its use would not be economical. The property to penetrate and continue to penetrate without rapid breakdown is called toughness.

fracture

While an abrasive must have hardness to penetrate and toughness to withstand continued usage and wear on the object to be abraded, of no less importance is the shape and type of sharp edge formed after the crude mineral is fractured or broken down through crushing to a desired grading. As an example, a high-point carbon steel tool has both the hardness and toughness to bore, drill, or cut a piece of ordinary steel to a given shape. But to do so, the tool must be hollow-ground to a cutting edge with allowance for chip clearance; so it is with abrasive mineral. The cutting edges left after crushing play an important part in the use of the abrasive. Each type and class of mineral has a natural formation or shape when crushed. Abrasive mineral fractures with sharp edges having a cutting action. The irregular sides of surfaces are generally dish-shaped, allowing for chip clearance, as is the case with the hollow-ground tool.

The relative hardness, toughness, and type of fracture of the five distinctly different minerals are as follows:

	Hardness	*Toughness (%)*	*Fracture*
Flint	6.8–7.0	20	Light wedges
Garnet	7.5–8.5	60	Light wedges
Emery	8.5–9.0	80	Round and blocky
Aluminum oxide	9.4	75	Heavy wedges
Silicon carbide	9.6	55	Sharp wedge and silvery

The measurement of toughness is based in a percentage table that shows the percentage of resistance toward breakdown under a given pressure.

14.3
HOW TO
SELECT THE
TYPE OF GRIT
FOR THE JOB

There are five distinct and different minerals used in the manufacture of coated abrasives (see Figure 14-3):

5 Minerals
Mineral does the job of cutting and the
five kinds in use today are:

1. Flint   ⎫ Natural
2. Emery   ⎬ minerals
3. Garnet   ⎭
4. Aluminum oxide ⎫ Synthetic
5. Silicon carbide ⎬ minerals

Flint
This mineral is quartz, white in color. Its appearance is similar to white sand.

Emery
Dull black in color. It is hard and blocky in structure.

Garnet
A reddish brown colored mineral of medium hardness with good cutting edges.

Aluminum oxide
An off-white to gray-brown colored mineral that is extremely tough, durable and resistant to wear. It is capable of penetrating almost any surface.

Silicon carbide
It is shiny black in color and due to its brittle qualities fractures into sharp, sliver-like wedges.

FIGURE 14-3   ABRASIVE MINERALS

1 /   Flint (or quartz)

2 /   Garnet (semiprecious mineral)

3 /   Emery

4 /   Aluminum oxide

5 /   Silicon carbide

Flint, garnet, and emery are natural abrasives mined from the earth's surface. Aluminum oxide and silicon carbide are products of the electrochemical furnace. Bauxite ore is processed to make aluminum oxide, and silica sand is processed to make silicon carbide.

14.3.1
FLINT

Flint or quartz mineral is the mineral used on ordinary sandpaper—flint paper, as it is known in the trade. Its type of fracture is well adapted in the fine grades to the finishing of finely finished leathers. Flint sandpaper is used by master painters, carpenters, and cabinetmakers. Obviously, owing to its lack of hardness and toughness, it is not an abrasive that will stand up under hard production usage.

14.3.2
GARNET

The table shows that garnet, being harder and tougher than flint, would be excellent for sanding wood, especially since it has a better cutting surface or fracture. Through the treatment of garnet grain by heat, the grain is toughened beyond its natural state and has just sufficient brittleness to break or refracture when in use, forming new but smaller cross sections of cutting edges. As stated, it is primarily a woodworking product, but it is also used in quantity for sanding between coats of finishing materials, such as enamel, paint, varnish, and shellac.

14.3.3
EMERY

Emery, a natural mineral, is found in large deposits in both this country and Turkey. Although of sufficient hardness to penetrate most objects and even those of extreme toughness, its fracture is the poorest of all the abrasives. Round and blocky with poor cutting edges and a total lack of concave sides for chip clearance, its use is confined for the most part to the price buyer, for industrial use, and to the smaller mechanics, who purchase it from hardware and other retail stores. Owing to its lack of sharp fracture, it will produce a higher polish when used with lubricants than will artificial minerals. With lack of free cutting it will generate heat and therefore a luster or color.

It can be appreciated that without chip clearance and with a dull fracture, it could not be used satisfactorily for woodworking purposes. However, when it is used with oil and under pressure it will produce a lustrous finish on a well-sanded surface.

14.3.4
ALUMINUM OXIDE

Aluminum oxide, fourth in hardness to the diamond, is capable of penetrating practically any commercial type of metal. It is extremely tough and therefore resistant to wear. These qualities in themselves defeat to some extent the possibility of developing a type of fracture with elongated edges and cupped sides. The crystals come from the electrical furnace as a dense mass and, when crushed for use in sandpaper manufacture, form blocky or regular heavy wedge-shaped crystals. Such shapes are ideal for cutting and tooling. The heavy shoulder supporting the short edges gives the mineral its toughness.

Aluminum oxide grain is used as the mineral of two types of products. The peculiar qualities of this mineral make it more effective than garnet for heavy-duty, high-speed machine sanding of wood or than emery or silicon carbide for general use in metal working.

Owing to the greater hardness and toughness of this mineral, even though it is less sharp in fracture, it is capable of standing up without refracture or breakdown under mechanical pressure or high speeds on belt, drum, disk, and other mechanical woodworking sanding devices. On hardwoods, the positive pressure of drum sanders can be met better with aluminum oxide grain than with garnet.

From this we may conclude that aluminum oxide, although more expensive than garnet, has found a definite place in the woodworking industry, where it is possible to carry the abrasive product to the full length of its cutting efficiency or life. Where it is not possible to do this, as, for example, in sanding gummy, sappy woods that cause excessive clogging or filling, in sanding softwoods, in sanding with machines running at low speeds, or wherever the nature of the work is such that the full life or production cannot be obtained, garnet continues to be popular for reasons that are obvious.

14.3.5
SILICON CARBIDE

Silicon carbide, third only to the diamond in hardness, fractures into crystals or grit sizes that have the longest edges of all minerals and best dish shape (concave sides). The crystals are very brittle, however, and although capable of penetrating any object other than diamond and boron carbide, their relative brittleness allows them to wear down rapidly. But it is an excellent abrasive for most low-tensile materials, such as softwoods and hardwoods. The life of the mineral for this purpose is quite satisfactory. Since the material itself is not resistant enough to break it down, the life of the coating is dependent upon its ability to resist filling or clogging.

It is also used in sanding or surfacing hard-finishing materials, such as lacquers or undercoats, and the hardness and sharpness of the mineral enable these media to be cut down smoothly with the least amount of time and without excessive refracture of the mineral itself.

14.4
HOW TO SELECT THE BACKING MATERIAL FOR THE JOB

Combining the abrasive material with a particular type of backing results in a variety of papers for a variety of applications. The following paragraphs examine the various materials used for sandpaper and identify the types of sanding operations usually performed with them.

The backings used for coated abrasives can be classed under the following four headings:

A / Paper
   1 / A weight, known as finished paper.
   2 / C and D weights, known as cabinet paper.
   3 / E weight, known as roll stock.

B / Cloth

    1 / Jeans: lightweight, flexible.

    2 / Drills: heavyweight.

C / Combination

    1 / Paper combined with lightweight cloth.

    2 / Cloth combined with fiber.

D / Fiber

The backing and type for the job is as important in many respects as the proper mineral in the selection of the product for a given job. If the work to be performed is on a flat, even surface, paper or combination, since these are lower in price, will answer the purpose. Where greater tensile strength is required, cloth should be used.

Accordingly, on all woodwork, for mechanical sanding of flat surfaces, paper or combination is generally used, especially if there is no tendency toward strain that would rip or tear the product from its side edge.

On irregular surfaces, curved shapes, etc., where the backing, of necessity, must be flexible to conform to the surface outline for mechanical sanding, cloth is used. The basis for the selection of the proper type will be explained later.

On regular and irregular surfaces, where an abrasive product is used by hand, paper or cloth is used, entirely dependent on the type of work. In light sanding on woodwork for turning, moldings, flutes, and for flat surfaces, paper is generally used in preference to cloth. Where, in general, heavier pressures are exerted due to the hardness of the wood, as in polishing wood stock in lathes, and the abrasive is used by hand on these mechanical operations, cloth is used. A cloth backing is a better all-around medium for shop requirements since it can be interchangeably used on sanding operations by hand or machine. However, paper, because of its lower price, is used quite often, especially for light sanding.

On the multitude of sanding operations in shops, selection of the correct type of backing for the job can be determined after better understanding of the backings themselves.

14.4.1
PAPER

Two kinds of fibers are used in making paper for coated abrasives. They are: (1) wood-pulp base fiber of which there are two classes, kraft and alpha-cellulose; and (2) hemp base (rope) pulp.

Pulp can be processed into two types of paper construction, fourdrinier or cylinder. The fourdrinier paper is one in which all the fibers from the sheet have been laid out in a single layer, then dried and calendered. Cylinder paper is one in which five separate thin sheets are formed from the pulp and then combined in the wet state, then properly calendered and dried.

Kraft-paper (fourdrinier) wood pulp is used for flint and emery sheet paper only. It is a cheaper product and is not as strong or as pliable as a refined grade of wood pulp or rope stock paper.

Rope stock, as the name implies, is generally a cylinder paper having thousands of tiny hemp fibers. This paper has great lengthwise tensile strength, which makes it very desirable for endless abrasive belts and drum sanding covers. It also has a necessary sheer strength and cross tensile strength to overcome brittleness and prevent tearing.

Alpha-cellulose paper, several grades of wood pulp paper, have been developed since 1935. These papers have resulted in backings for cabinet and finishing paper that are equal or superior in all respects to the rope stock fourdrinier paper formerly used for these abrasive items.

A-weight finishing paper is a lightweight flexible alpha-cellulose fourdrinier paper used chiefly for sanding by hand on finishing materials, since these materials are sanded with light pressure. The operator who sands these materials often needs to feel the imperfections of the surface as he is sanding, and the thinness of the paper allows this. Flexibility is desired in order that the backing conform to moldings, grooves, flutes, and narrow surfaces under light pressure without breaking up.

C- or D-weight alpha-cellulose fourdrinier backing abrasive paper has a heavier and less flexible backing. It is used for hand sanding on wood where greater pressures are used for stock removal and are coated with coarser grits than is the case with finishing paper. Accordingly, it must be stronger than finishing paper and have more body, as it must lie flat without buckling when being used. It must be flexible enough to follow the contour of irregular, rounded, molded, or fluted surfaces.

E-weight or roll-stock cylinder paper is a heavy paper with great strength lengthwise to withstand the tensile strains developed by motor-driven belt sanders and drum sanders. This paper also has an adequate crosswise strength, which tends to eliminate shearing or tearing across its width. Coated abrasives made on this type of backing are not flexible enough to be used on other flat or very mildly curved surfaces.

14.4.2
CLOTH

Abrasive cloth in sheet form is largely used for hand-sanding operations on materials other than wood. It must be flexible enough to conform to irregular surfaces under hand pressure. Accordingly, it is
made on a suitably filled jean or drill cloth in the fine and coarse
grits, respectively, and is given enough body so that it does not
wrinkle or buckle when put into use. Improperly filled cloth, too raggy,
would allow the sheet to wrinkle and buckle and tear with a poor
edge when used in narrow torn strips.

Where flexible cloth is desired and needed in roll form, jeans
(coded J) should be specified. For mechanical sanding, especially in
woodworking for moldings, flutes, and narrow, irregular shapes, jeans
cloth should be used because of its flexibility. Being a lightweight
cloth, it will stretch under excessive tension developed in heavy-duty
sanding operations. However, the bond will break, and thus will not
give the cutting life of a heavier-weight cloth.

Drill is a medium-weight, strongly woven, filled canvas cloth
backing. It is made in roll form and is used for belts, disks, or in any
place where mechanical sanding is required without a flexible backing. Although lacking sufficient flexibility to sand or grind intricate
or narrow curved, molded, or fluted surfaces, its greater strength and
greater resistance to stretch under high pressure and tension makes
it the product to use and recommend for medium and heavy-duty
grinding. Its lack of flexibility gives it greater body and a heavier and
stronger foundation for the abrasive mineral.

14.4.3
COMBINATION

Combination or laminated backings are made of two materials. Paper
combination—a thin cloth, not unlike cheese cloth, is laminated to E-
weight paper, the mineral being coated on the cloth side. This product
is stronger than paper and less expensive than cloth and is used where
the stress and strain is greater than E-weight paper is capable of
standing. It is available as garnet combination, silicon carbide combination, and aluminum oxide combination.

Fiber combination disks for flexible-shaft machines must be
flexible and yet have enough body to eliminate any tendency for the
edges to wrinkle or buckle, or the unsupported edges would catch and
tear on the work. To meet this requirement, thin but extremely strong

fiber is laminated to drill cloth backing on top of which the mineral is coated. This product is known as fiber combination and is furnished only in disk form.

14.4.4
FIBER

The newest addition to the backing types are the fiber backings. These backings are made of specially prepared rag stock which in the initial stages is made into a paper. Several layers of paper are often combined and are put through washing and drying operations. The resulting sheet is quite dense, relatively hard, and stiffer than ordinary papers.

14.4.5
OPEN-COATED AND
CLOSED-COATED
PAPERS

There are two types of mineral coatings: full or closed coat, and spaced or open coat. The difference between them is in the distance between the spacings of the bonded abrasive grits. Closed coated, as the name implies, describes the type of coating in which the mineral is closely coated, each grit being adjacent to the other or fully coating the backing. Open coated is descriptive of the type of coating in which each mineral grit stands by itself with a spacing or void between.

Spaced-grain coatings allow the material sanded to free itself without filling or clogging the surface. Closed coatings, with little spacing, form tight pockets to collect the material sanded and will fill more rapidly, especially on materials of low tensile strength.

Accordingly, with light pressure, where quick sanding is desired, especially on soft, gummy, plastic surfaces, the spaced-grain products are used. The reasons for using spaced-grain products in sanding varnish, shellac, and enamels are obvious, since this type of coating will eliminate rapid filling; and, as the medium itself presents a comparatively soft surface where light pressure is used, the coating will support the wear. It can be readily appreciated that spaced-grain coatings on cloth allow a more flexible material than full-coated; consequently, this type of material is used for operations that require extreme flexibility, such as sanding moldings, where the mineral grain cuts fast and smooth without burning. In sanding hardwood, *closed-coated abrasives* are best adapted. As these materials have high tensile strength, they do not fill or clog rapidly; and because of their heavier mineral coat, the abrasive will last longer. Where heavy pressures are used or in sanding nonfilling materials for rugged stock removal where a constant continuous cut is desired, full-coated types are used.

Open-coated abrasives are used for sanding finishing materials whose gum content would quickly load or fill a closed-coat material. They are also used for buffing and for stock-removal purposes in cabinetwork. Open-coated aluminous oxide fiber combination disks are recommended for paint removal in the refinishing of cabinets and other furniture.

One of the most important methods used to apply the abrasive coating is the electrostatic method. This is a patented process of coating minerals through the use of electricity. In the past, abrasive material has been coated to the backing by dropping it on the sheet coated with glue. Because the mineral chips landed haphazardly, their cutting edges were not oriented uniformly with regard to the item to be sanded. In the electrostatic method the grains stand on the sheet with their cutting edges oriented in the direction of the work. This makes for greater uniformity and a faster, longer-lived product than it was formerly possible to make. Both open and closed coats can be electrostatically applied.

The following materials are coated electrostatically: aluminum oxide metal working cloth sheets and utility rolls; aluminum oxide woodworking paper; combination rolls and cabinet and finishing paper; aluminum oxide woodworking cloth, jeans and drills; silicon carbide combination and finishing paper; and garnet finishing paper.

14.4.6
BOND

The adhesive or bond used to hold the mineral on a coated abrasive sheet is of several types, identified so that the cabinetmaker may select the proper type when polishing his cabinet:

1 / Water-soluble bonds:

    a / Glue bond

    b / Glue with filler bond

2 / Partly water soluble bond:

    a / Resin over glue bond

3 / Water-insoluble bonds:

    a / Resin bond (resin bond on nonwaterproof backing)

    b / Waterproof (resin bond on waterproof backing)

Only the highest-quality animal-hide glues are used in glue-bond abrasives. The glue is of higher quality than glues used for joining in the woodworking trade and for other commercial uses. For glue-with-filler-bond abrasives, the same grades of hide glue are used, with the addition of a carefully prepared filler that will modify the glue to produce a harder film, more heat resistance, and less effect by moisture than glue that is not so modified.

In the second group, the partly water soluble bond, there is construction resin over glue. Most abrasives have two coatings of adhesive, one on the backing into which the mineral coating is initially anchored, and the other a sizing over the abrasive particles. Resin-over-glue materials are meant to be used in dry sanding operations only. They are more heat resistant and perform more consistently over a wide range of humidities.

The water insoluble group of adhesives is divided into two groups: resin bond and waterproof. The term "resin bond" is generally associated with a phenolic resin adhesive coated on a backing that has not been waterproofed, as, for example, types C and D disks. Waterproof materials are designed to be used where wet sanding is desired. The backings on waterproof products are waterproofed. The primary use for waterproof paper is rubbing or sanding-out surfaces, undercoats, lacquers, varnishes, and enamels. It is used extensively in rubbing out lacquer finishes on furniture and works well in polishing the new plastic varnishes. Waterproof cloth is used in the metal, glass, ceramics, and plastic industries for wet sanding to eliminate dust, filling, and heating.

Waterproof examples are waterproof silicon carbide paper, waterproof aluminum oxide cloth, and waterproof silicon carbide cloth.

From the foregoing, an effort to select the proper and most economical abrasive for the type of work on which the abrasive is to be used has been examined. The limitations of the various abrasive materials, their backing, their coatings, and their bond type have been reviewed, and only by coordinating these conditions with the job can the proper sandpaper be selected. This foundation, added to your own experiences in use of the product, should result in a well-sanded product.

14.4.7
STORAGE

Both types of water-soluble adhesives, glue bond and glue with filler bond, absorb moisture and lose moisture with changes in the atmospheric humidity in which it is stored. The filler used with glue is nonabsorbent and, consequently, changes less with humidity than the glue bond. For best results both bonds should be stored and used at humidities in the range 35 to 55 percent relative humidity at 70°F. These conditions are optimum not only from the standpoint of the bond, but because the backings used on nonwaterproof abrasives are less brittle and more easily handled under these conditions.

14.5
HOW TO
SELECT THE
METHOD

From the decisions reached in the first two blocks of Figure 14-3, the various types of papers have been selected as best for a particular phase of sanding a cabinet. Now you must select the proper sanding method. Will it be the hand method or a machine method? If both methods are to be used, when should each be used?

14.5.1
HAND METHOD

The hand method of sanding implies the use of the hand and any vehicle that would allow the required force to be directed to the surface to be sanded. This means that a sanding block such as the one shown in Figure 14-4 may be used. This sanding block is a commer-

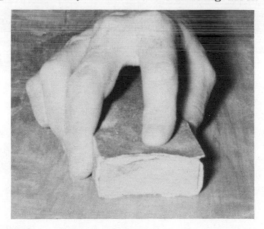

FIGURE 14-4   BLOCK SANDER

cial type that is available in local hardware stores. The home-shop (handmade) variety consists of a scrap piece of board 1¼ by 3 by 9 inches around which the sandpaper is wrapped. When other than flat surfaces are sanded by hand, the block identified above may be shaped to the curve in the cabinet or table. Finally, the sandpaper may simply be folded and held with palm and fingers. The A-type papers are best for this operation, since a feel for the finish, curves, angles, etc., is usually desirable.

14.5.2
MACHINE METHOD

Various sanding machines are available to the part- or full-time cabinet-maker.

BELT SANDER

The belt sander (portable) (Figure 14-5) is used primarily for heavy-

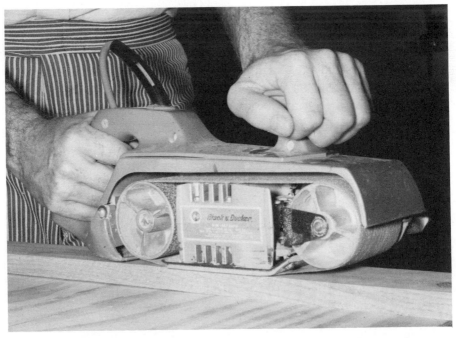

FIGURE 14-5   BELT SANDER

duty operations. There are a variety of types of papers available for different jobs. The following list will help you determine when to use the belt sander and what weight of paper and grit to use:

Stock lumber   Coarse (30–60); medium (80–100); fine (100–150) belts

Plywood   Medium (80–100); fine (100–150)

Veneers   Fine (120–150)

VIBRATOR SANDER

The vibrator sander (Figure 14-6) is a finishing sander. On most operations smooth finish paper will be installed. There are three separate operations for which this machine is especially useful. One is the final sanding before staining, another is the sanding operation required between finishing coats of varnish or lacquer, and the third is the polishing operation, which is usually performed after the last coat of finish has dried.

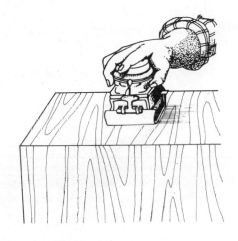

FIGURE 14-6   VIBRATOR SANDER

There are two varieties of vibrator sanders. One is the *orbital* type, where the moving plate revolves in an elliptical orbit. When this type of sander is used and fine to polishing-type paper is installed, the sander may be used in all directions. The other type is the *in-line* sander. The plate oscillates forward and backward. When using this type of sander, *always sand with the grain of the wood*, regardless of the type of paper being used.

DISK SANDER

The disk sander (Figure 14-7) is usually an attachment for an electric drill or flexible shaft. This type of sander is used in some operations of sanding wood. This would be, for instance, where curved materials are shaped and hard to get at. The disk is limited to a few operations because of the circular marks the paper makes in the grain of the wood.

FIGURE 14-7   DISK SANDER

The other type of disk sander is the fixed or stationary sander. It is usually mounted on the same machine base as the stationary belt sander (home-workshop variety). This type is ideal for the edge sanding of curved materials and ends of boards, 45-degree miters, and such. The variety of grit available for various operations is as follows:

Heavy stock removal   36–50 grit
Medium stock removal   60–100 grit
Light stock removal/polishing   120–150 grit

Drum Sander

The drum sander (Figure 14-8) may be either a stationary machine, where the drum or spindle rotates and oscillates up and down, or it may be an attachment for an electric drill (shown in Figure 14-8). This attachment may be installed in either a portable electric drill or a bench or floor-model electric drill.

Figure 14-8   Drum sander

The usefulness of this type of sander lies in its ability to be used in sanding inside curves that have small radii. The various operations that can be performed require paper of the same grit as that used in disk sanders.

14.6
HOW TO
SAND THE
CREDENZA

Let's apply to the sanding of the credenza what has been developed in Figure 14-3. The various types of materials—maple or birch and plywood—each need special attention.

The portable belt sander can be used with a medium belt, then with a fine belt. This may be done either before or after the base is added to the credenza. The trim for the top edge can be presanded before it is molded. This, too, would be done with a belt sander.

The next step in sanding the stock would be with the use of the vibrator and a paper with a 120, 150, or 180 grit installed. The flat surfaces could be done. It is possible to sand the top-edge molding with the vibrator. Set the sander to in-line sanding. Adjust or trim the paper to the exact outer edge of the base of the sander. Turn the machine on and *carefully* sand the flat and curved areas of the trim. Be extremely cautious where the trim is glued to the plywood. If the sander should stray onto the plywood against the grain it would make scratches that would show up after staining.

To sand the plywood surfaces, the vibrator can be used in in-line or in orbital position. If used in-line, sand with the grain of the wood only. Since almost all finished plywood is sanded at the factory with 120-grit paper, the grits to use would be 150, 180, or even 220. In all these sanding operations the finer the sandpaper that is used, the more control there is of the staining operation.

After the machine sanding has been completed, select a variety of papers similar to the grit used in the machine operations and hand-sand those portions of the credenza that could not be done by machine. Start with an appropriate grit and finish with the finest grit available.

As a final step, wrap a piece of fine paper around a block of wood and *very lightly* dress all sharp edges: for instance, around the door and drawer, on the bottom of the base, at the rear of the cabinet top and ends, and in the door and drawer openings.

Dust the entire cabinet, or vacuum clean if possible. With either a soft cloth or your hand, stroke all the surfaces and edges of the cabinet to verify that there are no fibers standing. The cloth will usually identify these areas more easily, because the cloth will snag on the fibers.

With this operation completed, the staining, varnishing, and painting phases, will begin. These are examined in Chapter 15, but since there is sanding in all these operations, they are discussed here so that the entire sanding operation can be read, studied, and understood without interruption. The final operation in sanding is sanding for a finish.

14.7 HOW TO SAND FOR A FINISH

Figure 14-9 illustrates the three decisions that must be made during the finishing process: (1) selecting the proper paper to smooth irregularities that occur during staining and finishing operations, (2) selecting the proper combination of sandpaper and liquid that will create a smooth surface, and (3) polishing with sandpaper for a gloss, satin, or dull finish.

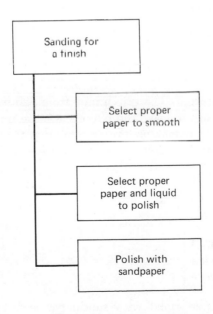

FIGURE 14-9   HOW TO SAND FOR A FINISH

14.7.1
How to Select
the Proper Paper

After the cabinet has been stained and dried, it is necessary to sand it. This becomes necessary because the liquid in the stain caused the fibers in the wood to swell and become erect. With the use of 180- or 220-grit type-A paper and *very gentle* pressure, these fibers must be sanded away. A very gentle pressure is stressed because heavy or uneven pressure will sand away some of the stained wood and result in light and dark or uneven colored areas.

At all times sand with the grain in a forward and backward motion. Be especially careful when sanding near the edges; the stain may be sanded away with one stroke. While sanding or after sanding, wipe the entire cabinet with the cloth to find all the rough spots. Re-sand these until they are smooth. Repeat this operation between coats of finish material. After the last coat of finish material is dry, the polishing may begin.

14.7.2
How to Select
the Proper Paper
and Liquid
for Polishing

The first sanding should be with water, so a water-insoluble-bond type of paper should be selected. The weight should be very light so that no scratching will occur. The grits range from 220 to 600.

The water tends to make the paper cut more smoothly and keeps the surfaces cooler so that no burning takes place. A substitute for water is paraffin oil. It is used the same as water. Liberally apply the oil to the surface to be sanded, then sand with the grain. Wipe away the excess oil when finished. Let the cabinet dry thoroughly (24 hours) and then polish it with wax.

14.7.3
How to Polish
with Sandpaper

Polishing can be performed with sandpaper and a solvent such as paraffin oil. By proper selection of grit, the addition of lubricant, and proper pressure and velocity, any desired effect can be obtained. The finer grits (400, 500, 600) result in more polishing and little cutting and a higher polished finish. The coarser grits (220 to 320) result in a more satin appearance because more of the sheen is removed from the top dressing.

In summary, in the decisions needed to sand a cabinet we find that a variety of types of sandpapers is needed. There are the types used in the various machines. There are different grits, 60–80 for coarse work to 500–600 for finishing polish work. There are lightweight, wet/dry, and heavyweight papers.

Sanding stock lumber must be done in a series of steps, starting with the rougher papers and progressing to the finer papers. Between coats of finish and after the final coat, other sandings must be done, with finer grades of paper and with the aid of lubricants such as water or oil.

A beautiful cabinet will result by proper application of sandpaper. But what about the different finishes—stains, shellacs, and others? Some ideas are presented in Chapter 15.

QUESTIONS |

1 / How does the selection of grit affect the wood's surface?

2 / Is toughness defined as the factor that determines the ability of the abrasive to penetrate the object to be ground or sanded?

3 / How many minerals are used in the manufacture of coated abrasives?

4 / What is another name for ordinary sandpaper?

5 / Can you name four backings that are used for coated abrasives?

6 / Is the backing and type of paper as important as the coating mineral in the selection of the abrasive for a given job?

7 / What is one type of finishing sander?

8 / Can you name two types of fibers used to make paper for coated abrasives?

9 / When sanding with a vibrating sander, should you always sand with the grain?

10 / Can water be substituted for paraffin oil in sanding?

15

HOW TO
FINISH
A CABINET

The third and final major phase of constructing a cabinet is to apply the finishes. This task is not an easy one. In fact, many cabinets are often reduced to storage bins in the garage because of a poor finishing job. Before beginning an examination of the principal factors and methods used in finishing, let's determine where we are by a review. Figure 15-1 shows in the smaller blocks those phases that were previously finished. They were the construction phase and the sanding phase. Recall that the study on preparing for a finish identified some sanding and polishing applications that will be noted again in this chapter. Only brief mention of these details will be given in this chapter, however, so should a more in-depth discussion be required, refer to Chapter 14.

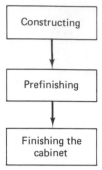

FIGURE 15-1   HOW TO CONSTRUCT THE CABINET

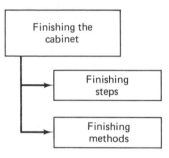

FIGURE 15-2   HOW TO FINISH THE CABINET

15.1
HOW TO
FINISH THE
CABINET

There are two principles to consider when finishing cabinets: (1) the steps to follow and (2) the methods to be used. Illustrated in Figure 15-2, both are concerned with detailing sequential operations as well as with defining principles about actions that are needed and reactions of finishes to materials. In the *finishing steps*, subjects such as filling, sealing, staining, coating, and polishing are examined. These steps are usually performed in each finishing task. There may, however, be certain cases in which some of the steps are combined. The study of *finishing methods* outlines the way(s) different types of finishing materials, such as shellac, varnish, and lacquer, are used. These methods will employ many, if not all, of the finishing steps. Further, the steps are indicated in outline form after the discussion of each method for easy reference during the finishing operation.

15.2
FINISHING
STEPS

Figure 15-3 illustrates in block diagram form the steps required to

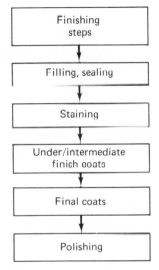

FIGURE 15-3   FINISHING STEPS

finish a cabinet. They are filling and sealing, staining, applying undercoats and/or intermediate finish coats, applying final finish coats, and polishing. Each step is treated separately, so that phase of the finishing process can be studied, reviewed, or referred to when the need arises.

15.3
HOW TO FILL

The pores or cells in certain wood used in making cabinets are very large. For wall paneling and certain other materials, applying a direct finish without filling would be satisfactory. In the finishing of most cabinets, however, a porous, uneven finish is not desirable. Therefore, a filler is applied that when dried and sanded creates a smooth, even surface for the application of top dressings.

For a filler to appropriately perform its function, it must contain a body that will readily fill the minute pores and cracks in stock, and the body must also be immersed in a vehicle that will evaporate and harden.

15.3.1	
How to Mix	
Paste Wood	
Filler	

Most commercial paste wood fillers are adequate for the job of filling stock, but there are a few brands, classified as liquid fillers, that contain little body and hence have little use. Paste wood fillers, whether bought commercially or homemade, have a silica base. The silica is combined with linseed oil, japan dryer, and turpentine in varying quantities, depending upon the type of application. As a base reference point combine 1 quart of turpentine with 1 pint of japan dryer and 2 to 3 pounds of fine silex. For a heavier-bodied paste, decrease the volume of turpentine and japan dryer proportionally or increase the silica content. For a lighter, thin base, increase the turpentine base. One quart of paste wood filler will cover approximately 70 square feet of board.

The filler may be applied to previously stained wood and to bare wood in its natural creamy color, or a color pigment may be added to tone it. If coloring is added, it should be slightly darker than the actual color of the stain that is to be used. This feature will cause the pores being filled to be slightly darker than the surrounding wood surfaces, thereby creating a pleasant effect. Use the following table as a suggestion for tinting the filling:

Cabinet Color /Wood	*Pigment*
Mahogany	Burnt umber
Walnut	Van Dyke brown
Oak	Touch of burnt umber
Maple	None required

If a lightener or darkener is needed, use zinc oxide to lighten the filler or ground black to darken the filler.

Finally, prepare paste wood filler to the consistency of cream—heavy or light depending upon the type of wood being filled and whether it is the first or second coat. If, as happens in some cases, the first coat does not completely do the job, a thinner mixture of the same paste can be applied as a second coat.

15.3.2
HOW TO APPLY PASTE WOOD FILLER

The prepared paste should be liberally applied to the cabinet surface. Use a stiff bristle brush 2 to 4 inches wide with medium-length bristles to vigorously rub the paste into the grain. This is usually accomplished by holding the brush perpendicular and using orbital or circular motions. After this brushing operation is complete, the paste may be (1) left as it is, or (2) stroked with the grain, or (3) brushed across the grain to prevent lifting the filler from the grain.

Within 10 to 20 minutes the paste will dull to a flat finish. When this happens the paste must be wiped away from the surface. Take a piece of burlap cloth or wood wool and vigorously wipe away the excess wood filler by stroking across the grain. If the filler has hardened too much to permit easy removal, soften it by adding thinner to the rag. A dowel tapered to a flat tip is very effective for removing excess filler from moldings and inside corners.

After you have gently (but firmly) removed the excess filler, wipe a final time with a smooth, soft cloth. Wipe with the grain. If the filler has been properly embedded, the rag will not pull it from the wood.

The filler can be applied most easily and thoroughly when the surface is horizontal. Once the filler has been applied, the position of the surface is relatively unimportant.

Allow the filler to dry thoroughly; 24 hours is generally sufficient. Then sand with paper of 180 to 220 grit. If there are pores or uneven places (hollows) within the grain that are not filled, a second coat of filler may be needed. If so, use either the same consistency as before where heavy coating is needed, or thin the filler and apply a light-bodied coat where it is needed.

15.3.3
SHELLAC AS A FILLER

On some not-so-porous woods a liquid filler will usually provide a good base for sealing the pores and evening the surface. Where this is the case, a coating of white shellac will usually solve the problem nicely. The shellac should be reduced to 1 part shellac to 6 parts denatured alcohol. When using this type of filler the stain is frequently applied first. But if you want to control the stain, filler, in addition to smoothing the surfaces, will reduce the penetration of the stain.

15.3.4
CELLULOSE FIBER
(WOOD DOUGH)
AS A FILLER

Commercially prepared cellulose wood fillers are available in most of the standard wood types and colors. There are natural, bleached, maple, oak, and walnut tones, to mention just a few. These fillers dry extremely fast and may be applied in more than one coat. Their usefulness is limited to cracks, pits, and filling between joints. In some instances coarsely end cut materials are filled with this type of filler.

There are two theories regarding when to apply this wood filler. Some people feel that there is less discoloration and better blending if the filler is applied after staining and the stain is sealed. If this method is used, the filler must be tinted before application. Other people apply the filler in natural color or tinted directly to unfinished wood. They feel that this method allows more freedom for sanding after the filler dries.

15.4
HOW TO SEAL

Sealing provides two important functions: (1) it protects the stain or wood from discoloration when the finishing material is added, and (2) it provides a base for controlling stains where a limited penetration of stain is desired or top staining is to be used.

One of the cheapest sealers is shellac. To use shellac as a sealer, reduce its strength by mixing it with four to six times its volume of denatured alcohol. The amount of porousness the wood has and the amount of control desired will dictate the desired reduction.

Lacquer can also be used as a sealer. An effective sealing coat is composed of 1 part lacquer to 3 parts lacquer thinner. Lacquer sealers are especially useful where lacquer will be the top dressing.

15.4.1
How to Use
Sanding Sealers

A fairly new product on the market is sanding sealer. This product usually can be purchased in clear form or in a variety of stain colors. It has a varnish base, so caution should be exercised where the final coats of finish are to be something other than varnish. This product requires good presanding and considerable postsanding. It is very much like a varnish stain except that it has some additional sealing qualities. There is very little control over tone and texture when using this product or any type of finishing product that combines steps of the finishing process.

15.4.2
How to Sand
the Sealer

The cabinet must be sanded thoroughly with a fine grade of paper after every sealing coat. Flint, garnet, or aluminum oxide paper in grits of 180 to 220 should be used. The paper can be installed in a vibrator machine or wrapped around a sanding block or used with the hand. Do not apply a great deal of pressure. The film coating is very thin, and pressure exerted while sanding may cut into the paste wood filler or stain.

15.5
HOW TO
STAIN

Although a variety of types of stain can be purchased commercially, such as oil, water, and varnish stains, oil stain is the most popular for use on cabinets.

Oil stain can be purchased in a variety of colors to match every type and color of furniture built for American homes, old or new. Certain precautions should be exercised when staining, and these will be discussed.

15.5.1
PIGMENT
OIL STAINS

Pigment oil stains are usually made from a mixture of ground powders soluble in naphtha or turpentine. The pigments are made from mixture of various oxides and silicates. The vehicle contains varnish, mineral spirits, and driers such as japan drier. These are combined with various oils such as linseed and tall oil and are added to mineral spirits, which makes up 80 percent of the volume of the container.

Oil stains are usually applied to sample (scrap) pieces of all materials to be stained. This gives the finisher a quick, reliable gage to use when he applies the stain to the cabinet. Since all woods take color differently, the various shades, depths, and tones will show.

Stain can be applied with a soft bristle brush 1½ to 3 inches wide or with a soft cotton rag (see Figure 15-4). There are two ways to stain: (1) apply the stain across the grain first, then with the grain, to even up the stain; or (2) brush or wipe with the grain at all times.

After the stain is applied, let it set briefly, from 2 to 10 minutes, until the desired depth of color is achieved. Wipe the end grain immediately; do not allow the stain to remain because it will become extremely dark. Begin to wipe the stain with a clean, dry, soft cloth,

FIGURE 15-4   **STAINING WITH A RAG**

starting with those pieces that take stain most easily. Continue wiping the surfaces until all the excess stain has been removed. Let dry 4 to 24 hours, depending upon the weather and the type of stain used. Penetrating oil stains are very similar to pigment oil stains but tend to react more quickly. Therefore, a wash coat of shellac mixed with 4 to 6 parts alcohol is usually applied to the cabinet before staining. The method af application is the same as that of the pigment oil stain.

15.5.2
SPIRIT STAINS

Spirit stains are composed of aniline powder, are soluble in alcohol, and are very difficult to use. Because they dry quickly, the colors may not be even. When shellac is added as a retarding agent, more control is obtained. This type of stain, however, is ideal for touch-up work when refinishing.

15.5.3
WATER STAINS

Water-soluble powder made from aniline dyes is the most desirable stain to use on a cabinet that will be exposed continuously to direct sunlight. It is the most penetrating of all stains, especially when used on base wood. The stain is sold in small packets as dry powder. The best results are obtained when the powder is added to very warm water, as it will then dissolve completely and mix more easily.

Since all colors are not available in powdered form, variations will have to be made by combining various water-soluble dyes. The amount of dye added to a basic color will have to be determined on a trial-and-error basis. Therefore, when making a mixture, be sure to make enough for the entire job. Some basic water-soluble dyes are: red (crimson), brown (tobacco), standard walnut, auramine yellow (lemon), nigrosine crystals (jet black), fuchsine red (scarlet), and malachite green (blue-green). As an example, a lighter brown can be obtained by adding yellow to standard walnut, a darker brown by adding nigrosine crystals, a reddish brown by adding crimson or fuchsine red. If a light walnut color is desired, just add more water, diluting the color.

Water stain is best applied with a brush that has long, fairly stiff bristles. Apply the stain in a sweeping motion back and forth with the grain. Continue brushing and staining until the entire surface is completely covered and appears to have the same density or volume of stain. As a last step before the stain sets, brush the entire surface with an empty brush until the stain is distributed evenly and the surface has a dull appearance. The best position for the surface to be stained is horizontal.

It is difficult to control the color because of the rapid penetration of the stain. Therefore, *do not* add additional coats of stain or double brush near the ends of each stroke. There is no way to stop this double dose of stain.

Be sure to seal the container if you wish to store any leftover stain. To recover the dyes, which may be used again, allow the water to evaporate, and recover the stain. When needed again, bring the water to a boil, add the dried dyes, and stir until dissolved.

15.6
UNDERCOATS
AND
INTERMEDIATE
FINISH COATS

The most foolproof method of applying finish coats is to start and finish with the same product. This will always assure compatibility because there will be no conflict in chemicals. In certain cases chemicals of different products will react with each other, and lifting, softening, opaquing, and dissolving are apt to result. A product that works well as an undercoating for certain finishes is shellac.

15.6.1
SHELLAC AS
AN UNDERCOAT

Shellac properly diluted is frequently used in finishing operations as a wash coat and an undercoat. If light-colored cabinets are being finished, white shellac is the better choice. If dark cabinets are to be finished, orange shellac is better. In either case the shellac must be diluted with denatured alcohol.

Since shellac is a derivative of varnish, it follows that the product will work well under most varnishes. Before using shellac, always refer to the instructions on the can of varnish. For instance, polyurethane varnish cannot be applied over shellac. However, when diluted properly (1 part shellac to 4 parts denatured alcohol), shellac can be used as a base coat for a lacquer-finished cabinet.

Shellac is ideal as a base coat because of its filling qualities and quick-drying capabilities. Some types of stain, such as oil and spirit stains, may bleed into the final finish and cause clouding or uneven coloring. By using shellac (when compatible with the final finish), a complete seal can be achieved, thereby preventing bleeding. It also provides a quick method for preparing for the final coat, because shellac when thinned will dry in 30 minutes to 2 hours, depending upon the drying conditions.

15.6.2
LACQUER AS AN UNDERCOAT

If lacquer is used as a final, top coating, it may also be used as a sealer and undercoat. Start with a very thin application of lacquer (1 part lacquer to 3 parts thinner) and watch for bleeding. The mixture will dry in seconds. Check the surface for any ill effects; if none, apply a second coat. If you use a brushing lacquer, make sure that the lacquer will dry slowly enough to permit even brushing. When thinning brushing lacquer, follow the manufacturer's suggestions by adding a *retarding* type of lacquer thinner. After one, two, or three coats have been successfully applied and are dry, sand the surface with a very fine paper (220 grit) using gentle strokes.

15.6.3
POLYURETHANE VARNISH AS AN UNDERCOAT

The *plastic* varnishes, as they are frequently called, usually cannot be applied over previously sealed surfaces because of chemical reactions. Therefore, if the cabinet is to be finished with a polyurethane type of varnish, an undercoat of the same material is most suitable. Thin the varnish to about 50 percent strength and apply with a brush or spray. When dry (usually 4 to 18 hours), sand with fine paper. Apply a second coat with a stronger concentration of varnish. Sand after the second coat dries (Figure 15-5).

FIGURE 15-5   HOW TO SAND TO SMOOTH IMPERFECTIONS

15.7
FINAL COATS

The next phase in finishing is that of applying the final coats or coat of finish. Whether these are shellac, lacquer, or special varnishes, they are usually applied in nearly full strength. There are certain requirements that must be met when applying each type, and these are identified below.

shellac	Apply succeeding coats only when the previous coat is dry.
lacquer	Apply all coats within the same time frame and do not, as a rule, allow more than 24 hours to elapse between coats.
varnish	Allow sufficient drying time between coats, depending on the type of varnish that is being applied. Do not allow more than 24 to 30 hours to elapse between coats of certain polyurethane varnishes.
waxes	Prepare special-purpose furniture waxes and apply each succeeding coat when the previous coat is thoroughly dry.

| oil-rub top coats | Liberally apply the mixture of oil (linseed usually) and brushing lacquer to the surface and rub well into the surface with even-pressure strokes. Wipe off the excess and let dry. Repeat oil applications until the surface is completely saturated and the desired depth is achieved. |

15.8 HOW TO COMPLETE THE FINISH

The final phase in the steps of finishing a cabinet is the polishing step (refer to Figure 15-2). The purpose of polishing is to develop a final sheen and to remove any and all imperfections that the final coats have picked up.

Recall from Chapter 14 that sandpaper with a grit from 240 to 600 may be used. The finer the grit, the more polishing and the less cutting will occur. In addition, rubbing abrasives such as pumice stone and rottenstone are used to develop special sheens. Finally, there are the waxes that will produce selected sheen and texture.

The top coats can be polished, rubbed, and cleaned. Each operation has a different purpose. They are:

polishing	A burnishing action that removes or blends fine scratches so they cannot be seen with the naked eye.
rubbing	An operation designed to remove irregularities that may have developed during the top coating.
cleaning	An operation that removes all foreign matter that results from polishing or rubbing.

15.8.1 How to Rub

Rubbing may be performed with fine sandpaper and/or pumice or a combination of sandpaper and pumice. To obtain the various sheens, perform the following actions:

dull finish Sand the cabinet with a grade 360 to 400 paper until the entire finish has been dulled. Follow with a good cleaning. No shine should be visible.

satin-sheen finish Sand the cabinet with a grade 360 to 500 paper, followed by a hand rubbing with a fine grade (type F or FF) of pumice mixed with water or oil.

high-satin-sheen finish Sand the cabinet with grade 500 to 600 paper until smooth, then follow with a rubbing of fine to extra fine (type FF or FFF) pumice mixed with oil. Clean.

Rubbing is usually required regardless of the type of top dressing. There is no practical way to prevent dust in the air from settling onto the surface, and there is no way to prevent foreign matter from entering the top coat, no matter how much filtering is done.

Machine rubbing may be very satisfactory for flat panels and surfaces. Generally in-line sanding will be required because scratching will result from across-the-grain sanding. Pumice, which is almost always rubbed by hand, should always be rubbed in-line. For those hard-to-get-at inside corners and moldings, a slurry mixture of pumice and oil applied and rubbed with a rubbing brush or stick will generally be effective. Sometimes a toothbrush is ideal. Pumice cuts fairly fast, so caution must be used. Occasionally, wipe the surface clean and dry it so that an examination can be made. Usually, though, two separate rubbings of pumice are required before the rubbing phase is complete. When wiping, be sure to wipe with the grain.

15.8.2
How to Polish

Polishing, which we have defined as a burnishing action, is the next-to-last phase in the finishing operation. Polishing may be performed to achieve a desired appearance but it is designed primarily to blend the slight imperfections created by the brush or sprayer into a glassy-like surface. A smooth, extra fine pumice may be used on satin-sheen surfaces. If a higher gloss is desired, a mixture of rottenstone and oil is used instead of pumice. Rottenstone, unlike pumice, will not scratch. Its cutting power is negligible. The polishing effect is achieved by the friction and heat generated during the rubbing. Heat will soften the top dressing sufficiently to allow the rottenstone to blend the slight imperfections and raise a polish. The same precautions should be made when polishing as those of rubbing. Two separate polishing steps are desirable, with a good cleaning between operations.

15.8.3
How to Clean

The purpose of cleaning is to permit examination of the surfaces previously rubbed or polished. Various substances may be used to clean: dry, lint-free, soft rags; water and a rag; mineral spirits and a rag. If water was used along with the pumice or rottenstone, then water can be used to wash down the cabinet after rubbing. Be careful that no wiping is done across the grain, or scratching may result. Wipe dry with a soft, lint-free rag.

If a slurry of oil and pumice or rottenstone was used in the rubbing or polishing operation, wipe away all excess slurry with a clean rag. Follow this initial wiping with another wiping, using a rag and mineral spirits. Finally, wash with water and wipe dry. Be cautious when using the spirits. Do not select a type that could affect the top dressing.

15.8.4
How to Wax

After the cabinet has been cleaned, examined, and the desired finish achieved, a good grade of furniture wax should be applied. Any of a number of commercial paste waxes and liquid waxes can be used for this operation. If desired, a wax mixture can be made from beeswax and turpentine. When the beeswax is thoroughly dissolved (usually in 2 days), color may be added to the wax.

Color pigment such as burnt umber, should be added to any clear wax when the wax is to be applied to any cabinet that has color (not bleached). The addition of color may prevent the possibility of wax smudges and discoloration in corners and crevices after the wax dries.

Apply a liberal coat of wax evenly with a small pad of soft cloth. Let it stand long enough to penetrate and give the finish an opportunity to show the proper luster. To do this, the wax must not harden before it is buffed, so it must be applied at moderate temperatures (68 to 80°F).

Next we shall discuss some of the shop methods used in the finishing of cabinets and furniture.

15.9
FINISHING
METHODS

Figure 15-6 illustrates four of the frequently used methods for finishing cabinets. They are (1) the shellac and wax method, (2) the varnish method, (3) the lacquer method, and (4) the oil-rub method. After a brief explanation of each method, a step-by-step procedure is provided in table form so that the book may be left open and easily read.

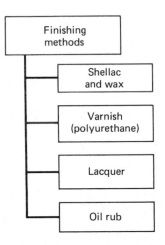

FIGURE 15-6   FINISHING METHODS

15.9.1
SHELLAC AND
WAX METHOD

In the shellac and wax method, shellac, denatured alcohol, sandpaper, pumice, rags, a good brush, and wax are needed. Where a shellac finish is selected, avoid using spirit stains and non-grain-raising stains, as these stains contain alcohol.

Prefinish the cabinet by sanding with final papers of 180 to 220 grit. Apply stain or proceed with a wash coat of shellac if control of stain is required. When the stain has dried, lightly sand with 280- to 320-grit paper. Seal with a mixture of shellac and alcohol in equal parts. Apply three to four additional coats of shellac, each one thinned as before. Follow each coating with sanding. Because it dries quickly, shellac must be applied rapidly. Avoid overlapping strokes by having the second brushful start before the first brushful has begun to set. Be fast in applying the shellac and be sure to cover the entire surface only once. Shellacking edges, turned moldings, and legs should be no problem because these areas are relatively small, and a single stroke of the brush will cover most small areas. When coating the sides of a cabinet brush from bottom to top. If spraying, be careful not to overspray.

Shellac can be treated as any of the other finishes during the rubbing operations. In the final polishing you may use fine sandpaper, pumice, and rottenstone. It is suggested that large flat areas be rubbed first. Then the styles and turned areas can be rubbed to match the flat surfaces. Clean off the slurry of pumice or rottenstone and oil with benzine or naphtha and a soft rag. Do all wiping with the grain. Follow these operations by washing with water and drying with soft, lint-free rags. *Water* should *not* be used when polishing with pumice or rottenstone. The results will be a too-dull surface finish. Follow the cleaning with waxing.

STEP 1 / Stain the cabinet *or* wash-coat the cabinet with 1 part shellac to 4 parts denatured alcohol.

STEP 2 / Seal the stain with 1 part shellac to 6 parts denatured alcohol.

STEP 3 / Fill the cabinet, if required, with paste wood filler or equivalent.

STEP 4 / Sand with 180- to 220-grit paper.

STEP 5 / Top-stain and accent-stain as required.

STEP 6 / Sand with 220-grit paper.

STEP 7 / Shellac with a mixture of 50 percent shellac and 50 percent alcohol.

STEP 8 / When dry, sand with 280- to 320-grit paper.

STEP 9 / Repeat steps 7 and 8 four or five times.

STEP 10 / Rub the cabinet with 400- to 600-grit paper, or type F or FF pumice, until the desired finish is achieved.

STEP 11 / Polish with type FF or FFF pumice, or a rottenstone and linseed oil slurry, using a felt pad wrapped around a block of wood.

STEP 12 / Clean with naphtha or benzene and a soft, clean rag.

STEP 13 / Wash with water and dry.

STEP 14 / Wax with tinted wax.

15.9.2
VARNISH METHOD

The polyurethane varnishes are much better to work with than ordinary spar varnish. They dry better, are lighter, and are easier to work with. The varnish method described here will explain how to use this type of varnish.

Polyurethane varnishes cannot as a rule be applied over shellac; therefore, shellac is not acceptable as a seal coat. The best method, according to several manufacturers of this product, is to seal the surface with a diluted solution of the same varnish. Methods of staining explained in the shellac method apply also to the varnish method.

There is a distinct difference in finishing with varnish and in finishing with shellac or lacquer. Varnish takes quite a long time to dry. The reason for the slow drying is the resins in varnish. These and the oils must harden after the thinner has evaporated. Both the turpentine and the humidity will vary the drying conditions.

Of the various finishing materials, varnish is one of the best methods of obtaining a satin-sheen finish. Because of its body, it covers completely and relatively thickly, thereby creating a suitable surface for rubbing with pumice. One precaution should be observed: allow the varnish to dry thoroughly before beginning the rubbing and polishing operations.

Of necessity, a dust-free work room or booth should be used when varnishing. A day before you are going to varnish, clean and vacuum the shop. On the day you are varnishing, do not raise any dust by using machines or doing any additional dusting.

For most cabinets three coats of varnish will provide adequate coverage. These may be applied with a spray gun or with a 1½- to 3-inch soft bristle brush. The soft bristles are needed to minimize the brush marks. Sand the sheen from each coat before applying the next coat to ensure a good binding surface.

STEP 1 / Stain the cabinet *or* apply a wash coat first if the stain needs additional controlling.

STEP 2 / Fill with paste wood filler tinted slightly darker than the stain.

STEP 3 / Sand with 180- to 220-grit paper.

STEP 4 / Apply a seal coat of varnish reduced by 50 percent.

STEP 5 / Sand with 180- to 220-grit paper.

STEP 6 / Varnish full strength or cut 10 percent.

STEP 7 / Sand with 220- to 240-grit open-coated paper.

STEP 8 / Sand between coats until three coats have been applied.

STEP 9 / Rub to a satin finish with 320- to 400-grit wet/dry paper and water, with 400 to 600 paper and water for a high sheen, or with 220 paper for a dull sheen finish; *or* rub with a slurry mixture of pumice types F, FF, or FFF and water or oil for the desired effect.

STEP 10 / Polish with rottenstone and oil.

STEP 11 / Clean with naphtha or benzene to remove all slurry. Wipe dry.

STEP 12 / Wax with tinted wax.

15.9.3
LACQUER METHOD

Lacquer, although available in both brush and spray varieties, is generally considered a spray finish. As with varnish, lacquer is available commercially in dull, satin, and high-gloss sheens. Tinted lacquer may be purchased, but it is generally used in the clear state. Used with a spray outfit whose pressure is between 25 and 50 pounds per square inch, lacquer is very easy to apply (see Figure 15-7).

Lacquer's primary advantage is its quick drying time. Depending upon the amount of retarding agent used, the drying time will vary from a few minutes to 20 minutes. This means that the entire finishing job for a small to medium-sized cabinet will take from 2 to 4 hours. Another advantage is that lacquer may be used for wash coating, sealing, and top dressing, thereby reducing the variety of equipment and supply that would be needed if another finish were selected.

Lacquer is a tough, durable finish that will not mar easily. If special conditions must be controlled, such as moisture, mildew, or fungus, special additives may be added that make lacquer more desirable.

FIGURE 15-7   HOW TO SPRAY LACQUER

Lacquer finishing can result in the *orange peel effect*, a buildup of lacquer that resembles the rough peel of an orange. If this happens during a spraying operation, it must be removed by rubbing and cleaning. Orange peeling occurs from insufficient thinner in the mixture that is being sprayed, or by using too much air pressure while spraying.

Another element to consider when using lacquer is its tendency to cause bleeding of the stained wood. This bleeding can cause serious problems if the lacquer is not mixed with a retarder. The fast drying of the material will trap moisture, cause the stains to interfere with the lacquer, and create streaking effects.

Lacquers are usually finished by rubbing with pumice, followed by polishing with rottenstone and oil, and a good cleaning. For the French polish effect seen on pianos, start with a high-gloss lacquer. Do not use pumice except in cases of orange peel, and burnish with rottenstone and an oil-soaked felt pad. Finish with a good application of wax.

STEP   1 /   Stain the cabinet *or* wash-coat the cabinet and sand with 180- to 220-grit paper, then stain.

STEP   2 /   Apply a wash or seal coat.

STEP   3 /   Fill with paste wood filler, if required. Sand when dry, with 180- to 220-grit paper.

STEP   4 /   Spray or brush lacquer. (If spray, dilute 10 to 15 percent with lacquer thinner; if brush, dilute 10 percent with retarder thinner.)

STEP   5 /   Sand between coats. Remove any orange peel or blushing (moist air trapped below surface). NOTE: *Blushing can be helped by lacquer thinner on a rag rubbed over the area.*

STEP   6 /   Repeat steps 4 and 5 until sufficient coats have been applied; 6 to 10 are usually sufficient for a fine job.

STEP   7 /   Rub with 400- to 600-grit wet/dry paper and oil or water *or* rub with pumice type F, FF, or FFF and oil or water.

STEP   8 /   Polish with rottenstone and a felt pad soaked with linseed oil.

STEP   9 /   Clean with benzene if oil was used, or wash with water. Dry.

STEP 10 /   Wax with a good grade of furniture wax.

15.9.4
OIL-RUB METHOD

Oil-rubbed finishing brings out the natural beauty of wood. The oil is allowed to penetrate the pores or cells of the wood until they become saturated and hardened. The process is a continuing one which starts with a daily application of boiled linseed oil, drier, and turpentine. After 1 week the applications are spaced at weekly intervals, then graduated to monthly applications. From then on the applications are dependent upon the use, and abuse, the cabinet receives. An inherent characteristic of this type of finish is its darkening. The older the finish is, the darker it will be.

Boiled linseed oil is diluted with turpentine, after which spar varnish and/or a drier may be added. A mixture of 2 parts boiled linseed oil to 1 part turpentine is the basis to which 10 percent varnish may be added. To work properly the mixture must be at room temperature or slightly warmer. Saturate a cloth with the mixture and rub small sections of the cabinet for periods of 10 to 15 minutes. Or brush on generously, let stand 5 to 10 minutes, then rub another 10 to 15 minutes. The oil must penetrate the cells. Pressure usually speeds the penetrating process. Wipe off excess oil and let dry 24 hours between coats.

If the oil-rub finish is used, no paste wood filler is usually required except on end-grain woods. The oil mixture will fill the pores.

After the basic coats have been applied, with sanding done between coats, the surface may be rubbed with rottenstone and an oil-soaked felt pad to bring additional sheen and luster to the surface.

STEP 1 /   Stain the cabinet.

STEP 2 /   Fill all sand cracks and blemishes as needed. (Paste filler is usually not required.)

STEP 3 /   Fill the end-grain stock with paste wood.

STEP 4 /   Apply a mixture of boiled linseed oil and turpentine with 10 percent varnish or drier; *or* apply a mixture of equal parts of boiled linseed oil, turpentine, and varnish.

STEP 5 /   Rub well, 10 to 25 minutes, in small areas.

STEP 6 /   Wipe off excess finishing compound and let dry for 24 hours.

STEP 7 /   Sand with 280- to 320-grit paper.

STEP 8 /   Repeat oil applications until desired depth, color, and tone are obtained. Sand and let dry.

STEP 9 /   Rub with a slurry of rottenstone and oil, using a felt pad or rubbing stick.

STEP 10 /   Clean with a lightly soaked rag of benzene if an oil–pumice slurry is used.

STEP 11 /   Wash all excess materials off the surface. Dry.

STEP 12 /   Wax with a light wax.

QUESTIONS

1 / What are the basic differences between finishing steps and finishing methods?

2 / How is a filler prepared?

3 / Why *isn't* birch or maple usually filled?

4 / Can you name three types of scales?

5 / What is meant by the term "wash coat"?

6 / What may happen when applying water stain if overstrokes with brushes are made?

7 / Will shellac prevent "bleeding"?

8 / Why is lacquer frequently used to finish cabinets?

9 / What are the steps in the cleaning operation?

10 / What are the specific steps used in applying a varnish finish?

11 / How can a dust-free room be obtained?

12 / What type of bristle brush is needed to apply varnish?

13 / What is the "orange peel effect" and what can be done to minimize it?

14 / Why can the filling operation be omitted when an oil-rub finish is applied?

UNIT V

Unit V provides a handy reference for items that are frequently referred to. They are gathered here to make it easy to locate them. Chapter 16 describes the various woods, both hard and soft, that are used in cabinetmaking. The Appendix consists of tables that provide data on screws, nails, drill sizes, lumber sizes, and average drying times for finishes. Following is a Glossary of the most common terms in our field of interest.

16

TYPES OF WOOD

16.1
HARDWOODS
(BROAD-
LEAVED
SPECIES)

16.1.1
AMERICAN BEECH

Properties /   One of the heavy woods, American beech (Figure 16-1) has an average weight of 45 pounds a cubic foot and, with a

---

The material in this chapter is reprinted from *Wood . . . Colors and Kinds*, Agriculture Handbook 101, Forest Service, U.S. Department of Agriculture (Washington, D.C.: Government Office, 1956).

specific gravity of 0.56, is classified as hard. It is rated high in strength and shock resistance and is readily bent when steamed.

Beech is subject to very large shrinkage and requires considerable care during seasoning if checks, warp, and discoloration are to be avoided. Heartwood ranks low in resistance to decay. The wood wears well and stays smooth when subjected to friction, even under water. Although ranking high in nail-withdrawal resistance, it has a tendency to split when nails are driven into it. When pulped by the soda process, beech yields a short-fibered pulp that can be mixed with longer fibered pulps to obtain paper of satisfactory strength.

Uses /   American beech is used for lumber, distilled products, veneer, railroad ties, pulpwood, cooperage, and fuel. The lumber is used largely in the manufacture of boxes, crates, baskets, furniture, handles, flooring, woodenware, general millwork, and novelties. Beech is especially suitable for food containers, since it does not impart taste or odor.

Description /   Heartwood is white with a reddish tinge to reddish brown. Pores are not visible but wood rays can be seen on all surfaces. On the end grain, the rays appear to be irregularly spaced, while on quartersawed surfaces they appear to be of different heights along the grain. On the plainsawed surfaces, the rays also appear to be of different height, but they look much narrower in this view. Beech is readily distinguishable from other native species by its weight, conspicuous rays, and tiny pores.

16.1.2
AMERICAN
SYCAMORE

Properties /   In weight, American sycamore (Figure 16-1) is ranked as a moderately heavy wood, averaging 34 pounds a cubic foot. A moderately hard wood, with a specific gravity of 0.46, it has a close texture and an interlocking grain. It is moderately strong, moderately stiff, and has moderately good shock resistance.

Sycamore has large shrinkage while drying, is inclined to warp, and is somewhat difficult to season. Also, it is not durable when exposed to conditions favorable to decay. The wood turns well on a lathe and keeps its shape well when bent to form after steaming. It is only intermediate in nail-withdrawal resistance but because of its interlocking grain ranks high in its ability to withstand splitting. Sycamore

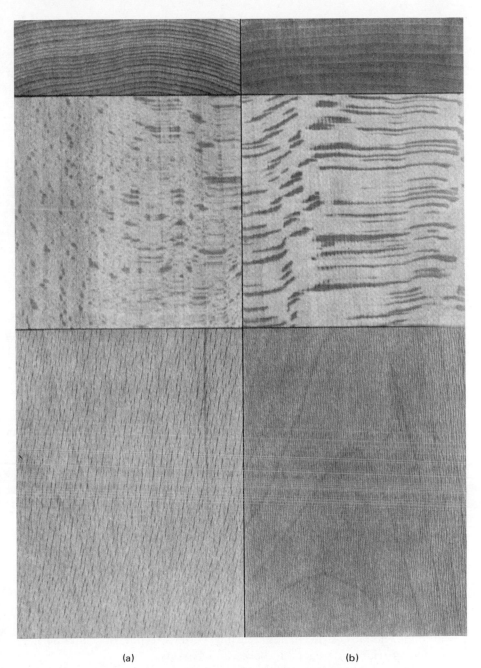

(a)   (b)

FIGURE 16-1   (A) AMERICAN BEECH; (B) AMERICAN
                   SYCAMORE

wood does not impart taste, odor, or stain to substances that come in contact with it.

Uses / The principal uses of American sycamore are for lumber, veneer, railroad ties, cooperage, fence posts, and fuel. The lumber goes largely into furniture and boxes. Considerable sycamore veneer is used for fruit and vegetable baskets and berry boxes. Although generally used for the cheaper grades of furniture, sycamore is used in one form or another in practically all grades. Other products made from the lumber include flooring, scientific instruments, handles, and butchers' blocks.

Description / Heartwood is reddish brown or flesh brown in color. Pores are very small and not visible to the unaided eye. Rays are visible on all surfaces. They appear uniformly spaced on the end grain and of uniform height on quartersawed surfaces. Plainsawed surfaces show rays that appear more numerous and more closely spaced than in beech.

16.1.3
ROCK ELM

Properties / Rock elm (Figure 16-2) is a heavy wood, averaging 44 pounds a cubic foot. The wood is classified as hard, with a specific gravity of 0.57. It is stronger, harder, and stiffer than any of the other commercial elms. With the exception of hickory and dogwood, rock elm has higher shock resistance than any other American hardwood.

Although rock elm undergoes large shrinkage when drying, it tends to shrink somewhat less than the other commercial elms. As with all the elms, care must be taken to prevent warp during seasoning. Rock elm is somewhat difficult to work with hand or machine tools, and the heartwood has low to moderate resistance to decay. However, all the commercial elms have excellent bending qualities.

Uses / Elm lumber is used principally for containers and furniture. In some cases, the different species of elm are employed indiscriminately, but when hardness or shock resistance is required to a high degree, rock elm is preferred. Rock elm veneer is used in considerable quantities in manufacturing various types of containers, especially fruit and vegetable boxes and baskets.

Large quantities of rock elm also go into crating for heavy articles, such as furniture, glass, and porcelain. The strength and toughness of this wood make it very serviceable for certain types of containers that

(a)   (b)

FIGURE 16-2   (A) ROCK ELM; (B) AMERICAN ELM

must stand rough usage, such as market baskets and bushel baskets for home use. Considerable quantities are used in the manufacture of furniture, especially the bent parts of chairs.

Description /   Heartwood is brown to dark brown, sometimes with shades of red. Summerwood pores are arranged in concentric wavy lines that appear lighter than the background wood. The springwood pores in rock elm are visible only upon magnification.

16.1.4
AMERICAN ELM

Properties /   American elm (Figure 16-2) is moderately heavy, averaging 35 pounds a cubic foot, and moderately hard, with a specific gravity of 0.46. It rates as moderately weak, but is moderately stiff and has good shock resistance.

The wood of American elm has large shrinkage and care must be taken to prevent warping as it seasons. Like all of the commercial elms, it has excellent bending qualities. Its heartwood has low to moderate resistance to decay. The wood is slightly below average in woodworking properties, but is among the top woods in ease of gluing. In nail-withdrawal resistance, it has an intermediate rank.

Uses /   American elm lumber is used principally in the manufacture of containers, furniture, and dairy and poultry supplies. Because of its excellent bending properties, the wood has been much used for barrels and kegs. Considerable quantities of veneer go into the manufacture of fruit and vegetable boxes and baskets. American elm also is used a great deal for crating heavy articles, such as furniture, glass, and porcelain products. It is used in sizable quantities in the furniture industry, particularly for the bent parts of chairs.

Description /   Heartwood is brown to dark brown, sometimes containing shades of red. Although the summerwood pores are not visible as individuals, they are arranged in concentric wavy lines within the boundaries of the growth rings. The wavy lines appear lighter than the background wood. American elm shows a springwood pore zone with a single row of large and easily visible pores.

16.1.5
BLACK WALNUT

Properties /   Black walnut (Figure 16-3) is classified as a heavy wood, averaging 38 pounds a cubic foot. The wood is hard, with a specific gravity of 0.51, is strong and stiff, and has good shock resistance.

Even under conditions favorable to decay, black walnut heartwood is one of our most durable woods. It can be satisfactorily kiln-dried or air-dried, and holds its shape well after seasoning. Black walnut works easily with handtools and has excellent machining properties. The wood finishes beautifully with a handsome grain pattern. It takes and holds paints and stains exceptionally well, can be readily polished, and can be satisfactorily glued.

Uses / The outstanding use of black walnut is for furniture. Large amounts are also used for gunstocks and interior finish, while smaller quantities go into railroad ties, fence posts, and fuelwood. In the furniture industry, it is used either as solid wood cut from lumber or as veneer and plywood. It also is extremely popular for interior finish wherever striking effects are desired. The wood of black walnut is particularly suitable for gunstocks because of its ability to stay in shape after seasoning, its fine machining porperties, and its uniformity of texture.

Description / Heartwood is chocolate brown and occasionally has darker, sometimes purplish, streaks. Unless bleached or otherwise modified, black walnut is not easily confused with any other native species. Pores are barely visible on the end grain but are quite easily seen as darker streaks or grooves on longitudinal surfaces. Arrangement of pores is similar to that in the hickories and persimmon, but the pores are smaller in size.

16.1.6
BLACK CHERRY

Properties / Black cherry (Figure 16-3) is a moderately heavy wood with an average weight of 35 pounds a cubic foot. The wood is also moderately hard, with a specific gravity of 0.47. Stiff and strong, it ranks high in resistance to shock.

Although it has moderately large shrinkage, black cherry stays in place well after seasoning and is comparatively free from checking and warping. It has moderate resistance to decay. The wood is difficult to work with handtools but ranks high in bending strength. It can be glued satisfactorily with moderate care.

Uses / Nearly all the black cherry cut is sawed into lumber for various products. Much goes into furniture and considerable amounts

(a)   (b)

FIGURE 16-3   (A) BLACK WALNUT; (B) BLACK CHERRY

are used for backing blocks on which electrotype plates, used in printing, are mounted. Other uses include burial caskets, woodenware and novelties, patterns and flasks for metalworking, plumbers' woodwork, and finish in buildings and railway coaches.

Description / Black cherry, which is not easily confused with other native species because of its distinctive color, has light to dark reddish brown heartwood. Although individual pores are not visible to the naked eye, their pattern is sometimes distinctive. On end-grain surfaces, the pores may appear to form lines that parallel the growth rings, while on plainsawed surfaces, they may follow the outline of the growth-ring boundary.

The wood rays of cherry are barely visible on end-grain surfaces and tend to produce a distinctive flake pattern on true quartersawed surfaces. They are higher along the grain than those of walnut and hence show more prominently on quartersawed surfaces.

16.1.7
HICKORY

Properties / The wood of the true hickories (Figure 16-4) is very heavy, averaging from 42 to 52 pounds per cubic foot, and very hard, with a specific gravity ranging from 0.56 to 0.66. It also is very strong as a post or beam, very stiff, and exceedingly high in shock resistance. Some woods are stronger than hickory and others are harder, but the combination of strength, toughness, hardness, and stiffness possessed by hickory has not been found to the same degree in any other commercial wood.

Hickory has very large shrinkage and must be carefully dried to avoid checking, warping, and other seasoning defects. It has low decay resistance but can be glued satisfactorily.

Uses / Nearly 80 percent of the true hickory used in the manufacture of wood products goes into tool handles, for which its hardness, toughness, stiffness, and strength make it especially suitable. Other uses include agricultural implements, athletic goods, and lawn furniture.

Description / Heartwood is brown to reddish brown. Pores are visible, but the zone of large pores is not sharply outlined as in oak and ash. Pores grade in size from one side of the annual ring to the other. Wood rays are very small and seen without magnification only on quartersawed surfaces. Tyloses frequently plug the pores, making their outlines indistinct. Under magnification, the end grain shows numerous white lines paralleling the growth ring.

(a)   (b)

FIGURE 16-4   (A) TRUE HICKORY: (B) WHITE ASH

16.1.8
WHITE ASH

Properties /   White ash (Figure 16-4) is a heavy wood with an average weight of 42 pounds a cubic foot. Ranked as a hard wood, it has a specific gravity of 0.55. It also is classified as strong and stiff, and has good shock resistance.

The wood of white ash is noted for its excellent bending qualities. In ease of working, tendency to split, and ability to hold nails and screws, it has moderately high rank. White ash lumber can be rapidly and satisfactorily kiln-dried, and it holds its shape well even under the action of water. The wood remains smooth under continual rubbing but is low in decay resistance.

Uses /   The use of white ash that dwarfs all others is its utilization for handles. It is the standard wood for D-handles for shovels and spades and for long handles for forks, hoes, rakes, and shovels. The wood is used too in the manufacture of furniture, where it is especially valuable for the bent parts of chairs. Its good bending qualities also make it useful for cooperage. White ash is used almost exclusively for many types of sports and athletic equipment, such as long oars and baseball bats.

Description /   Heartwood is brown to dark brown, sometimes with a reddish tint. As in black ash, the zone of large pores is visible and usually sharply defined. The white dots or lines that indicate summerwood pores are usually more prominent in white than in black ash. The small wood rays are generally visible only on quartersawed surfaces.

White ash is sometimes confused with hickory, but the two species are readily distinguishable. The zone of large pores is more distinctive in ash than in hickory. Also, the summerwood zone in ash shows white dots or lines that are visible to the unaided eye, but in hickory these dots or lines are visible only upon magnification.

16.1.9
QUAKING ASPEN

Properties /   One of the lightweight hardwoods, quaking aspen (Figure 16-5) averages 26 pounds a cubic foot. The wood is classified as soft, with a specific gravity of 0.35, and is weak, limber, and moderately low in shock resistance.

Although aspen has moderately large shrinkage, it can be

seasoned satisfactorily by air-drying or kiln-drying. In fact, few of the hardwoods shrink as little as aspen. The wood ranks low in decay resistance. It also is low in nail-withdrawal resistance, but has little tendency to split under the action of nails or screws. It is worked easily with hand or power tools and is fairly easy to finish to a smooth surface. Aspen glues easily with a variety of glues and under a wide range of gluing conditions. In painting properties, it ranks with the best of the hardwoods.

Uses / Aspen is used principally for lumber, paper pulp, excelsior, and matches. The largest present-day use of the lumber is for boxes and crates. It is probably most heavily used for pulpwood, chiefly in the manufacture of book and magazine paper and corrugating and insulating boards. Aspen has long been one of the preferred woods for the manufacture of high-grade excelsior.

Description / Heartwood is white to very light brown, with occasional brown streaks associated with defects. Pores are very small and generally not visible to the unaided eye. Growth rings are usually faint. Wood rays are small, uniform in height along the grain, and visible only on quartersawed surfaces. Aspen is similar to cottonwood, but cottonwood tends to have barely visible pores. The growth rings in aspen are generally narrower than those in cottonwood.

16.1.10
AMERICAN
BASSWOOD

Properties / Basswood (Figure 16-5) is a lightweight hardwood with an average weight of 26 pounds a cubic foot. The wood is weak, moderately stiff, and low in resistance to shock. Its specific gravity of 0.32 classes it as soft.

Although it has large shrinkage, basswood is fairly easy to air-dry or kiln-dry and stays in place well after seasoning. It has low nail-withdrawal resistance, but well resists splitting while being nailed. In decay resistance, it is low. The wood is easy to work with tools, takes and holds paint well, and is easily glued. When pulped by the soda process, basswood yields a soft, short-fibered, easily bleached pulp.

Uses / Most of the basswood cut in this country is first made into lumber for a variety of items. The laregst amounts are used for crates and boxes. The manufacture of sash, doors, and general millwork also accounts for much of the basswood lumber produced each year.

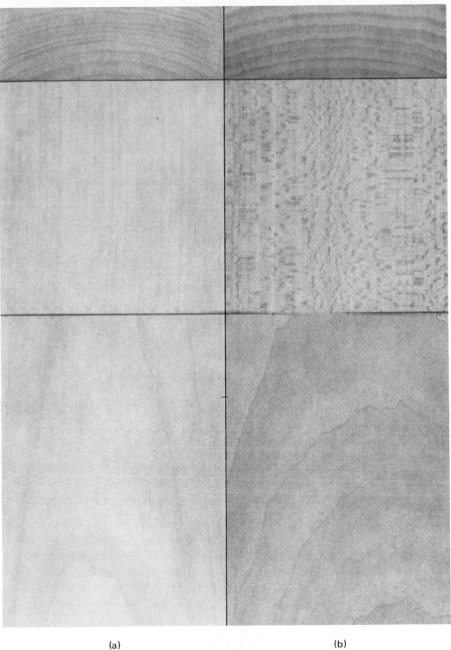

(a)   (b)

FIGURE 16-5   (A) QUAKING ASPEN; (B) BASSWOOD

In addition considerable lumber and veneer is used in the furniture industry, especially as core material overlaid with high-grade furniture veneers, such as walnut and mahogany.

Description /   Heartwood is creamy white to creamy brown or sometimes reddish. Pores are very small, as in aspen, and growth rings on plainsawed surfaces are generally faint. Wood rays are broader and higher than in aspen, and the two species can be readily distinguished by comparing their quartersawed faces. While the rays of aspen are low and uniform in height, some of those in basswood are distinctly higher than others and frequently darker than the background wood.

16.1.11

SWEETGUM

Properties /   Sweetgum (Figure 16-6) is a moderately heavy wood with an average weight of 36 pounds per cubic foot. The wood is hard, with a specific garvity of 0.46, moderately strong when used as a beam or post, moderately stiff, and has moderately high shock resistance.

Sweetgum has very large shrinkage in drying, and the sapwood and heartwood require different drying processes. The heartwood has low to moderate decay resistance. In nail-holding ability and in ability to resist splitting by nails and screws, sweetgum is rated intermediate. The heartwood requires special treatment before gluing can be done with best results.

Sweetgum ranks above average in turning, boring, and steam-bending properties but somewhat below average in the other machining properties. Its heartwood can be finished in a wide variety of color effects and the sapwood can be readily stained if a darker color is desired.

Uses /   The principal uses of sweetgum are for lumber, veneer, plywood, and slack cooperage. The lumber goes principally into boxes and crates, furniture, interior trim, and millwork. Veneer is used mainly for boxes, crates, baskets, furniture, and interior woodwork. Some sweetgum is used for crossties and fuel, and comparatively small amounts go into fencing, excelsior, and pulpwood.

Description /   Heartwood is reddish brown and occasionally variegated with streaks of darker color. Pores are so small that they are not visible except upon magnification. Growth rings are usually indistinct or inconspicuous. Rays are visible on quartersawed faces.

(a)   (b)

FIGURE 16-6   (A) SWEETGUM; (B) BLACK TUPELO

16.1.12
BLACK TUPELO

Properties /   A moderately heavy wood, black tupelo (Figure 16-6) has an average weight of 35 pounds a cubic foot. It is rated as hard, with a specific gravity of 0.46, and the heartwood is low to moderate in resistance to decay. The wood is moderately weak when used as a beam or post, moderately limber, and moderately high in ability to resist shock.

Black tupelo has large shrinkage and a tendency to warp while seasoning because of its interlocking grain. Considerable care is required in the drying process to produce straight, flat lumber. The wood generally requires special treatment before gluing to obtain the best results and it ranks below the average of 25 southern hardwoods in machining properties. In nail-withdrawal resistance and resistance to splitting under the action of nails, black tupelo has an intermediate rank. It can be readily pulped by the chemical and semichemical processes.

Uses /   Black tupelo is used mainly for lumber, veneer, and paper pulp, and to some extent for railway ties and cooperage. The lumber goes largely into shipping containers and furniture. Black tupelo has been used for many years in the manufacture of book and similar grades of paper.

Description /   Heartwood is pale to moderately dark brownish gray or dirty gray. Pores are very small, as in sweetgum. Growth rings are generally inconspicuous to moderately distinct. Rays are visible on quartersawed surfaces, but show up less prominently against the background color of the wood than the rays in sweetgum.

16.1.13
WHITE OAK

Properties /   The white oaks (Figure 16-7) are heavy woods, averaging 47 pounds a cubic foot, and are very hard, with a specific gravity ranging from 0.57 in chestnut oak to 0.81 in live oak. Led by live oak, they rank high in strength properties.

The wood of the white oaks is subject to large shrinkage and seasoning must be done carefully to avoid checking and warping. Pores of the heartwood, with the exception of chestnut oak, are usually plugged with tyloses, a frothlike growth that makes the wood impervious to liquids. The heartwood itself is comparatively decay resistant,

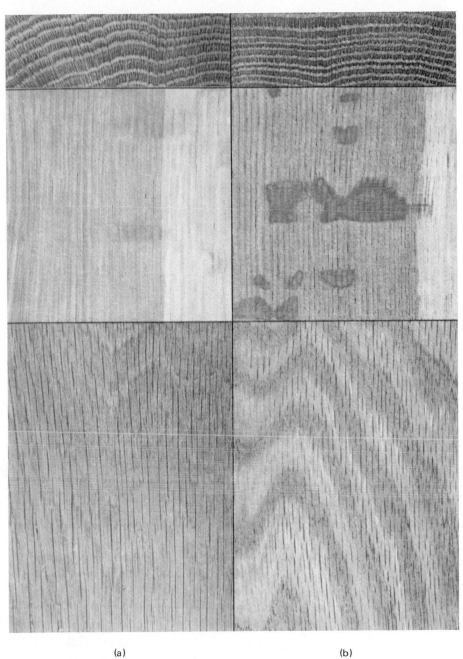

(a)   (b)

FIGURE 16-7   (A) WHITE OAK; (B) RED OAK

generally more so than that of the red oaks. White oaks are above average in all machining operations except shaping.

Uses / Most white oak is made into lumber for flooring, furniture, general millwork, and boxes and crates. Large amounts are used for flooring and furniture and it is the outstanding wood for tight barrels, kegs, and casks because of the nonporous heartwood. It has long been the leading wood for the construction of ships and boats.

Description / Heartwood is grayish brown. The outlines of the larger pores are indistinct except in chestnut oak, which has open pores with distinct outlines. On smooth-cut, end-grain surfaces, the summerwood pores are not distinct as individuals. Wood rays are generally higher than in red oak, the larger ones ranging from ½ to 5 inches in height along the grain. As in red oak, rays appear lighter in color than the background wood on end-grain surfaces and darker than the background wood on side-grain surfaces.

16.1.14
RED OAK

Properties / The red oaks (Figure 16-7) are similar in many properties to the white oaks. A major difference is that red oak, because it lacks tyloses in its pores, is extremely porous. A heavy wood, it averages 44 pounds a cubic foot and the average specific gravity of the more important species ranges from 0.52 to 0.60. The wood is hard, stiff, and has high shock resistance.

Red oak undergoes large shrinkage while drying, and seasoning must be done carefully to avoid checking and warping. It is considerably above average in all machining operations except shaping, and the heartwood ranks low to moderate in decay resistance.

Uses / Most of the red oak cut in this country is converted into flooring, furniture, millwork, boxes and crates, caskets and coffins, agricultural implements, boats, and woodenware. Considerable lumber is also used in building construction, and some is exported. The hardness and wearing qualities of red oak have made it an important flooring wood for residences. Preservative-treated red oak is used extensively for crossties, mine timbers, and fence posts.

Description / Heartwood is grayish brown with a more or less distinctive reddish tint. Pores are commonly open, and the outlines of the larger pores are distinct. On smoothly cut end-grain surfaces, the summerwood pores can be seen as individuals and readily counted when examined with a hand lens. Wood rays are commonly ¼ to 1 inch high along the grain. On end-grain surfaces, rays appear as lines crossing the growth rings.

16.1.15
YELLOW BIRCH

Properties / Yellow birch (Figure 16-8) is heavy, averaging 43 pounds a cubic foot, and hard, with specific gravity averaging 0.55. The wood is strong, stiff, and has very high shock resistance.

Yellow birch has very large shrinkage and must be seasoned carefully to prevent checking and warping. Like all commercial birches, it is low in decay resistance. Although the wood is difficult to work with handtools, it can be readily shaped by machine and ranks high in nail-withdrawal resistance.

Uses / Yellow birch is used principally for lumber, veneer, distilled products, and crossties. The lumber and veneer go mostly into furniture, boxes, baskets, crates, woodenware, interior finish, and general millwork. It is because of its pleasing grain pattern and ability to take a high polish, that yellow birch is widely used in the furniture industry. Spools, bobbins, and other turned articles are also important products.

Yellow birch is one of the principal woods used for hardwood distillation to produce wood alcohol, acetate of lime, charcoal, tar, and oils. It is used in smaller quantities for pulpwood and cooperage.

Description / Yellow birch heartwood is light reddish brown. Pores are very small, sometimes just barely visible on smoothly cut end-grain surfaces, and are uniformly distributed through the annual ring cross section. Pore lines are visible on longitudinal surfaces as very fine grooves that may even be seen through natural finishes. Wood rays may be seen only on quartersawed surfaces, where they appear to be of one size and of uniform height along the grain. Growth rings are moderately distinct on plainsawed surfaces.

16.1.16
SUGAR MAPLE

Properties / Sugar maple (Figure 16-8) is heavy, averaging 44 pounds a cubic foot, and hard, with a specific gravity of 0.56. Strong and stiff, it has high resistance to shock. Although it has large shrinkage

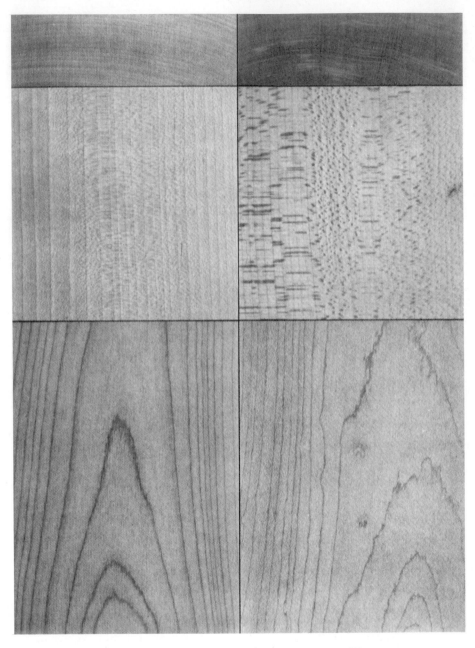

(a)   (b)

FIGURE 16-8   (A) YELLOW BIRCH; (B) SUGAR MAPLE

and presents some difficulties in drying, the wood can be satisfactorily seasoned. Its resistance to decay is low to moderate.

Sugar maple ranks high in nail-withdrawal resistance and intermediate in ease of gluing. The wood takes stain saitsfactorily and is capable of a high polish. Although generally straight-grained, sugar maple occasionally occurs with curly, wavy, or bird's-eye grain. The wood turns well on a lathe, is markedly resistant to abrasive wear, and is without characteristic taste or odor.

Uses / Sugar maple is used principally for lumber, distilled products, veneer, crossties, and paper pulp. Probably 90 percent of the lumber is manufactured into such products as flooring, furniture, boxes and crates, handles, woodenware, and novelties. It is especially suitable for bowling alleys, dance floors, and other flooring that is subjected to hard use. Sugar maple is one of the principal woods used in the hardwood distillation industry for the production of charcoal, acetic acid, and wood alcohol.

Description / Heartwood is light reddish brown and sometimes shows greenish-black streaks near injuries. Pores are extremely small and not visible on any surface. Wood rays may be seen on the end grain and especially on quartersawed faces, where the higher rays are distinctive because of their color and size and smaller rays appear as fine lines between them. The wood rays may also be seen on plainsawed surfaces as very small darker colored flecks that are parallel to the grain of the wood.

16.1.17
YELLOW-POPLAR

Properties / Moderately light in weight, yellow-poplar (Figure 16-9) averages 30 pounds a cubic foot. The wood is classed as moderately soft, with a specific gravity of 0.40, and is moderately low in bending and compressive strength, moderately stiff, and moderately low in shock resistance. Although it undergoes moderately large shrinkage when dried from a green condition, it is not difficult to season and stays in place well when seasoned. The heartwood is low to moderate in resistance to decay.

Yellow-poplar ranks intermediate in machining properties. Although low in nail-withdrawal resistance, it has little tendency to split when nailed. Also, the wood has an excellent reputation for taking and holding paint, enamel, and stain and can be glued satisfactorily. Yellow-poplar containers do not impart taste or odor to foodstuffs, and

(a)   (b)

FIGURE 16-9   (A) YELLOW-POPLAR; (B) COTTONWOOD

the wood can be easily pulped by the chemical and semichemical processes.

Uses / The principal uses of yellow-poplar are for lumber, veneer, and pulpwood. The lumber goes mostly into furniture, boxes and crates, interior finish, siding, fixtures, and musical instruments. The veneer is used extensively for finish, furniture, and various forms of cabinetwork.

Description / Heartwood is brownish yellow, usually with a definite greenish tinge. The wood rays, as seen on a smoothly cut end-grain surface, are somewhat more prominent than in cucumbertree. Positive identification of yellow-poplar and cucumbertree is best accomplished microscopically, but it is possible to separate them on the basis of gross features when both woods are at hand.

16.1.18
COTTONWOOD

Properties / The cottonwoods (Figure 16-9) are moderately light in weight, ranging from 24 to 28 pounds a cubic foot. With a specific gravity of 0.37, eastern cottonwood is classified as moderately soft, while black cottonwood's specific gravity of 0.32 classifies it as soft. The cottonwoods are moderately weak in bending and compression, moderately limber, and moderately low in shock resistance.

Moderately large shrinkage is a characteristic of cottonwood and it requires careful seasoning if warp is to be avoided. The heartwood has low decay resistance and the wood is rather difficult to work with tools without producing chipped or fuzzy grain. Cottonwood is low in nail-withdrawal resistance but does not split easily when nailed. The wood is classed among those that glue satisfactorily with moderate care. It has a good reputation for holding paint.

Uses / A large proportion of the annual output of cottonwood is cut into lumber and veneer and then remanufactured into containers and furniture. Both lumber and veneer are used in the furniture industry for core material, which is overlaid with high-grade furniture veneers.

Description / Heartwood of all three cottonwood species is grayish white to light grayish brown with occasional streaks of light brown. The annual rings are rather wide. Pores are barely visible on smooth cut, end-grain surfaces. Aside from the color of the heartwood, cottonwood is extremely similar to black willow. Separation of the two species is based mainly on heartwood color, which is light brown or reddish brown in willow, or on microscopic examination if only sapwood material is available.

16.2
SOFTWOODS
(CONE-
BEARING
SPECIES)

16.2.1
BALDCYPRESS

Properties / Baldcypress (Figure 16-10) is moderately heavy, with an average weight of 32 pounds a cubic foot, and moderately hard, with a specific gravity of 0.42. The wood is also moderately strong and moderately stiff. Its durability under conditions favorable to decay is outstanding.

Since green baldcypress lumber contains considerable moisture, it requires more care and time to kiln-dry than many other softwoods. However, the wood has moderately small shrinkage and slow air-drying is successfully practiced. It does not impart taste, odor, or color to food products.

Uses / The principal use of baldcypress is in building construction, especially where decay resistance is required. It is frequently used for posts, beams, and other members in warehouses, docks, factories, and bridges. Because of its high degree of resistance to decay, it is particularly valuable for greenhouses, stadium seats, cooling towers, and roof planks of dye houses.

Cypress is also used extensively for caskets and burial boxes and for sash, doors, blinds, interior trim and paneling, and general millwork. Containers, such as boxes, crates, vats, tanks, and tubs, require considerable quantities.

Description / Heartwood varies in color from pale brown to blackish brown and sometimes has a reddish tingle. The wood is without resin canals, and transition from springwood to summerwood is abrupt, as in redwood. Heartwood of darker specimens generally has a more or less rancid odor and longitudinal surfaces feel distinctly greasy or waxy.

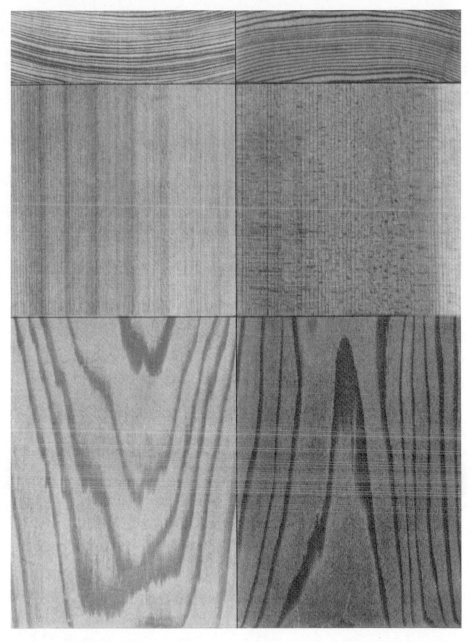

(a)   (b)

FIGURE 16-10   (A) BALDCYPRESS; (B) REDWOOD

16.2.2
REDWOOD

Properties / Typical virgin-growth redwood (Figure 16-10) is moderately light in weight, averaging 28 pounds a cubic foot. The wood is moderately hard, with a specific gravity of 0.38, moderately strong, and moderately stiff. Except for shock resistance, it has somewhat higher strength properties for its weight than would be expected.

Redwood is thought to owe its outstanding decay resistance to the reddish extractive in the tree, which colors the wood and accounts for its name. The wood has very small shrinkage, is comparatively easy to season, and holds its shape well after seasoning. Redwood has only intermediate nail-withdrawal resistance but takes and holds paint exceptionally well. Redwood, the cedars, and baldcypress make up the group of woods with the highest resistance to termites.

Uses / Probably from one-half to two-thirds of the redwood lumber produced is used in the form of planks, dimension, boards, joists, and posts. A large part of this material goes into framing for houses and industrial buildings, and into bridges, trestles, and other heavy construction. Much of the remaining lumber is remanufactured into house siding, sash, blinds, doors, general millwork, outdoor furniture, and tanks. Richly colored redwood paneling provides pleasing interior effects.

Description / Heartwood is usually a uniform deep reddish brown. The wood is without resin canals and has no distinctive odor, taste, or feel. Western redcedar may approach redwood in color, but the distinctive odor of western redcedar separates the two woods immediately.

16.2.3
INCENSE-CEDAR

Properties / A lightweight wood, incense-cedar (Figure 16-11) averages 26 pounds per cubic foot. The wood is moderately soft, with a specific gravity of 0.35, moderately weak, limber, and low in shock resistance.

Incense-cedar has small shrinkage and is comparatively easy to season with little checking or warping. It ranks among the most decay-resistant woods, along with cypress, redwood, and black locust. Also, the wood splits readily and evenly and is easy to work with tools.

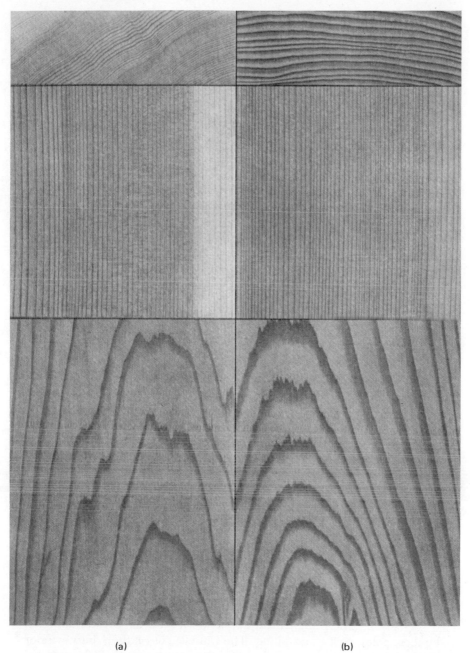

(a)   (b)

FIGURE 16-11   (A) INCENSE-CEDAR; (B) WESTERN RED-
CEDAR

Incense-cedar is one of the woods that holds paints longest and suffers least when protection against weathering becomes inadequate.

Uses /   The principal uses of incense-cedar are for lumber, fence posts, and crossties. Nearly all the high-grade lumber is used in the manufacture of pencils and venetian blinds. Since most incense-cedar lumber is more or less pecky, it is used locally for rough construction. The qualities of incense-cedar that adapt it particularly to pencil manufacture are straightness of grain, softness, and ease of whittling. Its decay resistance makes it well suited for fence posts and crossties.

Description /   Heartwood is reddish brown to dull brown, with an occasional tinge of lavender. Heartwood has a characteristic cedar-like odor and acrid taste. Shavings placed on the tongue for a few seconds give a slight burning sensation. Transition from springwood to summerwood is more or less abrupt and makes the growth rings prominent on flat-grained surfaces. It is easier to produce a smooth cut on the end grain of incense-cedar than on western redcedar. Although incense-cedar and western redcedar cannot always be separated with certainty on the basis of gross features, they can be readily distinguished under the microscope.

16.2.4
WESTERN
REDCEDAR

Properties /   Western redcedar (Figure 16-11) is light in weight, averaging 23 pounds a cubic foot. The wood is moderately soft, with a specific gravity of 0.31, weak as a beam or post, moderately limber, and low in ability to resist shock. In decay resistance, the heartwood ranks with the more durable woods.

The wood of western redcedar is not difficult to kiln-dry when proper methods are used, but requires more care in seasoning than other western cedars. After it has been properly dried, it stays in place well and has little tendency to warp. It is comparatively low in nail-withdrawal resistance but can be easily glued. Western redcedar takes and holds paint very well and is exceptionally weather resistant.

Uses /   The principal uses of western redcedar are for shingles, lumber, poles, posts, and piling. The lumber goes largely into exterior siding for houses, interior finish, greenhouse construction, flumes, and structural timbers, with smaller amounts being used in the manufacture of ships and boats, caskets, boxes and crating, sash, doors, and general millwork. Round western redcedar poles, most of which are treated with a preservative, are shipped to all parts of the United States for use as utility poles.

Description /   Heartwood is reddish or pinkish brown to dull brown. It has a characteristic cedarlike odor, but shavings placed on the tongue do not give quite the sensation that incense-cedar shavings do. Transition from springwood to summerwood is the same as in incense-cedar. The wood is sometimes confused with redwood, but the cedarlike odor of western redcedar separates the two species immediately.

16.2.5
SHORTLEAF PINE

Properties /   Shortleaf pine (Figure 16-12), a moderately heavy wood but ranking with the lightest of the important southern pines, has an average weight of 36 pounds a cubic foot. Typically, the wood is moderately hard, with a specific gravity of 0.46, moderately strong, stiff, and moderately shock resistant. The heartwood is moderately decay resistant.

Like all southern pines, shortleaf has moderately large shrinkage but tends to stay in place well after seasoning. In nail-withdrawal resistance, it ranks above hemlock, spruce, and Douglas-fir. And, like other southern pines, it produces a resinous substance from which turpentine and rosin can be made.

Uses /   Shortleaf pine lumber is used principally for building material such as interior finish, ceiling, frames, sash, sheathing, subflooring, and joists, and for boxes and crates, caskets, furniture, woodenware, and novelties. Considerable use is also made of shortleaf pine for crossties, telephone and telegraph poles, and mine timbers. In addition, the resin-rich heartwood is distilled to make wood turpentine, tar, and tar oils. Large amounts of this southern pine are used for paper pulp.

Description /   Heartwood ranges from shades of yellow and orange to reddish brown or light brown. Transition from springwood to summerwood is abrupt, with the annual rings prominent on all surfaces. Resin canals are large and abundant and are easily found in all annual rings. Summerwood bands are generally wider than those of ponderosa pine. In appearance, the wood of shortleaf pine closely resembles that of longleaf, loblolly, and slash, the other principal southern pines.

(a)   (b)

FIGURE 16-12   (A) SHORTLEAF PINE;   (B) PONDEROSA
PINE

16.2.6
PONDEROSA PINE

Properties / The wood of ponderosa pine (Figure 16-12) varies considerably in its properties. However, in the outer portions of trees of sawtimber size, it generally is moderately light in weight, averaging 28 pounds per cubic foot, and moderately soft, with a specific gravity of 0.38. This wood also ranks as moderately weak, moderately limber, and moderately low in shock resistance. It has moderately small shrinkage and little tendency to warp.

Ponderosa pine compares favorably with woods of similar density in nail-withdrawal resistance, is not easily split by nails, and glues easily. The heartwood has low to moderate decay resistance.

Uses / Pondersoa pine is used principally for lumber and, to a lesser extent, for piling, poles, posts, mine timbers, veneer, and hewn ties. The lumber has a variety of uses ranging from high-grade millwork to boxes and crates. For cabinets and millwork, the clearer, softer material is used, while the manufacture of boxes and crates consumes the lower grade lumber. Knotty pondersoa pine has come into wide use as paneling for interior finish.

Description / Heartwood is yellowish to light reddish or orange brown. Transition from springwood to summerwood is abrupt as in the southern pines, but the summerwood bands are narrow. Growth rings are generally most prominent on the flat-grained surfaces, which also frequently exhibit a dimpled appearance. This appearance is common in lodgepole pine too, but in lodgepole the dimples are smaller and more abundant. The resin canals of ponderosa pine are abundant and easily found in all anaual rings. They are larger than those in lodgepole pine, and the heartwood of lodgepole pine is lighter colored than that of ponderosa.

16.2.7
SITKA SPRUCE

Properties / Sitka spruce (Figure 16-13) is a moderately lightweight wood, averaging 28 pounds a cubic foot. The wood also is moderately soft, with a specific gravity of 0.37, moderately weak in bending and compressive strength, moderately stiff, and moderately low in resistance to shock. On the basis of weight, however, it ranks high in strength properties.

Although the wood has moderately large shrinkage, it is not

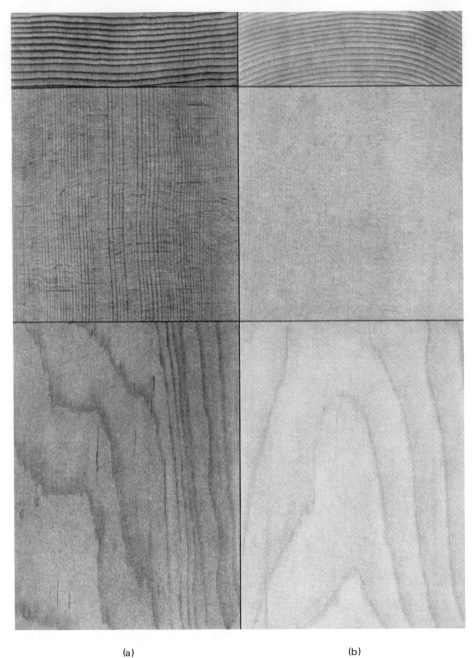

(a)   (b)

FIGURE 16-13   (A) SITKA SPRUCE; (B) ENGELMANN
                    SPRUCE

difficult to kiln-dry. It works easily, holds fastenings well, and can be obtained in clear, straight-grained pieces of large size and uniform texture with hardly any hidden defects. Its decay resistance is low. Although planed surfaces of Sitka spruce lumber may show a silky sheen, the wood has a tendency to produce wooly or fuzzy grain under the action of planer knives. As a pulpwood, Sitka spruce ranks high because of its long, strong fibers and the ease with which it can be pulped by any of the pulping processes.

Uses /   Sitka spruce is used principally for lumber, cooperage, and paper pulp. Some of the lumber is used for construction just as it comes from the sawmill, but the greater part is remanufactured into various products. At least half of the remanufactured lumber goes into boxes and crates. The other major uses of the lumber are for furniture, planing-mill products, sash, doors, blinds, and general millwork. Specialty uses include aircraft, ladder rails, and piano sounding boards.

Description /   Heartwood is light pinkish yellow to pale brown. Transition from springwood to summerwood is gradual, making the annual rings appear rather inconspicuous on flat-grained surfaces. Resin canals are usually more prominent than in the other spruces. On end-grain surfaces, the canals appear as small dots or very short lines that run parallel to the growth ring. Flat-grained surfaces are lustrous and frequently exhibit dimpling. The pinkish color of the heartwood distinguishes this species from all other spruces.

16.2.8
ENGELMANN
SPRUCE

Properties /   Engelmann spruce (Figure 16-13) is rated as light in weight, averaging 24 pounds a cubic foot. The wood is soft, with a specific gravity of 0.32, and is weak as a beam or post, moderately limber, and low in ability to resist shock.

Engelmann spruce can be readily air-dried with little tendency to warp. It has moderately small shrinkage and stays in place well when properly dried. The wood is low in decay resistance but glues easily under a wide range of gluing conditions. Engelmann spruce has excellent pulping and papermaking properties.

Uses /   Engelmann spruce is used principally for lumber and to a lesser extent for mine timbers, crossties, and poles. A large proportion of the lumber goes into building construction and boxes. Much of it is used for subflooring, sheathing, and studding. Some Engelmann spruce is pulped for paper.

Description / Heartwood is not distinct from sapwood and ranges from nearly white to pale yellowish brown. Transition from springwood to summerwood is somewhat more abrupt than in the other spruces. Resin canals are present, but are frequently difficult to find. They appear on very smoothly cut, end-grain sections as small white dots and on longitudinal surfaces as short, light-brown streaks or very fine grooves. The wood of all the spruces, with the exception of Sitka, is very similar in its gross and microscopic features and therefore almost impossible to tell apart.

16.2.9
SUGAR PINE

Properties / Sugar pine (Figure 16-14) is lightweight, averaging 25 pounds a cubic foot. The wood is moderately soft, with a specific gravity of 0.35, moderately limber, moderately weak, and low in shock resistance.

In decay resistance, sugar pine heartwood is rated low to moderate. The wood has very small shrinkage, seasons readily without checking or warping, and stays in place well. It is easy to work with tools, does not split easily in nailing, and has moderate nail-withdrawal resistance.

Uses / Sugar pine is used almost entirely for lumber in buildings, boxes and crates, sash, doors, frames, general millwork, and foundry patterns. It is suitable for all phases of house construction, with the high-grade material going into interior and exterior trim, siding, and paneling, while the lower grade material is used for sheathing, subflooring, and roof boards.

The wood also has proved very satisfactory for containers because of its light weight and color, nailing properties, and freedom from taste and odor. Sugar pine is widely used for foundry patterns because it meets the exacting requirements and is readily available in wide, thick pieces practically free from defects.

Description / Heartwood is light brown to pale reddish brown. Resin canals are abundant and commonly stain the surface of the wood with resin. Transition from springwood to summerwood is gradual, making the growth rings appear less prominent on flat-grained surfaces.

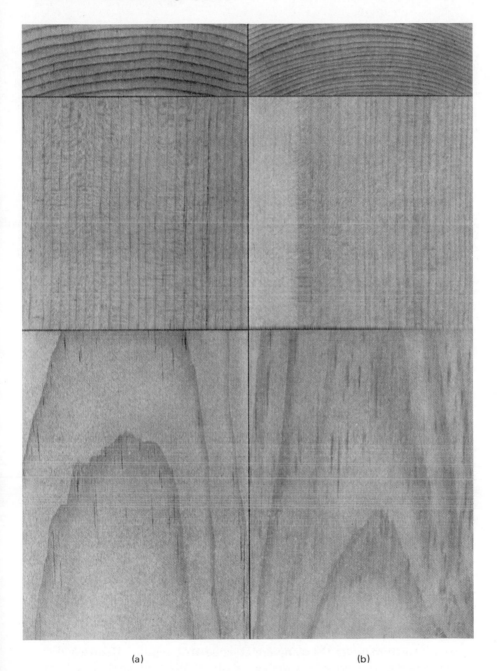

(a)   (b)

FIGURE 16-14   (A) SUGAR PINE; (B) WESTERN WHITE
PINE

16.2.10
WESTERN
WHITE PINE

Properties /   Moderately light in weight, western white pine (Figure 16-14) averages 27 pounds a cubic foot. The wood is moderately soft, with a specific gravity of 0.36, weak, moderately stiff, and moderately low in ability to resist shock.

Although the wood has moderately large shrinkage, it is easy to kiln-dry and stays in place well after seasoning. In decay resistance, it is ranked as low to moderate. Western white pine works easily with tools and glues readily. It does not split easily in nailing and occupies an intermediate position in nail-withdrawal resistance.

Uses /   Practically all of the western white pine cut is sawed into lumber. About three-fourths of this lumber is used in building construction. The lower grades are used for subflooring and wall and roof sheathing, while the high-grade material is made into siding of various kinds, exterior and interior trim, partition, casing, base, and paneling. Other uses of western white pine include match planks, boxes, and millwork products.

Description /   Heartwood is cream colored to light brown or reddish brown. Resin canals are abundant and transition from springwood to summerwood is like that in sugar pine. Separation of western white pine and sugar pine is generally accomplished on the basis of the resin canals, which are larger in sugar pine than in the other white pines. Microscopic characteristics, however, offer a more reliable means of differentiation than gross features.

16.2.11
WESTERN LARCH

Properties /   A heavy wood, western larch (Figure 16-15) has an average weight of 38 pounds per cubic foot. Also, it is moderately hard , with a specific gravity of 0.51, stiff, strong, and moderately high in shock resistance.

Western larch and Douglas-fir are frequently logged together and sold in mixture under the commercial name of "larch-fir." Heartwood of both species is moderately decay resistant. Western larch has large shrinkage in drying and presents seasoning problems because of the slowness with which it gives up its moisture. Although it ranks high in

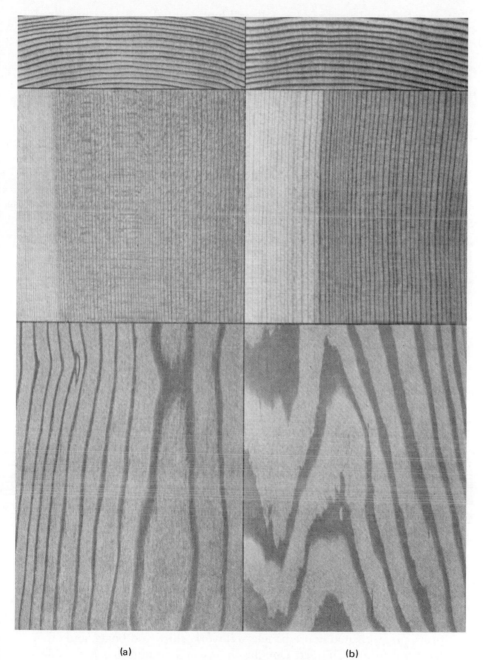

(a)   (b)

FIGURE 16-15   (A) WESTERN LARCH; (B) DOUGLAS-FIR

nail-withdrawal resistance, small or blunt-pointed nails are preferred to reduce splitting.

Uses /   Western larch is used principally in building construction as rough dimension, small timbers, planks, and boards. Considerable amounts also are made into crossties and mine timbers. Probably three-fourths of the lumber produced is used for structural purposes as it comes from the sawmill. Some of the high-grade lumber is remanufactured into interior finish, flooring, sash, doors, blinds, and other products.

Description /   Heartwood is russet brown and the color is best seen in summerwood bands on flat-grained surfaces. Resin canals are present, but are very small and difficult to find unless the resin has stained the wood surfaces or the exudation actually appears as very small droplets. Transition from springwood to summerwood is abrupt and there is little difference in color between the two zones. The heartwood lacks a distinctive odor.

16.2.12
DOUGLAS-FIR

Properties /   Most old-growth Douglas-fir (Figure 16-15) from the Pacific coast and northern Rocky Mountain States is moderately heavy, very stiff, moderately strong, and moderately shock resistant. It averages about 33 pounds a cubic foot. The wood is also moderately hard, with an average specific gravity ranging from 0.40 to 0.48. Wide-ringed second-growth Douglas-fir from the coastal States and material grown in the southern Rocky Mountain States tends to be lighter in weight and to have lower strength properties.

The wood of Douglas-fir can be readily kiln-dried if proper methods are used. Although it is more difficult to work with handtools than the soft pines, it holds fastenings well and can be glued satisfactorily. Dense heartwood has moderate decay resistance.

Uses /   The principal uses of Douglas-fir are for lumber, timbers, piling, and plywood. Remanufactured lumber goes mostly into sash, doors, general millwork, railroad car construction and repair, and boxes and crates. Plywood is now in wide use for sheathing, concrete forms, prefabricated house panels, millwork, ships and boats, and other structural forms. Chipped Douglas-fir sawmill residue has a considerable market at pulp mills.

Description /   Heartwood is orange red to red or sometimes yellowish. Resin canals, which are seen as brownish streaks in the summerwood, appear to be more abundant and more readily detectable than in western larch. Transition from springwood to summerwood is similar to that in western larch. The heartwood of Douglas-fir may be confused with that of the southern yellow pines, but resin canals are larger and much more abundant in southern pines. Most Douglas-fir has a distinctive odor.

16.2.13
Western Hemlock

Properties / Western hemlock (Figure 16-16) is moderately light in weight, averaging 29 pounds a cubic foot, and moderately hard, with a specific gravity of 0.38. It is also moderately weak and its shock resistance is fairly low. Although western hemlock has moderately large shrinkage, it is comparatively easy to season. Heartwood is low in decay resistance but the wood is easy to work with tools and has satisfactory gluing properties. Excellent for papermaking, it yields a tough, strong, and easily bleached pulp.

Uses / Western hemlock is used primarily for pulpwood and construction lumber and, to a limited extent, for containers, plywood core stock, crossties, and mine timbers. The pulp is used for newsprint and other printing paper, tissues, wrapping papers, and viscose and other cellulose derivatives. Although little western hemlock goes into heavy structural material, large quantities are used for sheathing, siding, subflooring, joists, studding, planking, and rafters in light frame construction.

Description / Heartwood of western hemlock is light reddish brown and frequently has a purplish cast, especially in the summer-wood bands. Transition from springwood to summerwood is gradual and on end-grain surfaces there is little color contrast between the two zones. The wood lacks normal resin canals.

Eastern hemlock heartwood is more roseate in color than western hemlock and the transition from springwood to summerwood is so abrupt that the two zones stand out distinctly. The coarser texture of eastern hemlock springwood tends to tear out in crosscut sawing and to produce a ribbed appearance on the end grain. A smooth cut is difficult to make on the end grain of eastern hemlock, even with a very sharp knife, while western hemlock cuts very easily and produces smooth surfaces.

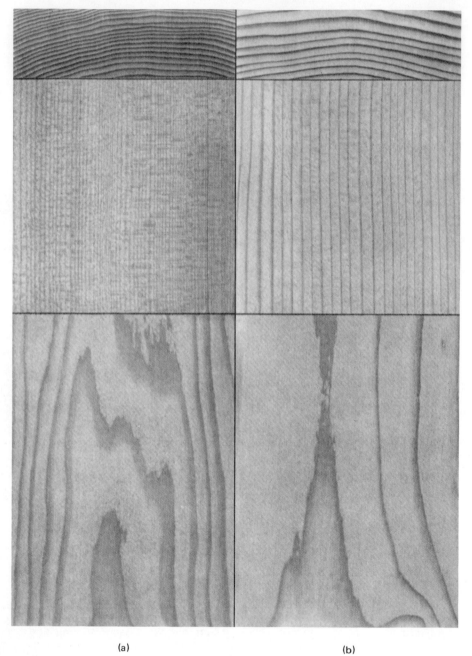

(a)   (b)

FIGURE 16-16   (A) WESTERN HEMLOCK; (B) WHITE FIR

16.2.14
WHITE FIR

Properties /   Commercial white fir (Figure 16-16) is light in weight, the various species ranging from 26 to 28 pounds a cubic foot. It is moderately soft, with an average specific gravity of 0.35, moderately weak, moderately low in shock resistance, moderately stiff, and low in nail-withdrawal resistance. It is difficult to season, a fact that retarded its use until satisfactory seasoning methods were developed. Also, its decay resistance is low, but gluing properties are satisfactory. White fir produces strong, high-quality paper pulp.

Uses /   White fir is used principally for lumber and pulpwood. The lumber goes largely into building construction, planing-mill products, boxes and crates, sash, doors, frames, and general millwork. Probably 75 percent or more of all white fir lumber is used for framing, subflooring, and sheathing of houses. Pulpwood is used chiefly in the manufacture of various grades of printing paper and high-grade wrapping paper.

Description /   Heartwood is nearly white to pale reddish brown and the wood lacks normal resin canals. Transition from springwood, like that in eastern hemlock, is more abrupt than in western hemlock. Also, color of springwood and summerwood on end-grain surfaces is more contrasting than in western hemlock. The balsam fir of the east is more uniformly white in color, with less contrasting rings than the western firs. Wood rays of the western firs frequently contain colored material that makes them stand out more on edge-grained surfaces than rays of the eastern firs, which are generally colorless.

QUESTIONS

1 /   What characteristic of pine lumber makes it so easily marred?

2 /   Define the difference between softwood and hardwood.

3 /   Which wood is very nearly the same as maple?

4 /   Why must oak lumber be filled when it is used for cabinetmaking?

5 /   Describe the characteristics of walnut lumber.

6 /   List three woods that are very dense.

7 /   Which woods would be used in the manufacture of Early American furniture?

8 /   Why is fir lumber not ideal for furniture and cabinetmaking? Select a characteristic to use as an example.

9 /   What properties of redwood and cedar make these woods desirable for outdoor use?

APPENDIX: TABLES

TABLE A-1
NAIL SIZES

Nails can be purchased in a variety of styles and sizes. The table establishes the average length of each size.

Size	Length	Common	Sinker head	Casing	Finish
3d	1¼ inches				
4d	1½ inches				
6d	2 inches				
8d	2½ inches				
10d	3 inches				
12d	3¼ inches				
16d	3½ inches				

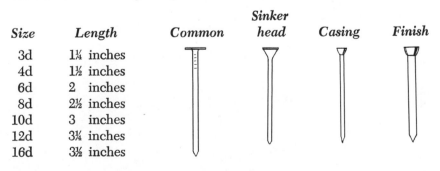

TABLE A-2

Charted below are screw lengths from 1/4" to 4" with shank dimensions from 0 to 20. These sizes are generally available and are the ones most frequently used.

LENGTH	SHANK NUMBERS																
	0	1	2	3	4	5	6	7	8	9	10	11	12	14	16	18	20
1/4 inch	0	1	2	3	4												
3/8 inch			2	3	4	5											
1/2 inch			2	3	4	5	6										
5/8 inch					4	5	6										
3/4 inch						5	6	7									
7/8 inch							6	7									
1 inch							6	7	8								
1 1/4 inch							6	7	8	9	10						
1 1/2 inch								7	8	9	10	11					
1 3/4 inch							6	7	8	9	10	11	12	14		18	20
2 inch								7	8	9	10	11	12	14	16	18	20
2 1/4 inch									8	9	10	11	12	14	16	18	20
2 1/2 inch									8	9	10	11	12	14	16	18	20
2 3/4 inch									8	9	10	11	12	14	16	18	20
3 inch													12	14	16	18	20
3 1/2 inch														14	16	18	20
4 inch															16	18	20
0 to 24 diameter dimensions in inches at body	0.060	0.073	0.086	0.099	0.112	0.125	0.138	0.151	0.164	0.177	0.190	0.203	0.216	0.242	0.268	0.294	0.320

TABLE A-2
SCREW SIZES

The table on page 386 is representative of round-headed screws, oval-headed screws, and cross-point or Phillips-head screws, in addition to the common screws shown.

TABLE A-3
WIRE BRAD SIZES

Wire brads are small flat-headed nails with sharp points in lengths of ½ to 1½ inches, in gage sizes from 20 to 14.

TABLE A-4
DRILL SIZES FOR PILOT HOLES

When drilling pilot holes in softwood, use a drill $\frac{1}{64}$ inch *larger* than those listed for hardwood.

Screw gauge no.	Pilot hole, hard wood
3	$\frac{1}{16}$
4	$\frac{1}{16}$
5	$\frac{5}{64}$
6	$\frac{5}{64}$
7	$\frac{3}{32}$
8	$\frac{3}{32}$
9	$\frac{7}{64}$
10	$\frac{7}{64}$
12	$\frac{1}{8}$

TABLE A-5
Proper Screws for Plywood Fastening

Plywood thickness	Screw size
¾-inch plywood	#8 1½-inch screw
⅝-inch plywood	#8 1¼-inch screw
½-inch plywood	#6 1¼-inch screw
⅜-inch plywood	#6 1-inch screw
¼-inch plywood	#4 ¾-inch screw

TABLE A-6
Standard Thickness and Width of Lumber

Soft woods

1-inch stock (actual thickness = ¾ inch)

Standard Width (in.)	Actual Width (in.)
2	1½
3	2½
4	3½
5	4½
6	5½
8	7½
10	9¼
12	11¼

2-inch stock actual thickness 1½ inches; width sizes are the same

Hardwoods

Sanded two sides:
1-inch stock = ⅞ to 1 inch full
2-inch stock = 1¾ to 1⅞ inches
Widths are random from 3 to 24 inches

Rough cuts:
1-inch stock = 1 to 1¼ inches thick, random width
2-inch stock = 1⅞ to 2⁵⁄₁₆ inches thick, random width
3-inch stock = 2¾ to 3¼ inches thick, random width

TABLE A-7
Average Drying Times for Finishes

Drying times vary with temperature and humidity.

Type	First coat	Second coat
Oil stain	1 hour	24 hours
Water stain	1 hour	12 hours
Spirit stain	None	None
Shellac	15 minutes	2 hours
Varnish	1½ hours	24 hours
Varnish (polyurethane)	½ hour	4–8 hours
Lacquer	2–15 minutes	5–10 minutes
Lacquer (brush)	10–25 minutes	10–35 minutes

GLOSSARY

ABRASIVES

Substances that are rubbed on wood to smooth it before or between applications of finish coats. Flint, garnet, aluminum oxide, and silicon carbide are common abrasives.

ADHESIVE

Material capable of holding other materials together, by surface attachment. Glues, cements, pastes, and mucilage are among the common adhesives.

Most of the definitions were supplied by courtesy of the Forest Products Laboratory, U.S. Forest Service.

AIR-DRIED LUMBER

Lumber that has been dried by storage in yards or sheds for any length of time. For the United States as a whole, the minimum moisture content of thoroughly air-dried lumber is 12 to 15 percent, and the average is higher.

BASE OR BASEBOARD

Board placed along the bottom of a wall next to the floor.

BASE MOLDING

Strip of wood used to trim the upper edge of a baseboard.

BASE SHOE OR SHOEMOLD

Strip of wood next to the floor on the interior baseboard. Called also a *carpet strip*.

BENZENE

Liquid obtained from petroleum. Used in dyeing, painting, and as a cleaning agent.

BEVEL

Angular surface across an edge of a piece of stock.

BLEEDING

Extension of the color of stain, paint, etc., beyond its desired edge or boundary.

BOARD

Yard lumber that is less than 2 inches thick and 1 or more inches wide.

BOARD FOOT

Board 1 foot square and 1 inch thick (or the equivalent).

BOILED LINSEED OIL

Linseed oil to which enough lead, manganese, or cobalt salts have been added to make the oil harden more rapidly when spread in thin coatings.

BRACE

Inclined piece of framing lumber used to complete a triangle and therefore to stiffen a structure. (There is also a hand tool called a brace.)

BUTT JOINT

Junction where the ends of two pieces meet in a square-cut joint.

CELL

General term for the very small units of wood structure, including wood fibers, vessel members, and other elements of diverse structure and function.

CLEAT

Strip of material, such as wood, fastened to another piece to strengthen it or to furnish a grip.

CLOSE-GRAINED WOOD

Wood with narrow, inconspicuous annual rings. The term is sometimes used to designate wood that has small and closely spaced pores, but in this sense the term "fine-textured" is used more often.

COARSE-GRAINED WOOD

Wood with wide conspicuous annual rings in which there is considerable difference between spring wood and summer wood. The term is sometimes used to designate wood with large pores, such as oak, ash, chestnut, and walnut, but in this sense the term "coarse-textured" is used more often.

CROOK

Distortion in a board that deviates edgewise from a straight line from end to end of the board.

CUP

Distortion in a board that deviates flatwise from a straight line across the width of the board.

DADO

Rectangular groove across the grain in a board.

DOVETAIL JOINT

Joint in which one piece has dovetail-shaped pins or tenons that fit into corresponding holes in the other piece.

DOWEL

Small, wooden pin used to strengthen a joint. Also, in a foundry, a pin placed between the sections of parted patterns or core boxes to locate and hold them in position.

FILLER (WOOD)

Heavily pigmented preparation used for filling and leveling off the pores in open-grained woods.

FINISH

Wood products to be used in the joiner work, such as doors and stairs, and other fine work required to complete a building, especially the interior.

FLAT-GRAINED LUMBER

Lumber that has been sawed so that the wide surfaces extend approximately parallel to the annual growth rings. Lumber is considered to be flat-grained when the annual growth rings make an angle of less than 45 degrees with the surface of the piece.

FLUSH

Even, or in the same plane (with reference to adjacent surfaces of two structural pieces).

GLUE

Adhesive, commonly used in joining wood parts.

GRAIN

Direction, size, arrangement, appearance, or quality of the elements in wood or lumber.

HARDBOARD

Man-made board of wood produced by converting wood chips into wood fiber, which is then formed into panels under heat and pressure.

HARDWOODS

Generally, the botanical group of trees that have broad leaves, in contrast to the conifers or softwoods. The term has no reference to the actual hardness of the wood.

JOINT

Junction of two pieces of wood or veneer.

KILN

Heated chamber for drying lumber, veneer, and other wood products.

KNOT

That portion of a branch or limb that has been surrounded by subsequent growth of the wood of the trunk or other portion of the tree. As a knot appears on the sawed surface, it is merely a section of the entire knot, its shape depending upon the direction of the cut.

LACQUER

Varnish-like solution used in the finishing of wood, metal, porcelain, and similar materials. Lacquers dry quickly and leave a tough, durable, flexible, lightweight film. They should not be used over oil-base paints because they contain solvents that will cut such paints. There are several types of lacquers. Cellulose lacquers have a base of nitrocellulose or pyroxyline; others have a resin base.

LAP JOINT
Joint composed of two pieces, one overlapping the other.

LAYOUT
Full-sized drawing showing arrangement and structural features.

LINSEED OIL
Yellowish drying oil obtained from flaxseed, widely used as a vehicle for lead-based paints. It is soluble in ether, benzene, and turpentine.

LUMBER
Product of the saw and planing mill, not processed other than by sawing, passing through a standard planing machine, cross-cutting to length, and matching.

MILLWORK
Generally, all building materials made of finished wood and manufactured in millwork plants and planing mills. Includes such items as inside and outside doors, window and door frames, blinds, porchwork, mantels, panelwork, stairways, moldings, and interior trim. Does not include flooring, ceiling, or siding.

MITER
Joint formed by two abutting pieces meeting at an angle.

MOLDING
Strip of wood, often decorative, such as that on the top of a base-board or around windows and doors.

MORTISE
Hole that is to receive a tenon; or any hole cut through a piece by a chisel or mortiser. Generally of rectangular shape.

MORTISE AND TENON JOINT
Joint made by cutting a hole or mortise in one piece, and a tenon, or piece to fit the hole, in the other.

OPEN-GRAINED WOOD
Common classification by painters for woods with large pores, such as oak, ash, chestnut, and walnut. Also known as "coarse-textured."

PANEL
(1) Large, thin board or sheet of lumber, plywood, or other ma-

terial. (2) Thin board with all its edges inserted in a groove of a surrounding frame of thick material.

PARTICLE BOARD
Man-made board composed of wood chips held together with adhesive.

PLAIN-SAWED LUMBER
Alternative name for flat-grained lumber.

PLYWOOD
Assembly made of layers (plies) of veneer, or of veneer in combination with lumber core, joined with an adhesive. The grain of adjoining plies is usually laid at right angles, and almost always an odd number of plies are used to obtain balanced construction.

POROUS WOODS
Alternative name for hardwoods, which frequently have vessels or pores large enough to be seen readily without magnification.

PUMICE
Extremely light, spongy, or porous material used in powder form to smooth and polish surfaces.

QUARTER-SAWED LUMBER
Alternative term for edge-grained lumber.

RADIAL
Coincident with a radius from the axis of the tree or log to the circumference. A radial section is a lengthwise section in a plane that extends from pith to bark.

RAISED GRAIN
Roughened condition of the surface of dressed lumber in which the hard summer wood is raised above the softer spring wood but is not torn loose from it.

RUBBING COMPOUND
Abrasive material used to produce a smoothly finished wood surface.

SAG
Unevenness or irregularity in a coat of paint, varnish, or lacquer. It results if too much of the liquid is allowed to collect in one spot or area.

SANDING
Rubbing sandpaper or similar abrasive over a surface before applying finish.

SHELLAC

Preparation made by dissolving lac in alcohol, and used commonly in the finishing of wood. Lac is a resinous substance secreted by a tropical insect.

SOFTWOODS

Generally, the botanical group of trees that bear cones and in most cases have needle-like or scale-like leaves; also the wood produced by such trees. The term has no reference to the actual hardness of the wood.

SOLVENT

Liquid in which things can be dissolved. Also, more loosely, a liquid in which tiny particles of a substance can be dispersed in suspension, without actually dissolving. Solvents commonly used in wood finishing are turpentine, alcohol, and petroleum and coal-tar distillates. The solvent in a finishing material usually evaporates, leaving the pigment or other necessary ingredients dry on the finished surface.

SPLINE

Thin strip of wood used to reinforce joints. Also known as a *feather* or *tongue.*

STAIN

Discoloration in wood that may be caused by such diverse agencies as microorganisms, metal, or chemicals. The term also applies to materials used to color wood.

STRENGTH

In its broader sense the term includes all the properties of wood that enable it to resist forces or loads. In its more restricted sense, "strength" may apply to any of the mechanical properties, in which event the name of the property under consideration should be stated: strength in compression parallel to grain, strength in bending, strength in hardness, and so on.

TACK RAG

Piece of cheesecloth or cotton rag moistened with thinned varnish. It is used to pick up small particles of dust.

TEXTURE

Term used interchangeably with "grain." Sometimes used to combine the concepts of density and degree of contrast between spring wood and summer wood.

TOENAILING

To drive a nail so that it enters the first surface diagonally and usually penetrates the second member at a slant, also.

TRIM

Finishing materials in a building, such as moldings applied around openings (window trim, door trim) or where walls join the floor and ceiling of a room (baseboard, cornice, picture molding).

UNDERCOAT

Coating applied prior to the final or top coat of a paint job.

VARNISH

Thickened preparation of drying oil, or resin and drying oil. When applied to a surface it leaves a hard, glossy, transparent coating. It may also be mixed with pigments to make enamels. Clear varnish is a slightly yellow, semitransparent liquid.

VENEER

Thin layer or sheet of wood cut on a veneer machine.

VESSELS

Wood cells of comparatively large diameter that have open ends and are set one above the other so as to form continuous tubes. The openings of the vessels on the surface of a piece of wood are usually referred to as *pores*.

WARP

Any variation from a true or plane surface. Warp includes bow, crook, cup, twist, or any combination.

WOOD SUBSTANCE

Solid material of which wood is composed. It usually refers to the extractive-free solid substance of which the cell walls are composed, but this is not always true. There is no wide variation in chemical composition or specific gravity between the wood substance of various species; the characteristic differences of species are largely due to differences in infiltrated materials and variations in relative amounts of cell walls and cell cavities.

WORKABILITY

Degree of ease and smoothness of cut obtainable with hand or machine tools.

INDEX